Lives in Solidarity

Muslim Minorities

Editorial Board

Jørgen S. Nielsen (*University of Copenhagen*)
Aminah McCloud (*DePaul University, Chicago*)
Jörn Thielmann (*EZIRE, Erlangen University*)

VOLUME 43

The titles published in this series are listed at *brill.com/mumi*

Lives in Solidarity

BDS *Activism among Europe's Muslims*

By

Jana Jevtić

BRILL

LEIDEN | BOSTON

Cover illustration: iStockphoto.com. Photograph by sleepyz.

The research and writing of this book were supported by the Open Society Foundations. The author received the Civil Society Scholar Award (CSSA) of the Open Society Foundations in both 2017 and 2018 cycles.

Library of Congress Cataloging-in-Publication Data

Names: Jevtić, Jana, author.
Title: Lives in solidarity : BDS activism among Europe's Muslims / by Jana Jevtić.
Other titles: Boycott, divestment, and sanctions activism among Europe's Muslims
Description: Leiden ; Boston : Brill, 2023. | Series: Muslim minorities, 1570-7571 ; vol. 43 | Includes bibliographical references and index.
Identifiers: LCCN 2023032709 (print) | LCCN 2023032710 (ebook) | ISBN 9789004544079 (hardback) | ISBN 9789004683099 (ebook)
Subjects: LCSH: Boycott, divestment, and sanctions movement. | Arab-Israeli conflict—1993—Foreign public opinion, European. | Muslims—Great Britain—London—Political activity. | Muslims—Bosnia and Herzegovina—Sarajevo—Political activity. | Muslims—Great Britain—London—Interviews. | Muslims—Bosnia and Herzegovina—Sarajevo—Interviews. | Solidarity. | Palestine—Foreign public opinion, European.
Classification: LCC DS119.76 .J477 2023 (print) | LCC DS119.76 (ebook) | DDC 305.6/970941—dc23/eng/20230810
LC record available at https://lccn.loc.gov/2023032709
LC ebook record available at https://lccn.loc.gov/2023032710

Typeface for the Latin, Greek, and Cyrillic scripts: "Brill". See and download: brill.com/brill-typeface.

ISSN 1570-7571
ISBN 978-90-04-54407-9 (hardback)
ISBN 978-90-04-68309-9 (e-book)

Copyright 2023 by Koninklijke Brill NV, Leiden, The Netherlands.
Koninklijke Brill NV incorporates the imprints Brill, Brill Nijhoff, Brill Schöningh, Brill Fink, Brill mentis, Brill Wageningen Academic, Vandenhoeck & Ruprecht, Böhlau and V&R unipress.
All rights reserved. No part of this publication may be reproduced, translated, stored in a retrieval system, or transmitted in any form or by any means, electronic, mechanical, photocopying, recording or otherwise, without prior written permission from the publisher. Requests for re-use and/or translations must be addressed to Koninklijke Brill NV via brill.com or copyright.com.

This book is printed on acid-free paper and produced in a sustainable manner.

Contents

Acknowledgements VII
Note on Transcription IX

1 Introduction 1

2 Palestinian Resistance and the Muslim Boycott 22

3 Europe, Islam, and the New Political Landscape 43

4 Private Lives, Public Duties, and the Generational Gap 60

5 European Hopes, Nationalist Desires, and the Urban–Rural Divide 87

6 Conclusion 123

Bibliography 135
Index 165

Acknowledgements

There are numerous collogues and friends who made the completion of this book possible, by sharing their thoughts and their time, and by being a source of guidance and inspiration to me during, before, and beyond the production of this book. I thank them all, starting with my mentor, Nadia al-Bagdadi.

I thank Nadia for her crucial input at times when I was getting lost in a torrent of boycott fatwas. Her provocations and conversations anchored and sustained me through every phase of this book—from its conception to its present form. I thank her and Aziz al-Azmeh for inviting me to participate in the Striking from the Margins Project that, while short-term, proved to be a stimulating context in which to meditate on the difficult question of religious authority and knowledge.

A special thanks goes to Charles Hirschkind, whose scholarship on Muslim ethics and practices served as an important signpost for developing and articulating my own ideas for exploring BDS activism in Tower Hamlets and Stari Grad. Both through his close reading of this book, and through his own writing, Charles widened my knowledge and ethnographic vision, for which I am beyond grateful.

Then there are colleagues and friends whose ideas and interventions made me consider a number of issues that would have otherwise escaped my attention. In this regard, I would like to thank Thijl Sunier, Laleh Khalili, and Cornelia Sorabji. I would like to thank Darryl Li for his assertion that I show the affective dimensions of BDS activism, an assertion that helped me rethink chapters 4 and 5 and write them anew, in their current form. To John Eade I am indebted for introducing me to a complex history of Tower Hamlets, and for nurturing and guiding my interest in the years to come. I am grateful to Nicolae Roddy for his patient but passionate elucidations, which proved to be a tremendous source of insight. I thank him for being an intellectual sparring partner—a sounding board—who pushed me to think more thickly about different conceptions of self that operate within the contexts of ethical and political action.

The research and writing of this book were supported by the Open Society Foundations. In particular, the Civil Society Scholar Award, which I was fortunate to receive twice, allowed me to conceptualize many of the ideas animating this book during my stay at the University of California, Berkeley.

I thank Nienke Brienen-Moolenaar, an Associate Editor at Brill, whose generous assistance in turning my thoughts into the final product and delivering this book to the reader was invaluable. I am also grateful for the suggestions and comments made by the anonymous reviewers for Brill.

Now, I want to thank my family. Zdravka Grebo Jevtić and Rade Jevtić—my mom and dad—for being supportive, tolerant, and patient with my research and writing, which at stages seemed endless. I thank them for encouraging my curiosity, for letting me live my passions, and for believing in me when I was beginning to doubt myself. I thank my sister Asja Jevtić Pezo—the one I love the most. Without her support, advice, and absolute confidence in my ability to succeed, many of the big decisions I made, like the one to write this book, would not have been possible. To Sid Jevtić and Maggie Smith Jevtić—my sidekicks and partners in crime—thanks for loving me and comforting me in any situation. During my time in Stari Grad, I benefited enormously from the kindness and hospitality of Muamira Smječanin, to whom I extend my heartfelt thanks. I am also grateful to my friends—Una Beganović, Damir Softić, Belma Čemalović, Asja Kratović, Mirna Dragaš, Jahmel Alexander Edwards, and others—who stuck by my side through years of fieldwork, exhausting revisions, and infinite struggles with formatting. To all of them I am deeply grateful.

Last but not least, my deepest gratitude goes to Bangladeshis and Bosniaks who, in various ways, supported or participated in this book. Thanks for generously sharing stories with me. I hope I did them justice.

Note on Transcription

In accordance with the guidelines by Brill, I have adopted a simplified system for transcribing words in Arabic and Bosnian. In general, I have limited the use of diacritics to bibliographic references, quotations, and colloquialisms. Pluralization of such words usually follows English standards rather than those of the original languages, for example, "fatwas" rather than "fatawa," unless noted otherwise.

I have done my best to use words in Arabic and Bosnian only to the extent necessary. When such words appear for the first time, they are italicized to draw the reader's attention. I also provide a translation in brackets, unless their meaning is widely known in English, or they are cognate words whose meaning can be easily discerned by English readers. For the sake of privacy, I have changed the names of informants except for those who wanted to be named.

CHAPTER 1

Introduction

In July 2005, more than 170 Palestinian civil society organizations and unions, including the main political parties, issued the call for boycott, divestment, and sanctions (BDS) against Israel until it fully complies with international law and basic principles of human rights. The call highlighted the fact that for nearly sixty years Israel has maintained a regime of settler colonialism, apartheid, and occupation over the Palestinian people. Governments, it argued, failed to hold Israel accountable. Corporations, at the same time, supported the establishment, maintenance, and expansion of Israeli settlements in the West Bank, where the violations of Palestinian rights were said to be pervasive and devastating, "reaching every facet of [...] life" (Office of the United Nations High Commissioner for Human Rights 2018). Against the backdrop of government complacence and corporate compliance, the absolute majority in Palestinian civil society called upon people of conscience around the world to impose boycotts and implement divestment initiatives against Israel, similar to those applied to South Africa during apartheid regime. The call garnered substantial visibility, moving from the margins of politics—college campuses and protest marches—to the United States Congress, the French National Assembly, and the German Bundestag, which passed a resolution describing boycotts and divestment initiatives against Israel as antisemitic.

Pushing back at charges of antisemitism, the BDS call espoused an approach anchored in human rights, "just as the civil rights movement did" (Barghouti 2011, 49). It defined three basic rights that constituted the minimum requirements of peace and called for ending Israel's corresponding injustices against the main segments of the Palestinian people—the refugees, the indigenous Palestinian citizens of Israel, and those under the 1967 occupation. Specifically, it urged Israel to end its apartheid, to end its occupation of all Arab lands, and to end its denial of the right of Palestinian refugees to return to their homes, which critics warned would "spell the end of a Jewish majority" (Halbfinger, Wines, and Erlanger 2019). Moreover, critics noted that insisting on the right of return for all refugees, which Israel was unlikely to ever accept in negotiations, was counterproductive to resolving the Israeli–Palestinian conflict. In response, supporters pointed out that the BDS call did not advocate for any particular solution to the conflict, but that its emphasis was on Palestinian rights and "regaining control of the Occupied Territories" (Mansoor 2020). One might say that by adopting a comprehensive rights-based approach, the BDS call set new parameters and clearer goals for what is now a growing movement made up of political parties, trade unions, student associations, and basically the entire spectrum of grassroots organizations around the world.

The BDS National Committee (BNC), which emerged out of the first Palestinian BDS Conference held in Ramallah in November 2007, functions as the Palestinian coordinating body and reference point for the transnational BDS movement. That said, the BNC does not dictate tactics or the choice of targets at the local level. These are "governed by the context particularities," political circumstances, and the readiness, "in will and capacity," of the BDS activists (Barghouti 2011, 60). The fact that BDS is not a "one-size-fits-all" type of movement, that it needs to be adapted to a local context, captures the very theme of this book. Focusing on two primary sites, one in England and one in Bosnia, I explore some of the ways in which BDS has become "localized," that is, has come to act as a catalyst around which various discourses on the demands of Islamic piety are articulated. Through ethnographic detail, I show that these discourses are tightly intertwined with local histories and social and political circumstances, and have as much to do with the plight of Palestinians as they do with the complexities and contingencies of daily Muslim lives in England and Bosnia.[1]

Tower Hamlets, an inner-London borough with a colorful history, is home to the largest youth population in Europe, and the largest Muslim population in England. Moreover, half of its population comes from minority ethnic communities. Long before Bangladeshis established themselves as owners of curry houses, Russian Jews ran bagel shops. French Huguenots made it famous for tailoring. Tower Hamlets also spawned the white working-class "cockneys," synonymous with chirpy "Englishness." The change and churn typical of London are vibrant here, along with some of its most striking inequalities. The most vulnerable are Bangladeshis, which is surprising given how socially networked they are. Debates about poverty, for example, were long dominated by secular nationalists of the first generation, who acted as power brokers between their community and the state. In the mid-1980s, their leadership was challenged by second-generation activists who formed an alliance with Labour activists engaged in radical anti-racist campaigns. This municipal radicalism signified a new activist framework whereby councils confronted global problems, from promoting economic justice to supporting liberation struggles. It is important to note that while councils did not bundle all of these ends together, "they often combined in an expression of left statecraft" (Cooper and Herman 2020, 43). Tower Hamlets Council, for example, positioned its proposal to boycott

---

[1] For the sake of brevity, Bosnia and Herzegovina is referred to as "Bosnia" in this book.

Veolia, a French corporation involved in Israel's violations of international law, within an "empowerment strategy" that included opposing privatization and promoting working-class culture.[2] This municipalist, left-of-center politics is now contested by a new generation of idealistic activists who reject secular concerns of their parents and instead show interest in issues they consider relevant to each and every Muslim. As a result, questions about the appropriate Muslim response to the Israeli–Palestinian conflict are easily linked to concerns about Afghanistan and Iraq, on the one hand, and unemployment, lack of public services, and poor housing conditions, on the other. Here, as will become evident to the reader, BDS points to a growing Islamic consciousness among younger generations, and a transition from local, secular municipalism to a transnational, Islamic horizon.

The central Stari Grad neighborhood of Sarajevo, at the same time, is a site of intense Muslim solidarity and western intervention(s), imagined as inhabiting a liminal space between east and west. Broader symbolisms of east and west are echoed in tensions between "cultured" locals and a range of newcomers, including "non-cultured" displaced persons from ethnically cleansed villages and a new wave of believers who took on a version of Islam associated with some of the Arabs who participated in the 1992–1995 war.[3] BDS is debated, interpreted, and adapted within these post-war Bosnian realities. For middle-aged and middle-class Bosniaks, with urban origins and high levels of education, BDS performs a creative merging of Islamic and European attachments and orientations. Against the backdrop of deep longing for Europe, BDS, with its vernacular of human rights and freedom, offers up a counterweight to what is identified as the primitive and "non-cultured" behavior of newcomers. In contrast, for young Bosniaks at the lower end of the social hierarchy, BDS emerges as an emotional response to the stigmatized and marginalized conception of Muslims vis-à-vis Europe, which arguably culminated in the Srebrenica genocide. Here, the popular theme of suffering connects Bosnia with Palestine, and shapes contemporary discourses of Muslim solidarity and

---

2   In February 2011, Tower Hamlets became the first municipality in England to pass a motion to "exclude Veolia from local procurement contracts" (Palestine Solidarity Campaign 2012). Further municipal BDS initiatives drew on affective ties with Palestine, "where friendship and solidarity were expressed through [...] acts of symbolic affinity, political sociability, and material support" (Cooper and Herman 2020, 49). In July 2014, for example, councilors visited the Occupied Territories as an expression of friendship and flew the Palestinian flag to convey solidarity with the people of Gaza "faced with escalating Israeli violence" (Cooper and Herman 2020, 49).

3   Under socialism, the Muslim "east" was just as likely to be viewed in less value-laden ways, "as fellow members of the Non-Aligned Movement and a destination for migrant workers or shopping" (Helms 2008, 105).

community. As I will describe in the chapters that follow, BDS is at once an expression of solidarity and a productive site for discussions regarding the very nature of that solidarity. These divergences on BDS cut across formal politics and state interventions, as well as everyday politics and micropolitics. It is at the intersection of these multiple levels of political practice that I situate the analytical focus of this book.[4]

The vast literature on BDS has focused on its (non)violent nature (Awwad 2012; Bakan and Abu-Laban 2009; Darweish and Rigby 2018) and lawfulness (Bot 2019; Cauffman 2018; McMahon 2014), the debate about the academic boycott of Israel (Beinin 2012; Butler 2006; Maira 2018; Marcus 2015) and the issue of antisemitism (Cannon 2019; J. S. Fishman 2012; Hever 2019; Kaplan and Small 2006; White 2020), with some attention to minority activism in Canada and the United States (Connors Jackman and Upadhyay 2014; Gertheiss 2015). But there has been no discussion on Muslims who show solidarity with Palestine, and recognize it as central to their ethical and political lifeworld. In this book, I am not interested in BDS per se, nor the economic, intellectual, and legal case for and against it. Instead, I treat BDS as a lens through which I grasp modes of action grounded in what Muslims in Tower Hamlets and Stari Grad perceive as Islamic values and ethics. As a result, I contribute not only to literature on pro-Palestinian activism, which tends to downplay and take for granted Muslim solidarity, but also to literature on solidarity activism more generally, which tends to treat questions of ethics as private, and questions of politics as necessarily public (Bellah et al. 1996; Wood 1994; Wuthnow 1991; cf. Lichterman 1996). My point in speaking about "ethics" is not to deny the importance of coalitions, networks, and autonomous reason to politics. Rather, my suggestion is that ethical attitudes and sensibilities are just as important. To dismiss them as irrelevant to politics is an analytical mistake. In this regard, I follow upon a growing recognition by scholars that our political discourses are not the product of critical deliberation alone but also the "way we come to care deeply about certain issues, feel passionately attached to certain

---

4   In this book, I use "Bangladeshi" instead of "Bengali" to distinguish between Islamic Bangladesh and Hindu West Bengal. For the purpose of analytical clarity, I also use the more official term *Bošnjak* (Bosniak), adopted in Bosnia's post-war constitution, instead of the former *Musliman* (Muslim), in use during the Socialist Federal Republic of Yugoslavia (SFRY). I make two exceptions. One in reference to the pre-war period when the term "Bosniak" had not yet officially replaced the term "Muslim," and an exception for quotations that specifically use the term "Muslim." That said, in ordinary conversations, "Bosniak" and "Muslim" are often used interchangeably. Importantly, "Bosniak," which applies to Bosnian Muslims only, should not be confused with "Bosnian," which denotes anyone from Bosnia regardless of ethno-national affiliation.

positions," as well as the traditions of practice through which such attachments and orientations become sedimented into our character (Hirschkind 2006, 30; see also Asad 2003; Mahmood 2012; Schielke 2009). In keeping with this language, one might say that the Muslim community or *umma* is articulated by political discourses that invoke a collective Muslim subject. This book discusses one specific dynamic in the shaping of an umma, that centered around pro-Palestinian activism. That said, I caution against privileging Islam as the singular basis for collectivity and political practice. Through an ethnography of BDS in Tower Hamlets and Stari Grad, I identify instead numerous strands and orientations in the lives of the men and women I came to know who considered BDS germane to one's life as a Muslim.

In short, chapter 2 outlines what I call the BDS "prequel." I combine historical and ethnographic sources to flesh out a method of mobilization in Tower Hamlets and Stari Grad. The six organizations I describe in this book insert their boycott calls into a long tradition of Palestinian resistance, on the one hand, and numerous examples of pan-Islamic resistance to colonialism and imperialism, on the other. Thus, they clearly differ from secular organizations mobilizing for BDS elsewhere. In chapter 3, I move away from historical precedents to reflect on modern-day sociopolitical landscapes in which BDS is grounded and comes to be seen as part of the larger project of realizing Islamic piety. Tower Hamlets has a reputation as the bastion of BDS in England. In a plethora of boycott calls, issued by churches and student associations, artists and trade unions, some of the most original ones come from Tower Hamlets and its Bangladeshi community, which has long suffered from unemployment, lack of public services, and poor housing conditions. Stari Grad, at the same time, has a fairly recent history of violence that has paved the way for strong symbolic ties with the Palestinian people. Here, the calls for boycott against Israel draw parallels between the Israeli–Palestinian conflict and the 1992–1995 war in which Bosniaks were the most likely to be murdered, violently expelled, or otherwise mistreated. In chapters 4 and 5, the attention turns to different imaginaries of BDS in Tower Hamlets and Stari Grad, presuming different relations to structures of social and religious authority, whether grounded in the authority of parents, state institutions, or neighborhood mosques. In Tower Hamlets, the movement is considered a token of devotion to Islam that instills in its participants dignity and pride in the context of local expressions of racism. In Stari Grad, the movement is an emotional response to anxiety that echoes through everyday post-war life, as well as through long history of international favoritism, hypocrisy, and double standards on human rights. The conclusion ties together the main themes of this book in a revealing comparison between Tower Hamlets and Stari Grad, and asks how we might think about the connections between the difficulties and challenges of "being Muslim" and the Palestinian struggle. In exploring the question of political struggle in a broader context, I shed light on important overlaps, and historic solidarity, between the civil resistance of BDS and a number of anti-colonial, anti-imperialist, and anti-racist movements around the world, notably Black Lives Matter.

This book comes at an inflection point for the BDS movement. Eighteen years since its launch, it has succeeded in causing significant furor. In city councils and supermarkets, on college campuses and in concert halls, the movement has awakened participation and given ordinary people the means to act responsibly toward distant others. But it has been less effective in creating a considerable economic dent or policy change. Of approximately 200 countries around the world, 160 have relations with Israel, including six members of the Arab League. That said, as I will argue in this introductory chapter, its effectiveness can also be measured in less instrumental ways and in more proximate places. By demanding freedom, justice, and equality for the Palestinian people, the activists and organizations I describe in this book contribute to the development of cultural dissent, political questioning, and economic change at "home." Here and throughout this book, I attend to these multiple levels of political practice, especially the ways in which other concerns, other parallel and tangential political issues, manifest in, and immanent to, everyday life are articulated through a movement focused on Palestinian rights. The first step is to reflect critically on anthropological debates on resistance and agency.

1   Resistance and Agency

The anti-colonial struggle and the 1989 revolution in Eastern Europe, Black Lives Matter and the "Arab Spring," have shown that resistance has become the operative term in modern political imagination and action. It has also defined a century of efforts to subvert the structures of power that oppress the Palestinian people (see Jamal 2005; Khalidi 2006; Norman 2011; Pappé 2004; Qumsiyeh 2011; Sayigh 2007). In his book, *Boycott, Divestment, Sanctions: The Global Struggle for Palestinian Rights*, Omar Barghouti, a co-founder of the BDS movement and the Palestinian Campaign for the Academic and Cultural Boycott of Israel (PACBI), argues that long before the South African movement's inspiration, "our own [Palestinian] history has had fertile roots of civil resistance against settler colonialism" (Barghouti 2011, 173). Similarly, Ramzy Baroud, a columnist and editor of the *Palestine Chronicle*, argues that pickets, protests, and strikes have long been the most tenacious "common threads in

Palestinian history," especially during the 1930s resistance against the Palestine Mandate (Baroud 2013a, 5). Baroud proposes that this legacy of civil resistance has found its new and evolved form in BDS. In the next chapter, I think more thickly about Baroud's argument, and attend to various discourses of resistance and their role in what I consider to be the "localization" of BDS in Tower Hamlets and Stari Grad. In this regard, I am less interested in "direct resistance" centered on countering the experience of colonial dispossession, and more on explicating the discourses, projects, and relations of resistance centered on the experiential contiguities between the Palestinian people and the men and women I came to know.

In the words of Michel Foucault, "where there is power, there is resistance" (Foucault 1978, 95–96). This also means that, as anthropologist Lila Abu-Lughod observes, "where there is resistance, there is power" (Abu-Lughod 1990, 42). In her rich ethnography of an Awlad 'Ali Bedouin community, she recommends that resistance be used as a "diagnostic of power." This in turn allows her to describe more precisely the operations of power with which her informants are confronted. Although Abu-Lughod makes an important analytical step away from partial or reductionist theories of power, she does not challenge the use of resistance to describe a whole range of human actions, including those which may be indifferent to the goal of opposing hegemonic norms. Anthropologist Saba Mahmood asks whether it is even possible to identify a universal category of acts, such as those of resistance, outside of "ethical and political conditions" within which such acts acquire their particular meaning (Mahmood 2012, 9). The women she studied in Cairo were interested in "living up" to the teachings of Islam not challenging them. This need not mean that they were reproducing their own subordination but rather that agency does not always equate to resistance. Whether one is cautious of resistance like Mahmood (see also Brown 1996; Sahlins 2002; Seymour 2006) or argues for closer attention to uncertainties within it (see Comaroff 1985; Fletcher 2001; Gutmann 2012; Kulick 1996; Moore 1998; Ong 1987; Ortner 1995; Scott 1990; Sivaramakrishan 2005; Speed 2008), the understanding of resistance as subjective as well as social encounter with power encourages us to think of the terms ordinary people use to organize their daily lives that are not simply a gloss for universally shared assumptions about the world and one's place in it, "but are actually constitutive of different forms of personhood, knowledge, and experience" (Mahmood 2012, 16).

In order to elaborate this point, I would like to examine Foucault's argument that power is productive, and we are never trapped by it. In other words, it is possible to modify its hold in particular contexts and following particular strategies. Resistance, in this view, must be carried out in more specific emplaced struggles against power exercised at an everyday, micro level of society. Foucault's "bottom-up" analysis locates power everywhere, but there is no primary or fundamental form of power that dominates society down to the smallest detail. He describes it instead as a field of "heterogeneous relations," exercised only over free subjects, "and only insofar as they are free" (Foucault 1982, 790). Free subjects, according to Foucault, are individual and collective subjects who are faced with a field of possibilities in which several ways of behaving, "several reactions and diverse comportments," may be realized.[5] Central to Foucault's argument is the paradox of "subjectivation"—the processes that secure a subject's subordination are also the means by which a subject becomes a "self-conscious identity and agent" (Butler 1993, 10, cited in Mahmood 2012, 17). Such an interpretation encourages us to conceptualize agency as a capacity for action that specific relations of subordination create and enable. In addition, Foucault cautions us about the emancipatory implications of resistance and resistance movements. His understanding of resistance as internal to power refuses the dream of emancipation and imagines instead more specific emplaced struggles against the tendency of power to tie subjects to their identities and interests in constraining ways. In keeping with this language, one might say that BDS and forms of resistance it engenders need not be based on fixed concepts of subjects' identities and interests. Indeed, for the men and women I met in Tower Hamlets and Stari Grad, BDS was simultaneously a secular movement for Palestinian rights and a political standpoint that was incumbent upon them as Muslims. I might note, in addition, that the appeal to identity overlooks the important differences in power and resources between subjects, and tends to make these differences a source of separation and conflict rather than resistance and change (on this, see Butler 1990; Lorde 1984; Sandoval 2000; Young 1990).

---

[5] Foucault's writings on the Iranian Revolution have been seen by some as denial of power in favor of ethics (see Beaulieu 2010; Dilts 2011). But Foucault does not deny power. He simply moves away from a conception of power in terms of transgression and prohibition to one that is creative and generative of identities and subjectivities. What is at stake in Iran, Foucault writes, is a "revolt of subjectivity" that cannot be explained only in economic terms (Foucault 1979, 8, cited in Afary and Anderson 2005, 255). The "soul of the uprising," according to Foucault, consists in the realization among the revolutionary Shi'ites that they have to change themselves—it is religion that provides this promise of a radical transformation of one's relation to the self, the state, the world, and the divine.

2 Spaces of Resistance

The question whether some alliances are more effective than others is a matter of careful analysis and not of priori theoretical contention. In other words, the basis for deciding which alliances are more effective than others should not be an abstract principle of "coming together" but rather a historical and contextual analysis of resistance. This, according to Foucault, paves the way for an "insurrection of [...] relations of power," which have been insufficiently elaborated in political theory (Foucault 1980, 82). In her influential essay, "Can the Subaltern Speak," Gayatri Chakravorty Spivak argues that relations of power at an everyday, micro level have their own trajectory, history, context, and content (Spivak 1988, 273). They have been, and continue to be, utilized, colonized, and transformed by the mechanisms of "macrological domination," that is, the connections between global capitalism and the state (Spivak 1988, 280; see also Guha 1983; O'Hanlon 1988; Prakash 1990; Stoner 1991). The goal, according to Spivak, is to create independent spaces of resistance, and to think of them as outside the confines of the state. This enables her to "free" power from the domain of political theory in much the same way as Foucault does.

I find it beneficial to think about a distinction between "power over," which speaks of change through the state, and "power to," which includes acts that bypass the state to implement change directly (Holloway 2002, 5; see also Dinerstein 2015; Rabasa 2010; Zibechi 2012). There is a binary antagonism between them, but these are not separate entities. As I hope to show in the chapters that follow, the localization of BDS entails a constant navigation between tactics of "power over" and "power to." These tactics resemble "repertoires of contention" that demand more or less explicitly the state to impose embargoes and sanctions against Israel (Tilly 1986, 2). But they also include an idea of self-managed change that focuses on questions of virtuous practice. Some are ambiguous acts confined to the private sphere of domesticity, family, and home. Others take form of pickets, protests, and strikes. Important here is that BDS is largely decentralized and diverse, allowing the activists and organizations I worked with to frame their goals, and to adapt their tactics, according to the social and political resources available to them.

The localization of BDS is based first and foremost on a recognition and elaboration of frames that connect the Palestinian struggle for freedom, justice, and equality to an international struggle to counter racism, poverty, and gender oppression, among other social and economic ills. Barghouti, for example, argues that the Palestinian boycott against Israel, "and its partners in crime," represent a small but critical part in the broader challenge to "neoliberal [...]

hegemony and the tyrannical rule of multinational and transnational corporations" (Barghouti 2011, 58). Baroud, at the same time, argues that although BDS has "indigenous roots within Palestine's history of resistance," it continues the legacy of other nonviolent movements against injustice and oppression (Baroud 2013a, 5). In the same vein, Raji Sourani, a human rights lawyer based in the Gaza Strip, argues that whether BDS be directed toward the end of apartheid in South Africa, military rule in Burma, or Israel's multitiered oppression of the Palestinian people, "it is a powerful tool utilized by civil society to ensure that systematic violations of human rights end," to bring about justice for the world at large (Sourani 2013, 61).[6]

This way of connecting a particular struggle to broader ones has many examples, such as the civil rights movement, Black Lives Matter, and the ongoing debate about "intersectional feminism." My insistence throughout this book, and one that draws on Spivak, is that the labor and practice of solidarity must be framed in reference to the corresponding social conditions in occupied Palestine, post-imperial England, and war-ravaged Bosnia, as well as the desires and aspirations of ordinary people who navigate these circumstances in their day-to-day lives. For my purpose, the value of comparison is that it helps elucidate distinct forms of experience, memory, and affect that make solidarity possible. For example, as chapter 4 will show, young Bangladeshis interpret BDS in light of their experience of exclusion and significant social deprivation along racial lines. It is important to point out that, while England essentially "exported" its racism to its colonies, which it plundered for wealth and cheap labor, there is a selective amnesia in England about its colonial legacy and a "noxious nostalgia" that taints its misunderstanding of that history (see E. King 2020; Younge 2020). It is in part the erroneous representation England has of its past, and its incapability to address the history of colonial exploitation, that enables the state to "exonerate itself from contemporary racial inequalities" (see Meghji 2020). The broad swaths of frustrated young Bangladeshis espouse forms of activism that revolve around Islamic piety precisely because they are seen as less complicit with mainstream institutions of the state. For young Bosniaks, at the same time, BDS emerges as an impassioned response to Israel's oppressive regime entrenched in European

---

6 In order that the claim I am making not be misunderstood, let me clarify one point. I recognize that BDS terminology, especially the use of "apartheid," is highly controversial and prone to debate. That said, within the frame of this book, the use of BDS terminology is inevitable as it focuses on the sentiments and commitments of two specific BDS campaign milieus—Tower Hamlets and Stari Grad.

hegemony that not only marginalizes Muslims but also accounts for the suffering of Palestinians. As I will argue, the affects and sensibilities of young Bosniaks chafe against the norms and regulatory institutions of the state, a friction that gives rise to new contestatory articulations of ethics, religion, and politics. For their elders, as I suggest earlier in this chapter, BDS represents a creative merging of Islamic and European commitments—a way to distance themselves from supposedly primitive, rural, and religiously radical newcomers, as well as parasitic political elites that use Islam to rationalize an unjust system of wealth and income inequality (see Arsenijević 2014; Mujkić 2016).

The examples I provide above show how BDS is modulated by, and refracted through, recent historical and sociopolitical circumstances. I am glossing over a number of different interpretations for the sake of brevity, but what I want to emphasize here is that BDS enables local concerns and conflicts to be codified through the lens of struggle for freedom, justice, and equality. This should not be taken to mean, of course, that BDS is limited to the kind of thinking and reasoning that I explore in this book. Rather, I highlight the connections between the Palestinian struggle and the contemporary plight of pious Muslims in a variety of national contexts that, I believe, are crucial for the realization of solidarity work in practice. BDS, in this sense, is both an iconic political struggle and a useful lens on the evolving notions of Muslim ethical and political commitment. It is both a resistance movement rooted in Palestine and a catalyst for thinking about political struggle in a broader context. Let me elaborate.

Rights frames, justice frames, and hegemonic frames readily visible in the arguments of well-known activists like Barghouti, Baroud, and Sourani are described as "master frames" (on this, see Carroll and Ratner 1996; Gamson and Mayer 1996; Snow and Benford 1992; Tarrow 1994). That said, a master frame's ability to resonate with different groups does not necessarily indicate a deep resonance—resonance can be superficial or "skin-deep." Greater frame resonance leads to greater mobilizing potential. In this book, I move from the most abstract and encompassing frames, in chapters 2 and 3, to more exclusivist frames that derive meaning from the workings of power and authority that are clothed in local history and culture, in chapters 4 and 5. As I move from one frame to another, I show that BDS lends itself to local interpretations that simultaneously address the goals of the Palestinian struggle and the complexities and contingencies of daily lives of Muslims in different sites.

Scholars from a variety of disciplines, such as anthropology, sociology, geography, and history, have pointed to the localization of transnational social movements, sometimes called "translocal," a term that aptly applies here. Although it has often been used as a synonym for transnationalism, translocality is actually an umbrella term that describes spatial connectedness or "more grounded transnationalism" (see Glick Schiller, Basch, and Blanc-Szanton 1992; Grillo and Riccio 2004; Guarnizo and Smith 1998; Levitt and Glick Schiller 2004; Pieterse 1995; M. P. Smith 2000). Differently put, translocality points to the creation of another type of transnational social space that is grounded in daily lives, activities, and social relations of ordinary people. It describes the ways in which ordinary people, their rituals and practices, "their feelings and understandings of their conditions of existence, [...] modify those very conditions" (M. P. Smith 1992, 493–494). This concept of translocality is one of a transnational grassroots politics, wherein ordinary people can create identities and agencies that challenge multiple levels of power—local, national, transnational, and global. They may, for example, hinder the forces of assimilation (Guarnizo, Portes, and Haller 2003; Kivisto 2001; Morawska 2004; Portes and Rumbaut 1996; Rouse 1992), build identities that were very difficult if not impossible to sustain at "home" (Johnson 1998; Stephen 1996), and challenge the state's administrative capacity to control their interests and movements (Favell 2003; Nagengast and Kearny 1990; Werbner 1997).

Translocality is typically the ethnoscape of migrants, social movements, and coalitions. Some prominent examples include feminist webs and indigenous rights movements in Latin America (Alvarez 1998; Brysk 2000; Thayer 2001), the border crossing of sanctuary activists from the United States (Coutin 1993; Cunningham 1999), and the new labor transnationalism in Europe (Evans 2005; Lillie and Greer 2007). This book draws on and contributes to a large and growing research on translocality. Drawing on ethnographic fieldwork and interviews, I explore some of the ways in which the BDS's narrative of oppression and resistance has been woven into daily acts that create distinct social and political imaginaries. In this regard, I emulate scholars who have used the concept of translocality to develop an agency-oriented approach to mundane, ordinary, and seemingly trivial consumption (see Ehn and Lofgren 2009; Hilton 2008). The sort of consumption that attracts great attention, and one I want to discuss here briefly, is the growing preference for objects that are produced in ways understood to be socially and environmentally good, or at least better than the alternatives on offer.

Originally a set of social and cultural turns caused by the deregulation of markets in the early 1980s (see Roseberry 1996), "ethical consumption" has recently been linked to images of sustainability, human rights, and environmental justice (see Berlan 2012; Goodman 2010; Grimes 2004; Leutchford 2012; Lyon 2009; Raynolds 2002). As it has become more popular, the label has been applied more to a range of activities. Those who go on an ecotourism resort for a holiday rather than a conventional one, who refuse to buy cosmetics that have been tested on animals, who take a train rather than a plane, all are considering the moral nature of objects when deciding whether or not to consume them. According to anthropologist James G. Carrier, "that moral nature springs from the objects' social, economic, environmental, and political context." Ethical consumers, then, "are those whose decisions about what to consume, the 'consumption' part, are shaped by their assessment of the moral nature of that context, the 'ethical' part" (Carrier 2012, 1). Although their goals are varied, ethical consumers have an important thing in common—their motivation and the basis for their assessment come from what they think the realm of economy and society are like, and what they think the relationship between them is and ought to be. As such, ethical consumption is inherently, if not always overtly, political (see Gudeman 2008; Micheletti 2003; Johnston 2008). Finally, since consuming ethically is a preference, it is not only about how to act. In adopting—even stressing—buying decisions as key to achieving goals, ethical consumption recognizes the market as essential to the acquisition and expression of agency through which dynamics of identity and community are organized. This point carries great relevance for my own analysis of the calls for boycott against Israel in Tower Hamlets and Stari Grad.

Defined as an attempt by one or more groups to achieve goals by instructing individual consumers to "refrain from making selected purchases in the marketplace" (M. Friedman 1985, 97), boycott has often been conceptualized and imagined as an act of collective resistance (see Bekin, Carrigan, and Szmigin 2007; M. Friedman 1991; Garrett 1987; Penaloza and Price 1993; Putnam and Muck 1991; Sen, Gürhan-Canli, and Morwitz 2001; Thompson 2004). This line of thought reinforces the dichotomy between private and public, between individual and collective, that has served as the ground on which much of the debate about solidarity activism has proceeded. One of my arguments in this book is that there is an interior economy to boycott that moves away from merely examining celebrations of its resistance and tries to understand the complex motives and reflexivity of its actors (see Clarke 2007; Colins 2012; Littler 2005). This in turn allows me to explore the rarely noticed outcomes of BDS. First, I argue that BDS does not only influence distant outcomes but also the more proximate social relations in Tower Hamlets and Stari Grad as it contributes to cultural dissent, political questioning, and economic change. Second, current debates about BDS are enmeshed in the thick texture of the lives of the men and women I came to know who interpret these debates in light of their struggles to lead moral lives and to be "good" Muslims. I should also point out, however, that many activists and organizations that spearhead

BDS in Europe and elsewhere categorize their practices as explicitly secular. Thus, my ethnographic tracings tend to differ from those of other scholars interested in BDS and context sensitivity (see Carter Haliward 2013; Feld 2014).

3   Self and Authority

One of the questions guiding this book is whether ethical practices of self-formation have consequences beyond the private sphere in which they are carried out. As I suggested earlier, there is a tendency among scholars to presuppose a distinction between public and private, in that, ethical practices are seen as private and thus ignored as consequential to politics. While I will discuss in chapters 4 and 5 some of the ways in which the activism of the men and women I came to know challenges our normative understanding of politics, here I want to point out that "what we take ourselves to be" is connected to how we treat others (Nehamas 1998, 64). In other words, how we understand ourselves, form ourselves, and relate to ourselves is the basis of our interaction with and treatment of others. Echoing Foucault, I argue that here lies an ethically meaningful idea of political practice.

My argument should be familiar to scholars who have alerted us to the inadequacy of "secular vocabularies" for thinking about "new constellations of religion and politics emerging in the world today" (Hirschkind 2006, 31; see also Asad 2003; Mahmood 2012; Schielke 2009). Much of their criticism is directed at the classical argument that religion should be confined to the private sphere, "as the passionate attachments that are said to characterize religious belief corrupt the rationality of political discourse" (Hirschkind 2006, 136). Indeed, religion was long considered a part of society's need for cohesion, but it was not recognized for its potential in challenging the status quo (see Hannigan 1991; C. Smith 1996). In the 1960s and 1970s, when religion was recognized as an antisystemic force, it was primarily through movements that appeared exotic and retreatist (see McFarland 1967; Robbins, Anthony, and Richardson 1978; B. R. Wilson 1970; Wuthnow 1976). The tide has turned a decade later with a growing recognition of religion's role in the success and failure of otherwise secular movements. For example, sociologist James A. Beckford has paid close attention to new spirituality that runs through ideologies of feminism and ecologism, and favors "synoptic, holistic, and [transnational] perspectives on issues transcending the [...] state" (Beckford 1990, 9). More recently, scholars have pointed out that although movements have to overcome a host of factors that can divide and disperse support, religion has the ability to transcend boundaries and supersede differences based on ethnicity and race, class and gender (see Hervieu-Léger 1997; Hondagneu-Sotelo et al. 2004). Religion, in this view, provides symbols and themes that can easily be appropriated by movement leaders (see Byrnes 1991; Barkun 1994; Jelen and Wilcox 2002). This is not to say that movement leaders "fake" religiosity, although some may use "moral issues for political purposes" (Bayat 2005, 903). Rather, as sociologist Asef Bayat argues, the goal has been to emphasize their use of religion for the cause of mobilization (Bayat 2005, 904). On this point, anthropologist James Toth has shown that in order to understand the rise of a radical religious movement in Egypt, and its subsequent transnational transformation, it is important to look at how those who lead it interpret the Qur'an against personal experience of corruption, poverty, and greed. Central to Toth's analysis is the idea that an "Islamically framed focus on social justice" not only gives a movement its particular sense of frustration but also resonates with key dimensions of everyday life in Egypt (Toth 2004, 131).

The relationship between religion and mobilization has also been examined by scholars interested in the transformative effects of "new media" on Muslim communities around the world. Some have suggested that younger generations turn to blogs, social media platforms, and other "cyber-Islamic environments" to infuse new life into concepts like *da'wa* (preaching or proselytizing of Islam), *fatwa* (religious decree), and most often *jihad* (which means both "holy war" and "effort directed at a specific goal") (see Anderson 2003; Bunt 2003; Herrera and Lotfy 2013; Karim 2002; van Bruinessen 2010). New media, to put it succinctly, allows younger generations to challenge more traditional interpreters of Islam in an unprecedented manner. In chapters 4 and 5, I look at a new generation of idealistic activists who confront mosque-based *imams* (those who lead the prayer) and *khatibs* (those who deliver the sermon during the Friday prayer) for their "endless" discussions of proper prayer techniques that say little about how to live piously in a secularizing context. Frustrated at being told "that is just the way it is," they not only reread and reassess the validity of Qur'an and other textual sources but also innovate by creating new public spaces in which supposedly "authentic" readings of Islam are transmitted. This is not a sign of their recent "emancipation" or "coming out" as some scholars have suggested (see Boubekeur 2007; Dassetto and Nonneman 1996; Leman 2000; Waardenburg 1996). Rather, it points to a longer and more complex process that has to account for the transformation and reform of Islamic traditions and the shifting configurations of power that affect generational change, migration, class, and gender.

In their study of "new veiling" in France and Germany, Schirin Amir-Moazami and Armando Salvatore define religious traditions as "institutionally and discursively grounded," and as a set of moral references, "which shape discourses and social practices" (Amir-Moazami and Salvatore 2003, 54). They build on the idea of "living traditions," as philosopher Alasdair MacIntyre calls them, which suppose a variety of moral dispositions on the basis of which traditions are molded and transmitted, formed and reformed. "Living traditions, because they continue a not-yet completed narrative, confront the future whose determinate and determinable character, so far as it possesses any, derives from the past" (MacIntyre 1981, 223). For this reason, the transformation and reform of Islamic traditions is considered a dynamic that cannot be reduced to social-structural fields but also has to account for the inherent search for "coherence of traditions," a force that produces an impetus to self-reform (Asad 1986, 14). If fragmentation occurs, which certainly seems to be the case, it is because traditions, their discourses and institutions, as well as the practices they authorize, have been exposed to "permanent internal interventions," not only in modern times but since their inceptions (Amir-Moazami and Salvatore 2003, 55).

A key background for concretizing these remarks is the process of reform that took place at the end of the nineteenth century and the start of the twentieth century in the most significant centers of the Ottoman Empire. "Upon the intervention of Muslim reformers," engaged as public intellectuals, educators, and government advisors, traditional forms of Islamic reasoning acquired a more public dimension (Amir-Moazami and Salvatore 2003, 55). Muslim reformers provided lessons that focused on the teaching and learning of Islamic scriptures, social practices, and broad issues related to social welfare, economic development, and the moral health and fortitude of the community as a whole. These disciplinary practices were considered germane to the cultivation of the ideal pious self. They also marked the de-facto subjugation of the *ulama* (religious scholars) and the disintegration of their monopoly on religious authority and knowledge. As a result, Islam could be interpreted in a more flexible and relaxed manner. Muslim reformers asserted their religious authority and knowledge via claims of commitment to Islam and correct moral dispositions. Both were understood as necessary in order to address and admonish a fellow Muslim and, in doing so, "rebuild a moral community of the faithful and contribute to its prosperity" (Amir-Moazami and Salvatore 2003, 57).

The rise of literacy, urban mobility, and new media since the 1960s has intensified a proliferation of a critical discourse on Islam. Simply put, Muslims are now more willing to take Islam into their own hands. They rely on their own readings and interpretations of the founding texts, or they follow scholars who question traditional dogmas. The ulama, at the same time, struggle to compete with a myriad of voices reading, debating, and effectively reformulating

Islam on the Internet, on satellite television, and in books and pamphlets. I want to suggest further that translocality, which I discussed at length earlier in this chapter, both enables this reformist discourse and provides spaces in which much of it is elaborated. Specifically, it enables Muslims to recognize, account for, and discuss power asymmetries within Islam, "which may be seen as a different type of hegemony," and provides them with an intellectual environment in which to develop a "counter-hegemonic discourse" (Mandaville 2001, 179; see also Eisenlohr 2012; Gonzalez-Quijano 2003; LeVine 2003; Mandaville 2003). As I will show, BDS is an opportunity for Muslims to not only formulate and enact what they believe to be the appropriate response to the Israeli–Palestinian conflict but also to engage with the question of who, what, and where the umma can be in the time of translocality.

4   Ethnographies of Resistance

My research, and this book, relies on and draws from many different disciplines. In particular, I have been influenced by sociologist Michael Burawoy's work on the "extended case method," which deploys participant observation to situate everyday life in its extralocal and historical context. In short, Burawoy's argument is that by "extending observations over space and time," we uncover unexplicated ways in which ordinary people understand their place within a larger scheme of things and actions they take to shape that place (Burawoy 1998, 17). They recreate, accommodate, and resist the complex webs that entangle them, and weld their resources to "reconfigure what is possible" (Burawoy 2000, 32).[7] An inquiry into the localization of BDS in Tower Hamlets and Stari Grad shows that a transnational discourse on Palestinian rights makes terrain in Tower Hamlets and Stari Grad by engaging the experiences of ordinary people who have long been rooted in their own traditions of resistance. In other words, more generic frames, such as justice and rights frames, resonate with memories and aspirations, fears and hopes, of the men and women I came to know. Through ethnographic detail, I draw attention to the interworkings of transnational ambitions and local realities, and show that, in so much as ways of "being Muslim" have been developed in the course of participation in BDS, the visions of power entailed and the types of resistance

---

7   Although it is common for ethnographic studies to "confine themselves to claims within the dimensions of the everyday worlds they examine" (Burawoy 1998, 5), Burawoy is not alone in "extending out" from the field. In fact, this was one of the hallmarks of the Manchester School of social anthropology (see Epstein 1958; Gluckman 1958; van Velsen 1960).

generated must be understood within the context of available, and often competing, styles and practices.

For five years, from 2009 to 2013, I conducted fieldwork in Tower Hamlets and Stari Grad.[8] In Tower Hamlets, BDS emerged in part out of a trenchant critique against mainstream Bangladeshi community politics of the 1980s and 1990s. Again and again in interview data, young Bangladeshis contrasted a sense of putative parochialism of Bangladesh's independence struggle with a set of welfare needs in Tower Hamlets and geopolitical issues they regarded as relevant to each and every Muslim. At the other end of my selection spectrum was Stari Grad. Here, the localization of BDS appeared to be strongly colored by the 1992–1995 war in which Bosniaks were the most numerous victims. Contrasting conceptions of BDS, as I will show in chapter 5, were articulated within a larger discourse on the current plight of the umma, which often culminated in references to the Srebrenica genocide. The point of such discourse was not victimhood itself but its connotation of innocence, "distance from responsibility," and thus morality, which in turn afforded a base for what anthropologist Elissa Helms calls "claims to legitimacy in the field of the social" (Helms 2013, 4; see also Maček 2007; Stefansson 2007). In this book, I extend Helms's analytic to Stari Grad by exploring how debates over the proper Muslim response to the Israeli–Palestinian conflict brought these local dynamics to light.

Before embarking on any physical journey into the field, I had to confront the issue of how and where to look for translocal connections and solidarity at the root of pro-Palestinian activism in Tower Hamlets and Stari Grad. Finally, I decided to include six organizations that occupied opposite ends of the BDS continuum, and thus pointed to different possibilities of thought and action available in Tower Hamlets and Stari Grad. In Tower Hamlets, I focused on the Palestine Solidarity Campaign (PSC) and Friends of al-Aqsa (FOA), two of the

---

8   In order to elaborate my methodological approach, let me spell out why I opted to do fieldwork in Tower Hamlets and Stari Grad. I noted earlier that in a plethora of boycott calls in England—a stronghold of BDS in Europe—most inventive ones came from Bangladeshis in Tower Hamlets. They described BDS as a marker of pride against social and economic exclusion, wherein Israel was seen as a part of the global North, and Palestine was seen as a notably poor and disposed part of the global South. The idea that boycott has become emblematic of "dissent by the dispossessed and impoverished" also applied to Stari Grad (Nash 2004, 3). Here, it intersected contexts of war and violence. Specifically, boycott calls evoked experiences of mass killing and forced migration, the same experiences that have rallied Muslims around Bosnia during and after the recent war, and in that way deeply connected to religious and ethical imperatives. Such an alignment expanded the tools available to activists and their solidarity work, and made Stari Grad a compelling case for ethnographic exploration.

largest and most effective organizations in England. Young Bangladeshis who gathered around these organizations aspired toward a middle-class status and saw in BDS a chance to confront what they described as an enduring victimization of their community. The idea of victimhood was constructed differently across generations, and it was precisely this generational twist that constituted an important factor in the localization of BDS. In Stari Grad, I concentrated on the Medjunarodni Forum Solidarnosti (MFS-Emmaus), Stand for Justice, Mladi Muslimani, and IslamBosna.ba. Young Bosniaks from poor and lower-income homes, who supported Stand for Justice and IslamBosna.ba, understood BDS to be essential to the restoration and strengthening of the Muslim community in the face of its increasing fragmentation. Although considerably different in their comprehension of BDS—and its role in crafting the Muslim subject—both organizations promoted forms of Islamic practice that stood in contrast to privatized and individualized notions of religion, popular among older Bosnikas from upper- and middle-income strata, who typically favored organizations like the MFS-Emmaus. In comparison to their counterparts in Tower Hamlets, these organizations were rather inactive. Nevertheless, they were the most significant sites in which BDS was situated in daily lives, activities, and social relationships of ordinary people. For this reason, it became essential to ethnographically approach them.

In methodological terms, their leaders were "gatekeepers" or key people I had to pass in order to enter the ethnographic field. To this end, I reached out to activists and scholars who were happy to vouch for me. The process took several months, mostly because key people in Tower Hamlets and Stari Grad put up resistance to being studied at close quarters. Once I was "in," I received invitations to community meetings, conferences, and roundtable discussions. I was asked to do volunteer work. I observed pickets, protests, and strikes. As Tower Hamlets and Stari Grad are both small, I soon became acquainted with a lot of people and heard about even more. The result was that many of the stories and people who told them became connected to each other. When conveying these stories in text, I used pseudonyms. The same pseudonyms are used consistently for the same people, allowing the reader to get to know the different informants, at least to some degree. I also used different writing styles, techniques, and voices, in this way connecting many of the stories and supplementing them with my own observation and participation.

This brings me to me. Naturally, the data I gathered was contingent on who I was—an educated, white, upper-middle-class woman. Bangladeshis in Tower Hamlets in particular had little reason to trust me or my capacity to represent their concerns accurately. I was born in Sarajevo, however, and have found this to be an important part of entering the field. Since April 1992, Sarajevo has become a mark of identity that I am most often identified with. Upon learning I was born in Sarajevo, and have lived through its four-year-long siege, all of the men and women I worked with, and many of the people I met in Tower Hamlets, asked all too familiar questions. "How did you survive?" "Did you lose a family member?" I should also point out, however, that resistance did not disappear on entering the field. After all, as Burawoy reminds us, "there is no escaping the fundamental divergence between observers, no matter how organic, and the interests of their declared constituency" (Burawoy 1998, 23). That said, it became clear early on that my experience of living under siege has made me seem more credible and persuasive. Again and again, I was told that it gave me insight and sensitized me to what was important—a spirit of resistance that flourishes under the most hellish of conditions.[9] In other words, my understanding of BDS in the eyes of those I met in Tower Hamlets was shaped by what I had gone through as a child living under siege.

I had no idea what to expect in Tower Hamlets, but I knew that my knowledge and experience would be conducive to rapport in Stari Grad, where staying in the besieged city has been turned into an unyielding moral hierarchy. For this reason, it mattered less that my name was "Serb-sounding," and thus alluded to my ethno-national background.[10] During the period of my fieldwork, I embraced my double role as a cultural insider—a person speaking the relevant language, familiar with a sense of loss and renewal in Stari Grad—and a professional outsider—an anthropologist with no actual ties to BDS. It is interesting to note that much of the literature on BDS has been produced by the so-called "activist scholars." Their insider positions have clear advantages, but I would argue that outsiders like myself provide valuable perspectives on the taken-for-granted assumptions of informants. I deliberately positioned myself as a question-asker and curious learner, someone with an incomplete knowledge of BDS who thus had to be taught. Although much of my data is affected by, and some even came about as a result of, these roles, I feel that I often engaged in situations where I could observe and listen or

---

9   For an excellent discussion of the impact of the anthropologist's personal biography on fieldwork and the relationships established in the field, see van der Geest, Gerrits, and Aaslid 2012.

10 Based on her fieldwork in Sarajevo, ongoing since the mid-1980s, anthropologist Cornelia Sorabji notes that, although certain surnames are distinctively Bosniak, Croat, and Serb, it is above all forenames that bear witness to one's background. That said, forenames might be subject to interpretations not intended by the name givers, as is often the case with mixed families like mine.

interact in a rather relaxed manner—watching television with my informants, sitting in a café, and so on.

An important part of my data stems from interviews. Some of the interviews had only one interviewee. Others were conducted in people's homes with much of the family and often also some friends present. The interviews were loosely organized by open-ended questions that allowed the space for unique and detailed stories to be told, but provided the flexibility when broaching difficult experiences and memories. Usually, I presented topics which I had found to be important when doing participant observation and which helped steer the conversation. Just as often, the conversation took unexpected detours, some of which became subject of further discussions and interviews with other informants. In total, I conducted forty taped interviews that lasted on average one and a half to two hours. After I had turned off the tape recorder, people typically kept talking for an extra thirty minutes or so. Throughout the book, I quote from both taped interviews and discussions written down post factum. I do not always indicate whether I am dealing with the one or the other, only stating it when I feel it is relevant.

Observations and interviews are the empirical backbone of this book. That said, in the next chapter, I turn to ethnohistorical sources to examine how current debates about BDS have been mapped onto the long and rich history of resistance in Palestine, on the one hand, and many examples of pan-Islamic resistance to colonialism and imperialism, on the other. This in turn allows me to highlight similarities and differences between the movement and other forms of popular resistance. "Extending out," more importantly, allows me to examine the specific sociopolitical climate in which the movement emerged. The failure of the Oslo Accords in general, and the violent suppression of the Second Intifada in particular, revived debates about the human rights violations against Palestinians, and paved the way for a new phase in the Palestinian struggle for freedom, justice, and equality. It is to these real events—conflicts and dramas that took place over space and time—that I now turn.

CHAPTER 2

Palestinian Resistance and the Muslim Boycott

Since its founding eighteen years ago, BDS has grown in prominence. "While it has chalked up only a few economic victories," it has garnered substantial visibility, supporters and also critics internationally (Mansoor 2020). BDS has exposed the subservience of Arab states that have broken their own boycott in search for open cooperation with Israel. Moreover, it has exposed the readiness of the Palestinian Authority (PA) to act as a "subcontractor for the Israeli occupation," criticizing its security and economic alliance with the occupation army (Barghouti 2011, 176). In keeping with this language, one might say that BDS has infringed on the position of the Palestine Liberation Organization (PLO) as the genuine representative and advocate of Palestinians around the world. Writing for *The Guardian*, Nathan Thrall, a Jerusalem-based analyst with the Middle East and North Africa Program of the International Crisis Group, argues that BDS has also "exasperated what is left of the Israeli peace camp" by nudging Palestinians away from an "anti-occupation struggle and toward an anti-apartheid one" (Thrall 2020). Moreover, he argues, in an era of corporate social responsibility, BDS has given "bad publicity to major businesses tied up in Israel's occupation," and has pushed other corporations out of the West Bank (Thrall 2020). It has scrutinized concerts, film festivals, and art exhibits, laying out guidelines for the cultural boycott of Israel, and has politicized academic and sports organizations, demanding that they take a stand on the extremely divisive Israeli–Palestinian conflict.

In England, BDS has brought turmoil to local councils, involving them in legal disputes over the right to boycott products from Israel and its settlements. In the United States, where over two dozen states have passed bills that penalize those who boycott, BDS has pitted Israel's allies against free speech advocates, including the American Civil Liberties Union (ACLU). It has ignited debates in Protestant churches, "some of the largest of which have divested from businesses that profit from occupation, colonization, and apartheid" (Thrall 2020). Moreover, it has become the bane of college administrators, "forced to adjudicate complaints from BDS-supporting professors and students that their free speech has been stifled, and claims by Zionist faculty, donors, and undergraduates that their campuses have become 'unsafe' spaces" (Thrall 2020). Above all, BDS has highlighted an issue that cannot be ignored indefinitely. Seventy-five years after its establishment, Israel flagrantly violates its "obligations under international law, depriving the Palestinian people from enjoying their inalienable rights, including the right to self-determination and the right of return" (Office of the United Nations High Commissioner for Human Rights 2022).

BDS has been recognized as a qualitatively different stage in the struggle against these pervasive violations of Palestinian rights, but it is neither a new phenomenon nor is it an alien one. In fact, many acts of civil resistance, such as boycotts, strikes, sit-ins, and demonstrations, have become a mainstay in Palestinian history. It is outside the scope of this book to engage in a thorough discussion of the long and rich history of Palestinian resistance and struggle for freedom, justice, and equality. That said, in order to provide some context for the chapters that follow, I present here a panoramic analysis of boycotts and other historical forms of struggle against Israel from within and outside the Middle East and the broader Arab world. Historical contextualization, in this sense, allows me to connect the ongoing BDS movement with the state-based Arab League boycott, the Beit Sahour tax revolt, transnational solidarity, and the call for jihad through consumer boycotts, issued by the class of religious scholars or ulama in the aftermath of Ariel Sharon's symbolic assertion of Israel's sovereignty over the Temple Mount. One of the key questions that follows from this panoramic analysis is how boycott has come to be thought of in religious terms.

1 The Palestinian Call for BDS and Transnational Solidarity

In March 2002, Israel launched Operation Defensive Shield in the West Bank—the largest military invasion into the territory since the 1967 Arab–Israeli War. All major Palestinian cities and nearby villages were reoccupied by the Israel Defense Forces (IDF) during the operation with strict curfews imposed, movements restricted, and international journalists, human rights monitors, and medical personnel denied entry to assess conditions and provide humanitarian assistance. In the middle of Israel's invasion, some of the leading Palestinian intellectuals and academic published a letter online, calling upon all those who oppose occupation, apartheid, ethnic cleansing, and war crimes, "those who are committed to justice and peace," to use the momentum they have generated to "break the conspiracy of silence among governments," and to demand they "end military assistance to Israel, suspend economic ties, and support the prosecution of war criminals" (Abdel-Shafi et al. 2002).

Five months later, a range of Palestinian civil society organizations, including the General Federation of Trade Unions in Palestine (GFTUP), the Palestinian Center for Peace and Democracy (PCPD), and the Palestinian Federation of Women Action Committees (PFWAC), published a new call for boycott against Israel that drew on the program of action prepared at the third World Conference Against Racism (WCAR) held in Durban in August 2001. This NGO document branded Israel a "racist apartheid state guilty of genocide," and called for an "end to its crimes against the Palestinian people" (on this, see Maisel 2003; Walden 2004). A year after Durban, with Israel still engaged in military occupation of the West Bank and Gaza Strip, Palestinian civil society organizations referred to Article 425 that declared a policy of "complete and total isolation of Israel" as in the case of South Africa, and the imposition of mandatory and comprehensive sanctions and embargos. For the sake of freedom and justice, Palestinian civil society organizations implored academic and cultural institutions, companies, political parties, and trade unions, as well as concerned individuals, "to strengthen and broaden the [...] Israel boycott campaign" (Palestinian Civil Society Organizations 2002). This call was part and parcel of a growing transnational solidarity movement at a grassroots and civil society level. Let me elaborate.

In the first months of the Second Intifada, students at the University of California in Berkeley erected mock checkpoints and wielded banners calling to "Divest from Israeli Apartheid." In the following year, the first formal divestment campaign was launched by Students for Justice in Palestine (SJP). In February 2002, in coordination with the San Francisco chapter of the American–Arab Anti-Discrimination Committee (ADC), SJP hosted the first national Palestine Solidarity Movement (PSM) conference. One of the resolutions adopted at the conference expressed an unreserved support for the Second Intifada. "We, the national student movement for solidarity with Palestine, declare our solidarity with the popular resistance to Israeli occupation, colonization, and apartheid." The PSM held four additional conferences at the University of Michigan, Ohio State University, Duke University, and Georgetown University. The conference originally announced for Rutgers University was held in a nearby motel after it had failed to get permission to use a university facility (see Carter Hallward and Shaver 2012; Downs 2006; Leibowitz 2007; J. K. Wilson 2008). In May 2002, a pro-divestment petition made rounds at Harvard University and the Massachusetts Institute of Technology (MIT). Six months later, faculty and students at Columbia University called for a divestment of funds from all companies that produce or sell arms and military hardware to Israel. Similar calls were made across the pond in England, as well as in France, Germany, and Australia, gaining the support of several Israeli academics and many Palestinians.

The calls for divestment were also on the rise among various faith-based groups. Several churches in the United States, such as the Episcopal Church, the Evangelical Lutheran Church, the Presbyterian Church, the United Church of Christ, and the United Methodist Church, made statements calling for economic pressure on companies that support or maintain Israel's occupation, contribute to the expansion or maintenance of illegal settlements, and assist any group that enables violent attacks against civilians (see Baumgart-Ochse 2017; Stockton 2015). In June 2004, the Presbyterian Church became the first to take up a phased, selective divestment as a means of supporting the Palestinian struggle for freedom, justice, and equality. The United Methodist Church, the United Church of Christ, the Church of England, and the World Council of Churches followed thereafter. This, according to Barghouti, confirmed that grassroots support, even in the western mainstream, "for the justness of the Palestinian cause was [...] robust" (Barghouti 2011, 54). The launch of the Palestinian Campaign for the Academic and Cultural Boycott of Israel (PACBI) by a group of Palestinian academics and intellectuals in Ramallah has helped to channel these early transnational efforts into a vibrant form of solidarity.

In July 2004, the PACBI called upon people of conscience in the international community of academics and intellectuals to comprehensively and consistently "boycott all Israeli academic and cultural institutions as a contribution to the struggle to end Israel's occupation, colonization, and system of apartheid" (Palestinian Campaign for the Academic and Cultural Boycott of Israel 2006). The call was based on two key premises. First, that academics from around the world have historically shouldered the moral responsibility to fight injustice, as manifest in their struggle to abolish apartheid in South Africa. Second, that Israeli institutions of higher education, and the majority of Israeli academics, have either contributed to maintaining, defending, and justifying the multitiered oppression of the Palestinian people, or have been complicit through their silence. These institutions, their products, and all the events they sponsor and support, therefore, had to be boycotted. Furthermore, the PACBI call urged artists and cultural workers to refrain from attending and taking part in conferences and lectures with complicit institutions. Although a number of academics, artists, and cultural workers, especially in the United States, supported the PACBI call, others like Cary Nelson, the former president of the American Association of University Professors (AAUP), criticized it for violating the principles of academic freedom and for encouraging censorship. Supporters, in turn, emphasized the incompatibility between insisting on the academic freedom of one group while denying and censoring "discussions about the fundamental human rights of another" (Barghouti 2010, 105, cited in Carter Hallward 2013, 28). They lauded the PACBI call for outlining the parameters of normalization as the participation in any project, initiative, and activity, in Palestine or abroad, "that aims [...] to bring together Palestinians [...] and Israelis, people or institutions, without placing as its goal resistance and exposure of the Israeli occupation and all forms of discrimination and oppression against Palestinians" (Palestinian Campaign for the Academic and Cultural Boycott of Israel 2011). While critics noted that the PACBI call discouraged bridge-building efforts between Israelis and Palestinians, it set up a coordinated boycott movement among Palestinian civil society organizations. More importantly, it recognized that a growing transnational solidarity movement needed to be anchored in the long and rich history of Palestinian resistance to Israeli oppression in all its dimensions.

Three days after the PACBI call was made, the International Court of Justice (ICJ) issued an advisory opinion on the legal consequences of constructing a wall in the Occupied Territories. The ICJ ruled that Israel's separation barrier was illegal and had to be dismantled forthwith, that Israel needed to offer reparations to those it had harmed, and that every signatory of the Geneva Convention relative to the Protection of Civilian Persons in Time of War was required to "ensure compliance by Israel with international law" (International Court of Justice 2004). Israel ignored the ruling, and neither the PLO nor the international community tried to enforce the court's ruling. In fact, several founding members of BDS have noted that had there been an attempt to implement the ICJ's ruling, there would not have been a BDS call (on this, see Baroud 2018; Thrall 2018). We might note, in addition, that BDS represented something of a last resort. "Coming after the collapse of the Camp David summit, Israel's reoccupation of the cities and towns of the West Bank and Gaza Strip shattered any remaining pretense that Palestinians had or would acquire something approaching sovereignty or real authority over any part of their land" (Khalidi 2020, 338). It exacerbated the political differences among Palestinians and underlined the absence of a viable alternative strategy, revealing that Oslo had failed, that the use of guns and suicide bombings had failed, "and that for all the casualties inflicted on Israeli civilians, the biggest losers [...] were Palestinians" (Khalidi 2020, 339; see also Rabbani 2006; Tessler 2009). Such political fragmentation, in combination with attacks carried out by the Israeli military against any form of collective resistance, reduced not only collective acts but also collective perception of resistance. Hamas, for example, offered young activists a greater sense of purpose to their resistance as a religious obligation, which in turn, challenged both the official discourse of the Arab League and the diplomatic course of the PLO that had done little to bring occupation to an end (on this, see Hilal 2012; Lybarger 2007; Mishal and Sela 2000; Roy 2011; Schanzer 2008; Seitz 2006).

Against the backdrop of post-Oslo hopelessness, and in the midst of political division and disarray, BDS indicated the rebirth of active solidarity with the Palestinian cause. It gave activists in Palestine and internationally a way to be on the offensive against, rather than simply reacting to, Israel's violations of international law and human rights. On the first anniversary of the ICJ's ruling against Israel's wall, more than 170 Palestinian civil society organizations endorsed the call for BDS, modeled after the earlier call by the PACBI. They spanned the political spectrum, including trade unions, refugee camp committees, prisoners' societies, and cultural centers. Importantly, their innovation was not in the strategies and tactics advocated. As I mentioned earlier, boycott and divestment campaigns were common in 2005, and even sanctions had been proposed. What was innovative was the merging of different campaigns for boycott, divestment, and sanctions around three basic rights that corresponded to the main components of the indigenous Palestinian population. First, freedom for Palestinians in the Occupied Territories. Second, equality for Palestinian citizens of Israel. Third, justice for Palestinian refugees, including the right to return to their homes and properties. While rooted and informed by almost a century of Palestinian struggle against settler colonialism, this comprehensive rights-based approach was inspired mainly by the anti-apartheid movement in South Africa (AAM). It is worth noting that the charge of apartheid, which had become prominent after the start of the Second Intifada, was not just a provocative analogy to South Africa but a legal claim, based on the crime of apartheid as defined in international conventions and the founding statute of the International Criminal Court (ICC). In the 2002 Roma Statute of the ICC, apartheid is defined as an institutionalized regime of "systematic oppression and domination by one racial group over any other racial group or groups," and committed with the intention of maintaining that regime. According to Barghouti, the use of the "apartheid" tag helped galvanize the Palestinian boycott movement, allowing it to set new parameters and clearer goals for the "growing […] support network, sparking or giving credence to boycott and divestment campaigns around the world" (Barghouti 2011, 56). That said, a genuine concern raised by solidarity groups around the world regarding boycott calls coming from Palestine has been the striking absence of an "official" national body behind them. In what follows, I want to focus on the formal Arab League boycott, discerning its characteristics, vulnerabilities, and potential legacies, all of which, I would suggest, hold importance for today's BDS.

2 The Arab League Boycott

In spite of their rivalries during the late 1940s and early 1950s, Arab states expressed what Avi Kober, a Senior Research Associate with the Begin-Sadat (BESA) Center for Strategic Studies, has called a commitment to "cooperation on the issue of Israel" (Kober 2002, 39). Regional alliances and coalitions formed on the back of secular Arab nationalism, in this sense, reflected a strong emotional commitment to cooperation but, more importantly, they were meant to counterbalance the perceived threat coming from Israel. This in perhaps best illustrated by organizations like the Arab League whose aim was to sustain relations between Arab states, and to participate in the coordination of their political plans and foreign policy. Although it lacked any binding power, the Arab League reflected a sense of dedication to the ideological and political project of Arabism as made obvious by its reaction to the Israeli Declaration of Independence in May 1948. Azzam Pasha, the then-General Secretary of the Arab League, told the *Jerusalem Post* that member states were fighting for an Arab Palestine. "Whatever the outcome," he explained, "the Arabs will stick to their offer of equal citizenship for the Jews in Arab Palestine and let them be as Jewish as they like. In areas where they predominate, they will have complete autonomy" (on this, see Caplan 2009; Diab 2012; Segev 2011). This position, according to Pasha, reflected an unjust decision by the United Nations to "give more than 50 percent of the Palestinian land to the Jews although they were legally entitled to 7 just percent." The Arabs were thus determined to act within a frame of alliances and coalitions when dealing with the newly formed state.

Pasha's statement was emblematic of a trend that was readily visible before 1948. For example, the Arab League passed a resolution in December 1945 that proclaimed "Zionist products and goods" undesirable in member states. "To permit them to enter [...] would lead to the realization of the Zionist political goals" (on this, see Joyner 1984; Losman 1972). Two months later, the Permanent Boycott Committee (PBC) was established in the interest of formally organizing the Arab League boycott, which in turn led to the establishment of the Central Office for the Boycott of Israel (CBO). In December 1954, the CBO announced a set of rules that clearly outlined the conduct of member states when dealing with Israel. These included travel bans and diplomatic embargos, but a bigger aspect of the Arab League boycott was a taboo of the Arab–Israeli commercial ties, which was difficult to break even after the Oslo Accords had been signed. This was because national boycott offices, which worked with the Ministry of Economy and Foreign Trade and representatives of the Boycott Central Bureau (BCB), monitored regional trade and reported their findings at the Arab League meetings. Those member states that traded with Israel, and thus rejected the principles of Arab solidarity, were exposed to harsh penalties and sanctions. For example, after the peace treaty between Egypt and Israel was formally signed in Washington in March 1979, Egypt was expelled from the Arab League and then boycotted in a move that several scholars have described as utterly ineffective (see Barnett 1998; Kaye 2001; Sarna 1986).

In this regard, it is worth noting that Egyptian leftists opposed the treaty for conceding Egyptian sovereignty over foreign and economic policies and, in so doing, enhancing the Israeli and American power in the region (see Aran and Ginat 2014; Starr 2009). This leftist critique known as "anti-normalization" was in fact an echo of a wider Arab discontent, especially as it became evident that Israel had no intentions of implementing the treaty's articles that pertained to resolving the Israeli–Palestinian conflict. As a reward for having made peace with Israel, Egyptian politicians not only faced harsh penalties and sanctions but found that the treaty gave them little leverage to contest "even the most egregious acts of Israeli aggression," notably the 1982 invasion of Lebanon (Colla 2006, 250). This in turn drove the wedge between Egypt and radical states like Syria even further, and paved the way for a shift in the politics of moderate states, suggesting that additional links in the chain would soon follow Egypt, and that the Arab League boycott would become a marginal issue in the long run (see Baumgarten 2005; Khalidi 2014; Louis and Shlaim 2012; Schulze 2017).

If the treaty rendered Egyptian politicians impotent to confront Israel, Egyptian writers, literary critics, and filmmakers could refuse to cooperate with those aspects not in the hands of politicians—cultural exchange, professional cooperation, and thus the normalization of relations between Egypt and Israel. The anti-normalization movement opposed normalizing the abnormal reality of "occupation, colonization, and apartheid" (Salem 2005, 104). It shook up the status quo. In addition, it proved to be a fertile space of resistance and solidarity with the Palestinian people, as manifest in the PACBI call I discussed earlier, as well as other earlier attempts to enact economic, political, and cultural boycotts. For example, the United National Leadership of the Uprising (UNLU), a coalition of political parties loyal to the PLO established during the First Intifada, was clearly influenced by the Egyptian anti-normalization efforts. Its pamphlets or communiqués—first of which was issued in January 1988—brought the Palestinian people to the streets and instructed them to reject all forms of normalization with Israel through sit-ins, strikes, petitions, demonstrations, and boycotts (see Mi'Ari 1999; Mishal and Aharoni 1994; Urban 1994). At the same time, local committees organized at the village level created an alternative infrastructure for providing basic services that had typically been administered by Israel. For example, women focused on home economics and planting their own gardens to help support their families at the time when many male breadwinners were imprisoned or otherwise unable to work (see Hiltermann 1991; Kuttab 1993). As a result, a more general boycott of Israeli goods and services was instituted. Some villages, like Beit Sahour, went as far as to institute a tax boycott.

In September 1989, this small village on the outskirts of Bethlehem employed the motto "No Taxation Without Representation," as individuals withheld taxes and several hundred businesses refused to pay the value-added-tax to Israel (see Aburish 1993; Grace 1990; M. E. King 2007; Robinson 1997; Stephan 2003). Israel's retaliation was swift and harsh. Beit Sahour was placed under siege, telephone lines were cut, and curfews were imposed. The IDF was brought in to stop and search people in the streets and to confiscate property. A number of well-known BDS activists, such as filmmaker Raed Andoni and visual artist Amer Shomali, along with Barghouti, Baroud, and Sourani, have claimed that this exaggerated military crackdown and show of force was Israel's attempt to "teach Beit Sahourians a lesson" and suppress their "war without guns." Beit Sahour, in their view, took civil disobedience to a whole new level by refusing to pay taxes and boycotting Israel's occupation and all of its institutions. Thus, it is not surprising that Beit Sahour has become a focal point of various discourses on Palestinian resistance. I want to suggest further that it has come to be conceived as a culmination of two overlapping histories. The first concerns the First Intifada. The second concerns an enduring tradition of Palestinian resistance that spans generations. "We are once again witnessing another chapter of that same history," Baroud has claimed. "This time it is being written with the help of thousands of solidarity activists around the world. This time the boycott is global, and unlike [its] tactics against Beit Sahour, Israel will no longer be able to isolate its enemies using tanks and helicopters. This time it is the one being isolated without guns or even a single bullet" (Baroud 2013b). From this perspective, the legacy of nonviolent resistance and its initiative by ordinary Palestinians has found its new and evolved form in BDS.

The mounting popularity of BDS described above stood in striking contrast to boycott campaigns organized by the Arab League. In the first eight years after Oslo, a quorum of the regional CBO had failed to meet, reflecting the indifference of member states toward Palestine and their new commitment to ending the secondary and tertiary levels of boycott.[1] The Second Intifada renewed the relevance of the Arab League boycott, at least on the surface. After a meeting held in Amman in March 2001, the Arab League declared that in light of Israel's clear suspension of the peace process, the interest in the CBO had been renewed. Seven months later, at a meeting in Damascus, nineteen of the Arab

---

1   A primary boycott prohibited direct trade and relations between Israel and the Arab League members. A secondary boycott was directed at companies from around the world that did business with Israel. "A third tier of the [Arab League] boycott blacklisted firms that traded with other companies carrying out business with Israel, or which maintained Israeli capital" (Grassroots Palestinian Anti-Apartheid Wall Campaign 2007, 17).

League's twenty-two member states discussed the internal structural issues relevant to the calls for the renewal of the CBO. Two years later, the Council of the Arab Inter-Parliamentary Union (AIPU) called for a termination of all forms of normalization with Israel through the CBO. Similarly, the Conference of Arab Regional Offices of Liaison Officers held in Damascus in April 2004, sought to inject new energy into the CBO. In his statement to the *People's Daily Online*, the then-General Commissioner of the Arab Regional Offices of Liaison Officers, Ahmad Khazaa, explained that the calls to reboot the CBO and the Arab League boycott "represent an active reaction to the barbaric policy of Israel, and a struggle of moral values" (cited in Grassroots Palestinian Anti-Apartheid Wall Campaign 2007, 25). In addition, a four-day-long meeting of the Arab Boycott Bureau held in Damascus in May 2006, defined the Arab League boycott as a peaceful means to bring about change, no doubt inspired by the rise of well-publicized BDS campaigns around the world. However, in spite of the repeated calls, statements, and promises, the Arab League boycott took on an increasingly rhetorical form, and seemed to have no impact in altering reality in which normalization continued to characterize relations with Israel.[2]

The PLO, in disarray for years, was completely silent in light of these exercises in rhetorical posturing for Palestine. The PA, with its circumscribed mandate and the constraints imposed upon by the Oslo Accords, was inherently incapable of supporting any effective resistance tactic, "especially one that evokes injustices beyond the 1967 occupation" (Barghouti 2011, 56). These large Palestinian factions, "[seemed] unable to recognize the indispensable role of civil resistance. Either by inertia or reluctance to evaluate critically their programs in light of a changed international situation, these forces became addicted to the military model of fighting the occupation, ignoring the troubling moral questions raised by indiscriminate forms of that resistance and its failure to achieve positive ends" (Barghouti 2006, 55). The status quo started to shift in August 2009, when the Sixth General Assembly of the Fatah Movement affirmed a strong commitment of Palestinian leaders to popular struggle as the main form of resistance against occupation, colonization, and apartheid (on this, see Barghouti 2011; Jacob 2009). Although much criticism has been leveled at the Fatah-dominated PA and its call for boycott, which came five years after

---

2 In November 2021, Qatar and Israel signed an agreement allowing Israeli diamond traders to operate in Doha, "and Qatari diplomats are the primary interlocutors with the Israelis on Gaza" (Cook 2022). Saudi Arabia, at the same time, is a virtual party to the Abraham Accords, the term used to refer collectively to normalization agreements between Israel and the United Arab Emirates and Bahrain.

the absolute majority in Palestinian civil society had called for BDS, there was a sense of vindication nevertheless. Even the PA recognized the power of non-violent resistance. This helped underline the consensus among Palestinians in support of boycott as a form of struggle against Israel's violations of international law and human rights. At the same time, for many Muslims around the world, boycott has come to mark a particular kind of religious obligation. It is to this interpretation of boycott that I now turn.

3 Resistance Online

In January 2002, around 130 religious scholars from Europe, Africa, the Far East, and the Middle East met in Beirut's famous Commodore Hotel for the Conference of the Scholars of Islam. At that conference—historically significant because it took place a few months after the September 11 attacks, "at a time when the pressure to recoil from the rhetoric of violent jihad had reached a high point"—representatives of Hamas and Hezbollah agreed that religious scholars should actively promote consumer boycotts of Israel as a lawful, easily defensible, and even moral means of supporting the Palestinian resistance (Halevi 2012, 45). In April 2002, religious scholars visited Cairo for a second conference at al-Azhar University, where they discussed the effects of the September 11 attacks on Muslims everywhere. They worried about the return of "culture war" and "clash of civilizations" to American politics. At the same time, they resented the pressure to reform religious institutions and enact a "liberal Islam." The September 11 attacks had set in motion a wave of "sedition by the people against their religion," and that kind of contention, religious scholars argued, posed a danger to Muslims everywhere (Halevi 2012, 46). For this reason, in addition to earlier calls that targeted Israel specifically, they called for a consumer jihad against the United States, which they considered an oppressive power that abetted the occupation of Palestine, and encouraged Muslims everywhere to boycott as a way to "fight in the path of God" (Halevi 2012, 47). Note that this framing of boycott as an act of jihad draws on a twentieth century tradition in which jihad has come to suggest both a spiritual struggle of conscience and an effort to transform wider society (on this, see Stephan 2009; Wagner 2008). In these arguments, these aspects of jihad are not just complementary but inherently conjoined dimensions of inner and outer transformations driven by moral actions undergirded by love and fear of God.

The defense of boycotts as jihadi acts spread among the ulama between October 2000, following Ariel Sharon's symbolic assertion of Israel's sovereignty over the Temple Mount, and April 2006, when the boycott of Danish products began to wind down.[3] That said, in the aftermath of the September 11 attacks, as suggested by the conferences in Beirut and Cairo, scholars joined the boycotting caravan en masse. Looking for a popular alternative to Islamic militancy and extremism, they promoted boycotts with urgency and issued fatwas that called on Muslims everywhere to forgo enemies' products and services. Boycott fatwas first appeared on the personal websites of more mainstream *muftis* (juriconsults or scholars who interpret and explain Islamic law), television scholars, and university professors, but were later reposted on several highly trafficked websites like IslamOnline.net, Muslm.net, and Sahab.net. What is important for a number of themes at the center of this book is that these fatwas were then translated into English by websites registered in the Middle East, such as AlMinbar.com and OnIslam.net, as well as websites registered in Europe, such as InMinds.com and IslamBosna.ba. Their goal was to resurrect the Muslim community politically, and to bring it behind the boycotting banner with a sense of unity, solidarity, and power. No one spoke about this more eloquently and persuasively than Egypt's Yusuf al-Qaradawi who tried again and again to rally the umma for a consumer jihad, first against Israel, then against the United States and Denmark.

3.1   *The Consumer Jihad from the Tobacco Protest to Fatwas Online*

Most scholarship on Middle Eastern boycotts dates back to the mid-1970s when historians and political scientists wrote about the 1973 oil embargo and the Arab League's official boycott (see Sherbiny 1976; Zacher 1979). They referred to an "Arab" rather than to a "Muslim" boycott in part because those who defended this political instrument as lawful, "by international [...] standards," did so using a secular, nationalist discourse (Halevi 2012, 46). In 1975, for example, the then-General Commissioner of the CBO proclaimed that the organization had neither a racial nor a religious nature. Such language continued to be used during the First Intifada, when Hanna Siniora, a member of the Palestine National Council (PNC), called for a boycott of Zionist products, urging all Palestinians to join a nonviolent movement of civil disobedience led by younger generations that believe "in a secular state and a secular ideology" (Siniora 1988, 3). Echoes of this secular, nationalist discourse could still be heard years later, in newspaper editorials, diplomatic statements, and faintly religious decrees. That said, the authors of these decrees also adopted a pan-Islamic rhetoric that coupled boycotting and jihad, and used new media in general, and the Internet in particular, to call on Muslims everywhere to join the struggle against a common enemy, notably Israel, the United States, and

---

3   Religious scholars called for a boycott of Denmark following the *Jyllands-Posten*'s publication of twelve editorial cartoons in September 2005, most of which depicted the Prophet.

Denmark. They also targeted, albeit sporadically, Russian, British, and Dutch products.

The historical roots of this online discourse lie not in the official Arab calls for boycott against Israel but in earlier, pan-Islamic efforts to resist imperial hegemony and Zionism through boycotts and embargos. Indeed, fatwas seeking to restrict commerce with the imperial enemy have a long tradition that stretches back to a decree attributed to Mirza Shirazi, an Iranian *marja'* (literally, "source of emulation"). In 1891, he warned Iranians that consuming tobacco, in concession to British commercial dominance, was equal to war against the "Imam of the Age" (see Keddi 1966; Lambton 1987; Moaddel 1994; Omid 1994). In his discussion of the origins, development, and popularity of boycott fatwas, historian Leor Halevi argues that early in the twentieth century, resistance movements established a strong association between "boycotting and jihad" (Halevi 2012, 49). For example, during the Constitutional Revolution of Iran, demonstrations against Russian and British products accompanied calls for jihad (see Abrahamian 1979; Afary 1996). In 1921, one of India's leading Islamic organizations issued a fatwa in resistance to British imperial rule. Signed by more than one hundred scholars, the Jamiat Ulama-i-Hind's fatwa banned "any commercial exchange by which the British may acquire strength" (Bamford 1925, 251–252, cited in Halevi 2012, 49). In 1935, a few years after he had persuaded the General Islamic Congress to support a resolution "against the purchase of Zionist products," Mohammed Amin al-Husseini, the then-Grand Mufti of Jerusalem, "issued a fatwa that condemned the sale of the Palestinian land to the Jews" (Kupferschmidt 1987, 244–245). In 1946, Hassan al-Banna, an Egyptian imam best known for founding the Muslim Brotherhood, summoned Egyptians to a jihad and urged them to "boycott Britain economically, culturally, and socially" (Mitchell 1969, 50).

Of all the actors to promote jihadi boycotts, none was more eloquent and persuasive than al-Qaradawi. In April 2002, at the al-Azhar conference I mentioned earlier, this renowned religious scholar delivered perhaps the most famous fatwa, "Boycotting Israeli and American Goods." He reached an audience of tens of millions through an Al Jazeera television program "The Sharia and Life," and he used his platform to call for a complete boycott of enemies' products and manufactured goods. "Each riyal and dirham," al-Qaradawi proposed, "that Muslims spend to buy Israeli and American goods becomes in the end a bullet to be fired at the hearts of our brothers and sons in Palestine." Thus, "it is an obligation not to help them [...] by buying their goods. To buy their goods is to support tyranny, oppression, and aggression" (al-Qaradawi 2002). On his personal website, three weeks later, al-Qaradawi described what he dubbed the "Muslim boycott" as a kind of passive resistance that adds to a balance of active resistance "our brothers carry out in the land of prophecies, the land of military outpost, and of holy war" (cited in Halevi 2012, 52). In his view, boycott was mandatory whenever the goal of weakening Israel and the United States could be achieved peacefully. Notably, al-Qaradawi advised that boycotting be accompanied not by violence but simply the sincere intention that gives religious significance to military jihad. He also paid homage to Gandhi's struggle and other movements "for freedom from colonialism," suggesting that boycott is in the hands of the nation and masses alone. "Let us use this weapon to resist our national and religious enemy, to make them know we are still alive, and that this umma will not die" (al-Qaradawi 2002). In short, in addition to supporting Palestinian resistance, al-Qaradawi put forth other, bigger goals. He saw the possibility of boycott by 1.5 billion Muslims as a way to rejuvenate the umma politically and "show its desire to protect what is holy."

According to al-Qaradawi, women played an important role in these boycott causes—one even more important that the role of men. "Women," al-Qaradawi argued, "manage the needs of the house and purchase the required commodities and utensils." This invocation of women's boycotting power stemmed in part from historical experience. For example, in the 1920s and 1930s, in support of nationalist movements for economic independence, Egyptian and Palestinian women formed committees to boycott foreign products (see Baron 2005; Fleischmann 2003). Inspired by this history, al-Qaradawi developed a markedly gendered take on boycott. In chapter 5, I will discuss the calls for boycott against Israel that relegate women to the private sphere of domesticity, family, and home. It is important to note, however, that neither al-Qaradawi, nor boycott leaders in Stari Grad impressed by his teachings, reduce the role of women to "mistresses of the house." In fact, as al-Qaradawi's fatwa makes clear, women are understood to nurture boys and girls in the spirit of jihad, and educate them in what they must do for their community, on the one hand, and what they must do to their community's enemy, on the other. "When the children gain awareness, they will commit to the cause and will carry on the boycott enthusiastically. Later, they will lead their own fathers and mothers" (al-Qaradawi 2002). In its charter, Hamas also referred to connected and complementary roles for women in the struggle against Israel's multitiered oppression—those of mothers and those of pious Muslims. "Women have a no lesser role than that of men. They produce men and play a great role in guiding and educating the new generation" (cited in Ward 2009, 111; see also Hammami 1997; L. Hudson 1994; Jad 2005; Peteet 1997).

In chapter 4, I will show that this "generational," and markedly gendered, approach to boycott is typical of first-generation Bangladeshis who consider it a form of instruction transmitted from one generation to the next. But they also emphasize the duty of children to take over and make sure that the boycott continues when parents get old. That said, BDS and its boycott measure cannot be interpreted as a linear process or a one-sided transmission. It can also work the other way around. What I am suggesting here is that many of the young Bangladeshis who make up the backbone of BDS in Tower Hamlets claim to have encouraged their parents to join the movement as a way of reflecting over the meaning and implication of their commitment to Islamic piety.

One of the points that I insist on throughout this book is that BDS, while indebted to a century of Palestinian resistance, articulates local struggles over authority, legitimacy, and representation for which issues of class, gender, and generation are important. From the standpoint of my argument here, it is interesting to note that mainstream and radical tendencies in Tower Hamlets and Stari Grad agree that boycotts are incumbent upon every virtuous Muslim in light of governmental inaction. In his fatwa, al-Qaradawi honed in on this inability of governments to break relations with Israel and the United States. "They do not listen to us. For this reason, we turn to people, that they might boycott. [...] No weapon remains with us except for the boycott," he contended (al-Qaradawi 2002). Radical scholars like Saudi-born Hamoud al-Aqla al-Shuebi, who gained notoriety for his defense of the September 11 attacks, similarly highlighted the necessity of consumer boycotts. In a fatwa issued in June 2001, al-Shuebi argued that when the coordination of armed jihad is prevented by the careless Muslim rulers who "lack zeal for the war against the states of the infidels," with which they engage in intimate liaisons, boycott becomes an alternative way of striving in the path of God (cited in Halevi 2012, 53). The apparent failure of the Arab League boycott, from this perspective, paved the way for a nonviolent vision of jihadi resistance that seldom envisioned leaders or state institutions playing a positive role.

Fatwa by Saleh al-Fawzan, a member of Saudi Arabia's highest fatwa-issuing council, also confronted the issue of leadership. In February 2006, during a lecture at the Imam Turki bin Abdullah Mosque in Riyadh, an individual asked him, "If the ruler of a Muslim polity does not commend us to boycott Israeli commodities nor prohibits us from doing so, may I boycott, knowing that they will be harmed by the boycott in support of the Prophet?" In his response, al-Fawzan proposed that when the ruler "commands the boycott of a nation," boycotting is obligatory. "Obedience is due to the ruler, because this act contributes to the common good [of the Muslim community] and damages the enemy. However, when the ruler does not command boycotting, then the people have a choice. They can boycott or not boycott, doing whatever they want as individuals" (al-Fawzan 2006). Notably, in al-Fawzan's view, the boycott was not incumbent upon the community as a whole, as suggested by al-Qaradawi, but rather a matter of individual choice. In spite of their obvious differences, al-Qaradawi and al-Fawzan, as well as others who issued boycott fatwas, including Ahmad bin Hamad al-Khalili, the Grand Mufti of the Sultanate of Oman, and Faysal Mawlawi, the Deputy Chairman of the European Council for Fatwa and Research (ECFR), considered the boycott to be essential to one's life as a Muslim. This made for an internationally relevant discourse that was actually rooted in local concerns, notably the feelings of anxiety among trade unions due to a number of free trade pacts signed between the United States and Middle Eastern states like Egypt and Jordan.

It is no coincidence, therefore, that trade unions formed the backbone of the boycotting movement. They constituted the readership of boycotting websites, disseminated boycott fatwas online, and distributed lists of banned products at protests and demonstrations. The association between labor activism and an assertive rhetoric of jihadi boycotts gave rise to a particular economic ethic. During a live fatwa session in October 2000, Fuad Mukhaymar, an Associate Professor of Islamic Studies at al-Azhar University, delivered the opinion that Muslims can triumph in "their jihad against industrialized nations by favoring their own national products [...] and by putting fellow Muslims to work" (Mukhaymar 2000). In this sense, one can say that the Muslim boycott had a precedent in the core tenants of economic nationalism, which were defined in religious terms. Notably, Mukhaymar argued that after the boycott is imposed, governments have a task of creating jobs for those who worked in factories ran by the Israeli and American companies. Although workers will be less paid, Mukhaymar explained, the issue will be "easy for them to accept if they consider it a form of jihad that is exerted for the sake of their religion and homelands." Similarly, in an interview for daily newspaper *As-Safir* in December 2002, Muhammad Hussein Fadlallah, a prominent Lebanese cleric, argued that the United States wishes to transform the world into a consumer market for its products, "especially the Islamic world" (cited in Halevi 2012, 53). The only counter measure, according to Fadlallah, "is to purchase Muslim-made products." Mukhaymar and Fadlallah enjoyed massive popularity precisely because they appealed to workers and sprinkled their fatwas with references to the activities of trade unions, as well as popular councils and anti-normalization committees.

3.2 *Boycotting Websites from Mecca to Sarajevo*

For centuries, muftis have addressed the concerns of ordinary people seeking their specialized knowledge (see Gaffney 1994; Hooker 2003; Messick 1996;

Skovgaard-Petersen 1997). Thanks to new media, however, fatwas have become increasingly popular nowadays. They do not replace traditional modes of argumentation but rather point to a new set of conditions within which "older commitments and themes have been given a new direction, shape, and form" (Mahmood 2012, 82). In other words, fatwas no longer appear at a lonely junction on the information highway, where one fatwa consumer can meet one fatwa producer in isolation, for thousands of other fatwa consumers quickly converge at the same spot. In an instant, the junction becomes very crowded, "and the great number of fatwa consumers [arrive] with pressing demands for more information" (Halevi 2012, 62). Boycott fatwas I explore in this chapter present an interesting example of demand far exceeding supply, as evidenced by the fact that they are often reposted and recycled. In this regard, one can say that new media allows fatwa consumers to play a greater role than ever in the dissemination and proliferation of new Islamic knowledges and ethical materials. How fatwas circulate among Muslim publics, and the kind of appropriations that take place, ultimately lie outside of the muftis' control.[4] By creating websites dedicated to the Muslim boycott, ordinary people helped to disseminate, and to revisit and revise, the theological-juridical discourse I discussed earlier.[5] These boycotting websites also published news, cartoons, and multicolored logos of the blacklisted companies and products, and thus played an important role in circulating the emotive information and shocking photographs that fueled the boycotting movement.

Under a photograph of the burning twin towers of the World Trade Center, Palestine-Info.com, a news website registered in the al-Rimal neighborhood of Gaza, published the following question, "Who could be behind an atrocity on such a scale. [...] Could it be the same entity behind the bombing and destruction of USS Liberty in 1967 to widen the conflict" (cited in Bunt 2003, 91). Elsewhere, Palestine-Info.com, more commonly known as the Palestinian Information Center (PIC), published statements like "terror is our common enemy," in this way suggesting that Palestinians empathized with Americans, in spite of their "strong opposition to [America's] blatant bias toward Israel." In its "Today's News" section, moreover, Palestine-Info.com suggested that "Israeli, Jewish, and Zionist media have taken advantage of September 11 to embark on a campaign of vilification against Islam and Muslims around the world." In

---

4   For a detailed debate on the uncertainties of the fatwa production, see Caeiro 2011.
5   This is a recent turn of events because, as many scholars have noted, Arabic speakers made limited use of the Internet in the last decade of the twentieth century (see Abdulla 2007; Hofheinz 2005; Warf and Vincent 2007).

response to this perceived Islamophobia, and in light of the cycle of violence during the Second Intifada, Palestine-Info.com often reported on jihadi acts in Israel. For example, after a suicide bomber killed twenty-nine people in a hotel in Netanya in March 2002, Palestine-Info.com published a statement by Muhammad Deif, the Commanding General of Hamas's Qassam Brigades, that was laced with references from the Qur'an. "Fight them, and God will punish them by your hands," Deif proposed. He then proceeded to describe the suicide attack on Barak Hotel as "one in a series against the terrorist Sharon and his Nazi government."

Six months later, Palestine-Info.com lost its .com status after a number of activists and organizations from the United States pressured service providers to close websites associated with Hamas and al-Qaeda (on this, see Bunt 2003; Lipton and Lichblau 2004). It had originally registered a .co.uk domain, but it subsequently launched an entirely new website, available at Palinfo.com. The type of content that has emerged after 2002 focused almost entirely on consumer boycotts as a means of supporting the Palestinian resistance peacefully. For example, in a video published in April 2015, Palinfo.com called for a boycott of Israeli products and goods to the tune of Queen's "We Will Rock You." Men and women sang, "They have got blood on their hands, it is not too late to end support for the apartheid state. We will boycott Israel" (Palestinian Information Center 2015). Other calls, while not as creative, also made the case for consumer boycotts as peaceful instruments of passive resistance, drawing inspiration from earlier pan-Islamic efforts against imperialism, notably the Tobacco Protest of 1891–1892.

AlMinbar.com, a Mecca-based website dedicated to *khutbahs* (sermons), familiarized its users with the long and rich history of the "politics of passive resistance and abnegation" in a similar manner (Halevi 2019, 216). At the time of writing, the website was saturated with content from Mecca, Medina, and al-Aqsa. The al-Aqsa section highlighted a sermon from Yusuf Abu-Sunaynah, an imam who delivered his lectures on the Voice of Palestine, an official radio station of the PA. It called on Muslims everywhere to "wake up from their heedlessness," and unite their ranks in an extensive boycott against "not only the most obvious targets but also Britain, for its role in the creation of the criminal entity that occupies Palestine, and Russia, for trying to fortify itself from Islamic organizations within its territory and for defending Israel" (Abu-Sunaynah 2008). Moreover, according to Abu-Sunaynah, the pressure on the Palestinian people to end their resistance "coincided with a shameful betrayal from the Arab leaders." The considerable collection of sermons within a searchable format on AlMinbar.com, in short, gave credibility to different Islamic organizations active in the West Bank and Gaza Strip, and it emphasized the importance of the Israeli–Palestinian conflict for Muslims everywhere.

The perhaps most popular boycotting website out there is IslamOnline.net. Registered in Doha in June 1997, it features sections in English and Arabic on "Cyber Counseling," allows users to submit questions via its "Ask the Scholar" section, and hosts live fatwa sessions in which scholars answer questions about practical problems of everyday life. The website's main religious scholar is al-Qaradawi and, at the time of writing, his fatwas dominated a section on international relations and jihad. Importantly, he criticized all attacks on "helpless [...] civilians who have nothing to do with the decision-making process and are striving hard to earn their daily bread." In his view, the September 11 attacks were a "heinous crime in Islam." He called for "intelligent rage" through passive resistance rather than "senseless violence" (al-Qaradawi 2001). Other scholars whose fatwas frequently featured on IslamOnline.net include Mawlawi, Mukhaymar, and al-Shuebi, whom I discussed earlier in this chapter, as well as Monzer Kahf, a prominent scholar of Islamic banking, finance, and economics, Ibrahim Salih al-Husseini, the Grand Mufti of Nigeria, and Sayyid Muhammad Nuh, an expert on *hadith* (the collection of the Prophet's actions or speeches). Moderates among them promoted the idea that jihad could be fulfilled without violence through consumer boycotts. Even the more radical ideologues like al-Shuebi stood as important proponents of jihadi boycotts, arguing for them both before and after the September 11 attacks.

In October 2010, after a clash with the Qatari financiers over editorial independence, the team behind IslamOnline.net launched OnIslam.net. This new website focused on the institution of family, "especially the challenges facing Muslim families in a secularizing context" (cited in Ali 2016, 240). For example, in a section called "Reading Islam," OnIslam.net described ways of being Muslim compatible with the daily realities of European life. Although it favored organized forms of social engagement, such as giving meat to the poor during Eid al-Adha, OnIslam.net also adopted a strong, anti-imperial rhetoric, thus revising the Muslim boycott in new sociopolitical contexts. In the weeks prior to its closure in October 2015, due to technical difficulties, OnIslam.net published al-Qaradawi's fatwa on duties of Muslims in Europe, which was first published in March 2006 on IslamOnline.net. Muslims in Europe, according to al-Qaradawi, "have a duty to adopt and champion the rights of their umma." Such duty includes supporting the cause of Palestine, "with the sincere intention to return back the usurped rights to their legitimate owners. [...] Muslims must help with whatever power they have. The vehicle of this help is a boycott of enemies' products and manufactured goods" (al-Qaradawi 2006).

One of the more fruitful ideas to emerge from al-Qaradawi's fatwa on duties of Muslims in Europe has been to describe the boycott against Israel as an emergent form of Islamic public engagement that fits the secular state framework according to circumstances, interests, and policies. This discourse of "public Islam," as some scholars have called it (see Gasper 2001; Mandaville 2003; Salvatore 2004), also informs the practices and arguments of the activists and organizations I worked with. As I hope to show in chapters 4 and 5, it gives them a means to speak about the struggle of Palestinians to realize their rights but frame it in a way that attracts recruits looking for a new approach to Islam that emphasizes social responsibility and active participation in Europe's political life.

Another contribution I want to draw the reader's attention to has been al-Qaradawi's reading of Islam such that it speaks directly to the circumstances of being Muslim in Europe. Websites like Leicester-based InMinds.com that highlight al-Qaradawi's work and the work of other scholars popular among young Muslims, such as Malaysia's Chandra Muzaffar and Iran's Abdolkarim Soroush, have served to further reconfigure the structures and sources of religious authority. I situate BDS within this mediatic context. In a section called "Fatwas Given by Islamic Scholars on the Boycott of Israel," for example, InMinds.com suggests that every leading ulama from every school of thought in Islam "is united in their support for a boycott of Israel and those that support Israel" (Innovative Minds 2006). This section includes fatwas issued by al-Qaradawi and Fadlallah, as well as fatwas issued by Ayatollah Sistani, an Iranian marja' in Iraq, and Sayyid Ali Hosseini Khamenei, the Supreme Leader of Iran. One might say that this testifies to a shift in the locus of religious authority in Europe, especially as regards the question of where young Muslims are looking to find new ideas and interpretations of Islam. Importantly, the kind of translocal Islam that emerges out of the challenges and difficulties of life in Europe is contrasted with the Islam of mosque-based imams and parents that supposedly holds little hope of providing a solution. In this regard, it is worth noting that al-Qaradawi's "Boycotting Israeli and American Goods" has served as the blueprint for InMinds.com's call upon younger generations of European Muslims to leave the sectarianism of their parents behind and "join people of conscience around the world in the boycott of products and companies that support the Zionist entity" (Innovative Minds n.d.).

In December 2008, the InMinds.com's call that I mentioned above was recycled by IslamBosna.ba, registered in Sarajevo. Many of the products listed by InMinds.com, such as Dr Pepper and Shreddies, were not available in Sarajevo at the time. This suggests a rather wide circulation of new Islamic knowledges and ethical materials that leads to inconsistencies of action and a lack of coherence with local situations and conditions. That said, six years later, IslamBosna.ba published a new and revised call for boycott. It noted that, although the boycott against Israel and its supporters is discussed on Islamic forums and message boards, users often lack a clear religious instruction, "making any discussion pointless." For this reason, IslamBosna.ba identified six points that underpin the boycott against Israel, thereby citing authoritative fatwas issued by al-Qaradawi and al-Fawzan. The sixth point pertained to its outcomes. "Those who call for boycott share lists of products and companies that have ties to Israel. [...] To boycott them all is a difficult task and has little—if any—chance of hurting Israel. For the boycott against Israel to succeed, we have to concentrate on what hurts Israel the most. This calls for professional advice." IslamBosna.com then instructed its users to join the BDS movement, and in doing so learn how to target Israel more effectively, concluding emphatically, "God knows best" (Islam Bosna 2014).

In the next chapter, I point to specific sociopolitical contexts in which BDS has come to be understood as a religious obligation. I show that ordinary people in Tower Hamlets and Stari Grad who have taken on BDS frame their decision in terms of varied experiences of social and economic exclusion. Thus, their decision to boycott has to be locally contextualized, taking also into consideration the contingences and predicaments of Muslim political participation in secularizing societies and spheres. BDS, as I will make clear, effectively brings together the secular discourse of citizenship and nation with the discourse of Islamic piety.

CHAPTER 3

Europe, Islam, and the New Political Landscape

When a wave of demonstrations in support of Palestinians during the Gaza War descended into attacks on Jews in France, defacement of cemeteries in Greece, and arson in Sweden, an alarmist discourse accused Muslims in Europe of a "new antisemitism" (see Bunzl 2005; Klug 2004; Silverstein 2008; Taguieff 2004). In June 2003, European politicians met in Vienna to discuss the fact that "antisemitism is surging [...] to an extent unprecedented since the end of the Second World War" (Organization for Security and Cooperation in Europe 2003). They emphasized that this antisemitism was not a history lesson but a contemporary phenomenon "rooted in the same kind of extremist thinking that lies behind the international terrorism that is threatening our civilization." Their concern, in other words, was with antisemitism coming out of the Middle East. The notion that this new antisemitism that Muslims in Europe were accused of was an import of a "hermetically sealed ideology" that the Middle East inherited from Europe, and then preserved completely intact from the mid-1930s to the late 1970s (Holz and Kiefer 2010, 111), however, failed to situate the apparent phenomenon in the context of continuing social, economic, and political exclusions in Europe.

It is outside the scope of my interest in this book to go into the antisemitism charge that all too often cloaks the debate around BDS (see Butler 2006; Hever 2019; Maira 2018; Marcus 2015). My goal here is simply to suggest that many of the men and women I met and, over a period of five years, came to know participate in BDS not because of their prejudice or hatred of Jews but because they oppose Israel's oppressive regime that is perceived as part and parcel of European hegemony that not only marginalizes Muslims in Europe but, in their view, also accounts for the suffering of Palestinians. In previous chapters, I traced different discourses of resistance and struggle that have informed the ongoing BDS campaign, with close attention to how and by whom these discourses were produced and circulated. We might remind ourselves that, between October 2000 and April 2006, a whole spectrum of differentiated and otherwise competing voices in Islam used new media, especially the Internet, to appeal to Muslims everywhere to support Palestinian resistance through consumer boycotts, and thus accomplish their duty of jihad peacefully. In the process, they not only expanded on earlier, pan-Islamic efforts to resist European hegemony and Zionism but also paved the way for new syncretic and complex links between morality, virtue, politics, and consumption. When it comes to Muslims in Europe, I was especially interested in the calls for a more public engagement in the name of Islam, facilitated in part by Islamic pedagogical materials discussed earlier, and their bearing on the practicalities of everyday life. Many voices on the Internet, besides that of al-Qaradawi, claimed that boycotts as acts of passive resistance fit the secular state framework according to policies, circumstances, and interests but were nevertheless rooted in a true sense of belonging to an Islamic tradition.

In this chapter, I focus on how and by whom these ideas were received and made use of locally. In other words, I recontextualize resistance and root it in the thick texture of my informants' lives. I begin with a highly condensed portrait of historical happenings in Tower Hamlets. The Labour Party's two-tier legislation on race and migration, together with the Conservative Party's attempts to rein in spending on public resources, as I will show, created greater room in the borough's political arena for the expression of localized links with an Islamic umma. As a result, questions about the appropriate Muslim response to the Israeli–Palestinian conflict could more easily be connected to concerns about education, employment, and housing in Tower Hamlets. In Stari Grad, at the same time, war-related population movements and migrations brought about an array of tensions between "cultured" urban locals and rural newcomers with supposedly inferior cultural habits and knowledge. Hierarchies of class, gender, and generation debated BDS amid these post-war tensions. To account for the importance attributed to urban values in Stari Grad, that is, to be regarded as refined, educated, and knowledgeable, I will also explore the stigmatized and marginalized conceptualization of European Muslims vis-à-vis Europe.

1   Tower Hamlets

The East End of London has long captured the public imagination. Whereas the tree-lined avenues and high-end condominiums of London's West End are known for their proximity to economic and political power, the East End conjures images of crowded alleys and docks, "a mongrel conurbation of hard toil, poverty, and criminality" (de Hanas 2014). Throughout history, the East End has absorbed waves of migrants, starting with thousands of Huguenots who fled Louis XIV's persecution after the Revocation of the Edict of Nantes in 1685. Following the Huguenots, there was an influx of Irish who escaped the 1840s potato famine. Mass migration of Jews persecuted in the Tsarist Empire had begun in the late nineteenth century, and reached a climax after the great pogrom of Kishinev in 1903 (see W. J. Fishman 1975; Kadish 1992;

Lipman 1990).[1] "Petty France" became "Little Jerusalem," as the number of Jews swelled to over 120,000. A Bangladeshi community established itself in the late 1950s. The area around Brick Lane has thus been branded as "Banglatown." Anne Kershen (2012) notes that for successive waves in the East End it was in part religion—though not necessarily religiosity—that provided cultural stability, political unity, and the institutions of community life. The building on the corner of Fournier Street illustrates this point nicely. Originally built as a Huguenot church in the eighteenth century, it became a Methodist chapel and then a Jewish synagogue before its incarnation in the 1970s as the Brick Lane Great Mosque.

These relatively distinct waves of migration have set Tower Hamlets, which covers much of the traditional East End, apart from other diverse places in England, such as the neighboring borough of Newham or the city of Leicester, where migration has been more variegated. Migrants to districts that now make up Tower Hamlets have tended to settle in enclaves, giving Wapping a "Catholic" character and Stepney a "Jewish" one. Muslims of predominantly Bangladeshi descent account for "more than half the population near Brick Lane and Whitechapel," where I worked extensively (Tower Hamlets Council's Corporate Research Unit 2015). The discrimination and disadvantage they face have been documented. According to Metropolitan Police figures, for example, there have been more "anti-Muslim hate crimes" in Tower Hamlets than in any other borough from the mid-2012 to the late 2014 (Measuring Anti-Muslim Attacks 2014). A study by Trust for London and the New Policy Institute, at the same time, has found that Tower Hamlets has "the highest rate of poverty, pay inequality, and unemployment of any London borough." The unemployment rate among Muslim males is almost three times the national average. When employed, "they earn approximately 20 percent less than white males" (Trust for London 2017). A Joseph Rowntree Foundation's report has confirmed that Muslim women, and especially Bangladeshi women, "remain among the most excluded and lowest-paid sections of the labor force" (Chouhan, Speeden, and Qazi 2012, 23). The framing of BDS in religious terms that I explore in this book must be located within these complexities and contingencies of daily Muslim lives.

1.1 *Representation, Race Relations, and Resources*
The origins of Bangladeshi settlement in Tower Hamlets can be found in the arrival of around 5,000 migrant workers from a Muslim majority district of

---

1 Historians now appreciate the mixture of forces at work. Opportunism and chain migration were also at work, it seems (see Gidley 2009).

Sylhet between 1954 and 1956 (on this, see Anwar 1998; Gardner 1995; Gardner and Shakur 1994; Kabeer 2000). Initially, their representatives were ex-sailors who had established themselves as travel agents and owners of cafés and restaurants. In a familiar pattern of chain migration, "people came from particular localities within Sylhet itself so that competition between entrepreneurs for control of voluntary organizations and other positions of community responsibility was fought out through kinship and village networks" (Eade 1991, 59). The intense struggles for positions in the Bangladesh High Commission and the locally dominant Labour Party, for example, were stimulated by the tightly knit nature of settlement in the borough's western wards. The largest concentration of Bangladeshis was in Spitalfields, although substantial numbers were also established in the neighboring St. Mary's and St. Katherine's wards.

The first key exploration of the Bangladeshi first generation's experience of migration was produced by Caroline Adams who worked in Tower Hamlets' schools and youth services. Her *Across Seven Seas and Thirteen Rivers: Life Stories of Pioneer Sylheti Settlers in Britain* is divided in two sections. The first provides a history of Sylhet, the lascars' journeys from the Bengal delta, and the emergence of a community. Adams draws these threads together in the final somber paragraph.

> The Bangladeshi community in Britain began to take root on the territory marked out by the first few casual pioneers who have found the way "across seven seas and thirteen rivers" from Sylhet to Aldgate. Here at last was the memorial to those thousands of nameless sailors who died in cold water and blazing engine rooms. The Empire had finally come home.
> ADAMS 1987, 66

The second section is comprised of interviews with Bangladeshis who opted to seek work and make a life in Tower Hamlets. These predominantly male elders were joined by their wives and children in the late 1970s and early 1980s, resulting in the rapid rise in Bangladeshi numbers from 5,000 to around 24,000 (on this, see Eade 1991; Forman 1989). Despite the high concentration of Bangladeshis in the borough's western wards, families gradually moved eastwards, weakening the tightly knit character of the early community. The vast majority of workers among the first generation took low-paid, unskilled, or semi-skilled jobs, especially in the local garment trade, retail shops, cafés, restaurants, hotels, and hospitals. Many of them, however, were unable to find full-time jobs and were thus dependent on public resources in competition with members of the white working-class.

In 1981, the establishment of the London Docklands Development Corporation by Michael Heseltine, the then-Secretary of State for the Environment, resulted in a massive redistribution of resources, a movement from industry to services, and the reimaging of the derelict dock area (on this, see Bird 1993; Brownhill 1990; Colenutt 1991). Both white and Bangladeshi members of the working-class were excluded from this redevelopment. The high-rise offices on the edge of Spitalfields, as well as the Manhattanesque skyline of Canary Wharf and Isle of Dogs, were staffed with white middle-class commuters and those who bought the expensive new housing along the river. Large swathes of housing intended for demolition, at the same time, were allocated to "troubled families," typically Bangladeshi. The remnants of the white working-class clung to the former council estates, often benefitting from Margaret Thatcher's "right to buy" policy. Introduced in October 1980, the policy radically transformed the previous pattern of housing tenure. In Tower Hamlets in the 1970s, there were something like 40,000 council tenancies (see Carr 2011; Eade 2007). One decade later, the number dropped to 25,000. The move away from policies and promises of inclusion, well-being, and belonging to those based on need resulted in an increasingly racialized issue of housing in Tower Hamlets.

The white working-class, whose existence was under a threat from the slum clearance schemes, bitterly resented migrants in general, and Bangladeshis in particular, whom they saw as competing for scarce housing and other public resources. The British National Party (BNP) gained a brief electoral success in 1993 "on the back of this resentment" (Eade 1997, 130). The Labour Party returned to power in 1994 and had to confront a powerful mix of diminished public resources and high expectations from working-class residents who were confronted in their day-to-day lives with the social and economic polarization fostered by the Docklands redevelopment. However, it did little to address the implicit racism connected to distinct senses of national and local identity thrown into crisis by the settlement of previously colonized people (see Eade 2000; Marriott 2006; Sinha 2008; Visram 2002).

The ways in which the past impacts upon the more recent tensions between a resentful white working-class and Bangladeshis is explored by historian Georgie Wemyss. She contends that the same patterns that establish the British empire as a source of national pride—as it supposedly signals exceptional work ethic, philanthropy, and civilizational values—also drive the creation of highly racialized politics of belonging in Tower Hamlets. Specifically, patterns of discriminatory amnesia regarding previous injustices in the name of empire, which are essential to Britain's view of its past, "work to ensure that people whose ancestors were subject to British rule in the Asian subcontinent,

Africa, and the Caribbean remain near the base of [...] an unstable hierarchy of belonging" (Wemyss 2008, 53). These particular bundles of silences, in other words, construct a sense of white belonging but marginalize British Bengali belonging, "as links between Britain and Bengal, and the violence and oppression of British colonialism, are obscured" (Wemyss 2008, 55). Because there is little social mixing between "ordinary members of the Bangladeshi community and white neighbors," histories, such as those of the thousands of lascars, subjects of the empire, which could bring a critical eye to Britain's view of its past and destabilize the highly racialized politics of belonging, remain excluded from dominant discourses (Dench, Gavron, and Young 2006, 231, cited in Wemyss 2008, 65).

The contingent and itinerant nature of racism in Tower Hamlets is also discussed by sociologist Alan Hudson (2006). He connects it to "Labour Party's peculiar two-tier legislation on race and migration," which first produced a climate of hostility to migrants in general, and Bangladeshis in particular, and then led to their incorporation into local government. The first tier put in place was a system of controls that turned Bangladeshis into second-class citizens. According to Hudson, "this was an open invitation to [...] racists to vent their anger on the newcomers." The second tier, which expanded on the framework for race relations devised in the mid-1960s, prescribed the code of conduct to be applied toward "the body of people made inferior in status by previous migration controls" (A. Hudson 2006; see also Latour 2017; Turner 2008). It resulted in the demonization of dispossessed sections of the white working-class, on the one hand, and the establishment of ethnic identity as a condition for the allocation of public resources and the inclusion of a narrow branch of ethnic minority as a new leadership to supervise resource allocation, on the other.

Bangladeshi entrepreneurs, many of whom ex-sailors who had established themselves as travel agents and owners of cafés and restaurants, initially provided community leadership, acting as power brokers between their compatriots and local state officials. However, in the mid-1980s, their leadership was challenged by a second generation of activists who found jobs in local government, social and welfare services, schools and colleges. These aspiring leaders, who emerged from diverse youth organizations established during the late 1970s in response to discrimination in education, employment, and housing, used the language of socialism and class struggle in their highly effective alliance with white left-wingers (see Eade 1997; Purdam 1996). They challenged their elders as community representatives, especially those leading the Bangladeshi Welfare Association, whose activities were seen as influenced by more traditional Bangladeshi "village politics" (see Back et al. 2009;

Begum and Eade 2005; Eade and Garbin 2002; Garbaye 2005). Many of these second-generation activists were born in Sylhet during the mid-1960s and came to Tower Hamlets during the late 1970s and early 1980s. Therefore, they were exposed to both the Bangladesh War of Liberation and the discrimination on the streets and schools of the borough. During the anti-discrimination struggle, the expression of both experiences was essential to forging a link between Bangladeshi national heritage and cultural identity, on the one hand, and the mobilization of class and ethnic identity, on the other. Perhaps more importantly, second-generation activists espousing secular nationalist views still regarded themselves as Muslims, observed public rituals with their fellow Muslims, and expressed their religious identity through different observances at home. They were also prepared to work alongside mosques and other faith-based organizations in order to gain or remain in power, a phenomenon the next chapter explores at some length.

Until the mid-1980s, mosques and other faith-based organizations in Tower Hamlets had little influence on community politics. However, with the opening of the East London Mosque in July 1985, they gained more legitimacy, and the issue of religion started to appear at the center of debates on "community needs." The participation of the East London Mosque's leaders in anti-drug and youth projects had legitimated their claim to represent the Muslim community in an area dominated by secularists for decades. In this regard, it is worth noting that the East London Mosque's leaders repeatedly voiced concerns about "un-Islamic" practices promoted by second-generation secularists, such as the celebration of the Bengali New Year, that could encourage younger generations to think nationally but not Islamically. Muslim identity, rooted both in the code of conduct that Islam has to offer and in the "authenticity" of moral values, was thus contrasted with a set of syncretic national and cultural practices (see Eade and Garbin 2006). The East London Mosque has also formed successful partnerships with national and local governments, and its expansion, which resulted in the opening of the highly popular London Muslim Centre in June 2004, has strengthened its position at a time when funding for secular organizations notably declined. The East London Mosque is now seen as a key power broker in the local political sphere, so much so that every politician is obliged to speak to its leaders if they want to stand a chance of being elected (see Glynn 2008; McLoughlin 2005; Peace 2013).

During the 2005 general election campaign, the Respect Party as a whole, and George Galloway in particular, made a point of working closely with the East London Mosque and organizations that have sprung from it after a factional conflict, notably the Islamic Forum of Europe (IFE) and its youth wing, the Young Muslim Organization (YMO). Both were instrumental to Galloway's success in an area long considered to be a Labour heartland (on this, see Peace 2013; Tatari 2014). The IFE, for example, commented that although Galloway was unlikely to establish a caliphate in Tower Hamlets, "he has passionately campaigned for Muslims far more than some [...] community elders [...] still living in the days of maharajas in British India" (cited in Hussain 2006). Importantly, young Muslims gathered around the IFE, who saw first-generation entrepreneurs and second-generation community leaders as archaic as the political left, were drawn to Galloway's criticism of England's military presence in Iraq and Afghanistan. It is worth recalling that four years prior this generation born and raised in Tower Hamlets had formed the backbone of the Stop the War Coalition. Galloway mobilized around other political issues close to their hearts like the Israeli–Palestinian conflict, and he famously promised to fly the Palestinian flag on the roof of the Tower Hamlets Council offices if he was elected. These key mobilizing themes were combined with a strong focus on local welfare issues, such as opposition to privatization policies, higher taxes for businesses, safeguarding the National Health Service (NHS), and raising the minimum wage (Respect Party 2005). Galloway's success in spite of the stiff electoral competition from more established candidates must be understood in light of his grassroots approach, on the one hand, and his ties with mosques and other faith-based organizations in Tower Hamlets, on the other. As I hope to show in chapters 4 and 5, this innovative merging of community participation with faith-based organizing is absolutely vital for activists and organizations that mobilize for BDS.

When Galloway was elected as the Member of Parliament for Bethnal Green and Bow, overturning a Labour majority of over 10,000, the London Muslim Centre hosted an event in his honor. Galloway expressed gratitude to volunteers who "gave their blood" for him. Meanwhile, Muslehuddin Faradhi, the IFE's leader, claimed that he had made sure that Tower Hamlets' young Muslims were able to "make an informed judgment and cast their vote without fear," further commenting that the impact of Galloway's success would be "felt for years to come" (cited in Hussain 2006). Indeed, the Respect Party as a whole has brought to the fore a new generation of idealistic activists concerned with community participation and public representation of Muslims in Tower Hamlets. For decades, the municipal socialism of the Labour Party and its second-generation allies have stayed at the forefront of discussions about race, ethnicity, and discrimination. However, the kind of translocal and transcultural Islam that I have discussed in previous chapters, proffered by organizations that have sprung from the East London Mosque, has given many of the newly politicized Muslims I knew in Tower Hamlets the arguments to loosen the grip of their elders and change the terms of debate. As a result, tendencies toward community participation, social responsibility, and greater activism carried out in the name of Islam have been contrasted with secular politics of the first generation that drew its support from kinship and village networks in Sylhet. In the next chapter, I will discuss how three generations of Bangladeshis debated BDS in light of this changing character of political exigencies in Tower Hamlets.

2   Stari Grad

During the course of its siege, Sarajevo became one of the last strongholds of multiethnic unity and tenacity. City voices claimed that, before the war, "we did not know who was Serb or Croat or Muslim, we were all just friends" (Sorabji 1993, 33). However, this is not an accurate description of the situation in which people were very aware of who was what. Other people's customs and traditions, such as colored eggs brought to school by Croat and Serb children and Ramadan baklavas by Muslim, were understood as signs of difference. In addition, despite the oft-noted number of intermarriages, most marriages were made within the ethnic group (see Bringa 1995; Hayden 1996; Sorabji 1994). This does not imply that different groups hated each other and were waiting for a chance to get even. For the most part, the existence of different customs and traditions was not perceived as a threat but as one aspect of life in Sarajevo. In this life, more energy was spent on working and socializing than on mulling over the merits or menaces of different customs and traditions. Other people's practices were normal, sometimes a matter of curiosity, and often used as a route for the expression of good will and cooperation. It is precisely this practice of daily *suživot* (literally, "life together") that defined the spirit of Sarajevo (see Donia and Fine 1994; Karahasan 1994; Malcolm 1994; Pinson 1993).

Sarajevo's city center has long been a domain in which different groups met and interacted at work and school, in the markets and cafés. Urbanization throughout Yugoslavia, at the same time, has meant that the city's population has grown steadily since the 1960s. The area known as "New Sarajevo," a wasteland of dreary apartment blocks subsidized by large conglomerates, such as Energoinvest and Hidrogradnja, were inhabited by workers and their families so that "Muslims, Serbs, and Croats lived alongside each other" (Sorabji 1994, 112). In spite of the massive scale of displacement taking place during and after the recent war, socially owned apartment blocks, such as Grbavica and Velešići, have not become ethnically homogenous. This relative diversity has allowed the residents to emphasize their loyalty to the model of a cosmopolitan community that under socialism had symbolized modernity as well as a political ideology of *bratstvo i jedinstvo* ("brotherhood and unity") (Lofranco 2017, 45).

In contrast to the city center and New Sarajevo, neighborhoods of Stari Grad known as *mahalas* are felt to be, and preserved as, Muslim in a way that the rest of the city's space is not.[2] A mass of steep cobbled streets lined with houses, their courtyards and gardens hidden from the street by high fences and gates, mosques dotted around, mahalas are places where Arabic and Turkish greetings, such as *es-selamu alejkum*, *merhaba*, and *akšam hajrula*, are often used instead of the more typical "greetings […] of the city outside" (Sorabji 1994, 112). Furthermore, while solidarity among residents of New Sarajevo has been established by participating in the same workplace, neighborly ties of mutual assistance and respect, sometimes referred to as *komšiluk*, have considerable social status in mahalas (see Pickering 2006; Sorabji 2008; Stefansson 2010). Their old women in *dimije* (flowing, baggy trousers) sit by the window observing, ready to ask, *čija si* (meaning, "what family do you belong to"), when you come barging into their komšiluk equipped with a camera, tape recorder, and notepad.

In the intimacy of mahalas, the terms *nacija* (nationality) and *vjera* (faith) are often used interchangeably. In this conception, Muslims are at once members of larger national community and smaller community of believers who vary in their levels of observance. There are those who pray five times a day and fast the entire month of Ramadan, those who fast token days of Ramadan and participate in some religious practices and rituals, and those who drink openly and never pray and fast. For this majority, the lack of strict observance says little about the role of Islam in self-perception. As Sorabji has astutely observed, "The consumption of alcohol no more prevents a Muslim being a Muslim than petty thefts stop a Catholic being a Catholic" (Sorabji 1993, 34). What this illustrates is that Islam is not only understood as a set of traditional guidelines to *hajj* (pilgrimage to Mecca), *salat* (daily prayer ritual), and *saum* (fasting). It is also understood as a set of loose moral imperatives, such as cleanliness, courtesy, and generosity, that are essential to the practical organization of everyday

---

2   According to the 1991 survey, New Sarajevo had 95,089 residents—34 percent Muslim, 35 percent Serb, and 9 percent Croat. At the same time, Muslims made up 72 percent of Stari Grad's mahalas. The percentage went up to 85 according to the unconfirmed survey of 2013. I use the term "Bosniak" instead of "Muslim" in various chapters of this book, but readers should bear in mind that before the war "Muslim" was the correct terminology, and that even today it is common in ordinary conversations.

life. This widely held understanding of Islam is readily visible in mahalas above Baščaršija where many of my informants come from.³

2.1   *Movement, Memories, and Moral Claims*

In socialist Bosnia, many self-confessed believers whose families had Party links could easily assert that, after all, Islam and socialism upheld and encouraged the same modern virtues—hard work, cooperation, and obedience to state authority. These sorts of accommodations have been noted by anthropologists working on other parts of the socialist bloc (see Hann 1988; Humphrey 1983; Kligman 1988). They were born of necessity under unsympathetic or openly oppressive regimes, but they should not be viewed as "bogus concessions" to the authorities, "made through guilty self-delusion or with fingers crossed behind the back" (Sorabji 1993, 34). As an abstract system of principles and values with direct bearing on daily conduct, Islam was easily related to other abstract systems, and this process did not end with the decline of one-party socialism. Even the loose Islamic revival movement of the mid-1980s, comprised of men and women in their teens and twenties, relied on Islam's nature as an abstract system of values. Many of those who led the revival were, or had been, students at Sarajevo's *madrasas* (secondary religious schools or colleges for the study of Islam, although this may not be the only subject studied) and the Islamic Theological Faculty. Some were urbanites attracted to Islam who came from wealthy families and tended to have higher levels of education than their peers. Others came from poor rural families attracted to free accommodation, subsidized meals, and stipends that religious schools could offer in a way that secular ones could not.

In and around Sarajevo's madrasas there soon emerged a community of committed young Muslims keen on acquiring or improving their knowledge of the Qur'an, hadith, and such ancillary fields as Arabic grammar and philology. Some of the women had adopted headscarves and long dresses, while others avoided the revealing sorts of fashions, such as short skirts and sleeveless tops, typically favored by their fashion-conscious peers. That said, what dominated their conversations and behaviors were not religious rules or guidelines but broader moral questions of shyness, modesty, and fear of God. It was on this axis that they "stressed their association with the umma" (Sorabji 1994, 110). For example, Turkish boys were deemed expert Qur'an reciters because family relations of obedience and respect had provided them with an appropriate environment for religious learning and training.

---

3   Baščaršija is Sarajevo's old bazaar and the historical and cultural center of the city.

With the decline of one-party socialism, the old Islamic revival appeared to be joined by new enthusiasts. Younger reformed Muslims who stressed their association with the umma struggled to find common ground with older Muslims who, "although often believers in bits of what the young saw as superstition, sometimes illiterate and certainly not schooled in Arabic or Islamic theology," nonetheless prayed five times a day and fasted the entire month of Ramadan (Sorabji 1994, 118). That said, these struggles over the motives and meanings of Islamic practice between the reformed, on the one hand, and the religiously non-reformed, on the other, had no implications for the majority of those enjoying the new religious freedom, who saw their religious activities as closely related to their new European future. The increased religious activities provided ammo to Serbian and, to a lesser extent, Croatian propagandists warning of Muslims' desire for a "fundamentalist" state. Muslims themselves, however, greeted them as the opening of a door to freedom and democracy closely related to Europe.

The restructuring of the Islamska Zajednica Bosne i Hercegovine (the Islamic Community of Bosnia and Herzegovina), the highest representative body of Muslims in the region, echoed this feeling. In a constitution that was passed in January 1990, the Islamska Zajednica adopted Arabic names for many of its structures—*mesihats* and *rijasets*, for example, replaced the Serbo-Croatian *starešinstvos*—and thus legitimated itself vis-à-vis the umma. The election of the first non-Bosnian *reis-ul-ulema* (the highest official of religious law) supported its new transnational "tone and aims" (Sorabji 1993, 34–35). Above all, however, the new constitution foregrounded the concept of democracy, and of giving voice to Muslims at the lower ranks of the establishment. Given the popular connotations of democracy, this move was meant to stress the Islamska Zajednica's relationship to Europe. This association of Muslim identity with European-style values was also apparent in attitudes toward the possibility of war.

In the summer of 1990, when Belgrade-registered cars were reported vandalized on the Adriatic coast and Serbs feared to go there, "Sarajevans felt free to take their seaside holidays, and were happy to enjoy the reduced prices" (Sorabji 1993, 35). As war loomed and then began between Serbia and Croatia, the urban locals, most notably Muslims, believed that, while Serbs and Croats might fight, "Muslims were too 'cultured' and rational to fight," and would remain calm in the face of it all (Sorabji 1993, 36). This attitude was one deemed in keeping with Europe, which Muslims wrongly believed would safeguard Bosnia's territorial integrity and constitutional order, and in keeping with Islam, which they considered to be the religion of peace and tolerance. With war approaching Bosnia itself, the notion of European-style values was interpreted as pertaining to Bosnians en masse, rather than Muslims in particular. In April 1992, when the shelling of Sarajevo began, a third understanding emerged. Rather than Muslim civility versus non-Muslim aggression, or Bosnian civility versus non-Bosnian aggression, this was a conflict between urban civility and rural aggression (see Maček 2007; Stefansson 2007). This important division between urban and rural, on which the urban locals, most notably Muslims, commonly drew when assessing the nature and character of war, is ingrained in the Yugoslav cultural and sociological project of modernization, deserving of some attention.

A number of scholars have observed that Yugoslavia was an agrarian, underdeveloped country for much of its history (see Bougarel 1999; Donia and Fine 1994; McCarthy 1993). When industrialization and economic modernization occurred, development came rapidly. The Communist Party, which came to power in the aftermath of the Second World War, turned this rapid development into a cornerstone of its political project. From the 1950s onward, at the time when cities like Belgrade, Sarajevo, and Zagreb witnessed an influx of migrants from the countryside, communist leaders sought to bring Yugoslavia out of its "backwardness" by imposing education and the "right," European *kultura* (culture) onto the masses (see Kolind 2008). In doing so, they demonized the latest newcomers, and turned them into a collective scapegoat. In other words, those coming from the countryside became a symbol of mentality and lifestyle that Yugoslavia was to leave behind. This socialist project of modernization was accompanied by the cultural construction of the rural "other" as a negative pole in neighborly relations. Those whose parents moved to the city from the countryside hid this image tarnishing fact from their peers, and distanced themselves from the latest newcomers. Meanwhile, those born in the city, or simply *Sarajlije*, as they are most commonly known, saw their lifestyles polluted by "primitive peasants," and soon a cleavage of identification evolved in which education became the main distinguishing factor (see Ramet 1996; van de Port 1998). In short, modernization in general, and urbanization in particular, moved the traditional antagonisms between the city and the countryside into the cities themselves and made them even more pronounced.

As I argue in this book, the cultural construction of the rural "other" by the urban locals, particularly those closer to the *dobra, stara porodica* ("good, old family") end of the spectrum, intensified during and after the recent war. It was sparked by the massive population displacement, experienced as forced "de-urbanization," "de-modernization," and "de-Europeanization."[4] The academic

---

4   In socialist Bosnia the concept of the "good, old family" was an important one. Part of its significance lay in the characteristic Bosnian, and wider former Yugoslav, disdain felt by

notions of "peasantization" and "ruralization," in this sense, capture a widespread feeling among the Sarajlije I met in Stari Grad that those who migrated to "their city" during and after the recent war kept their rural mentality instead of transforming themselves into decent, "cultured" urbanites (see Jansen 2009). The shifting boundaries, and forced mobility across them, were accompanied by the impoverishment of large sections of Sarajevo's middle and upper-middle classes that, although aware that their situation was far better than that of most displaced persons, seemed more concerned with what they have lost. For example, before the war, many had felt themselves to be upwardly mobile. Regaining economic ground lost in the war was now seen as an aspiration for younger generations. This economic hardship was coupled with the lasting sorrows of war, such as grief, broken relationships, and lost ambitions. On this loosely sketched background, one can begin to understand the antagonisms between Sarajlije and newcomers, urban and rural people, and economic elite and lower classes, all of which, as I will show, undergird the localization of BDS in Stari Grad.

The antagonistic attitudes of Sarajlije toward the newly arrived groups of people are already implied in the terminology used to describe them. The most common collective term is *došljaci* (literally, "those who have arrived," but the term carries negative connotations). More overarching terms are *seljaci* (peasants or villagers) and *seljačine* (a form of the same word but more exaggerated), *papci* (literally, "hooves," meaning bumpkins or hillbillies) and *primitivci* (primitives). In addition, specific groups of newcomers are labeled according to their specific regional origins, as in *Hercegovci* (people from Herzegovina), *Krajišnici* (people from Krajina), and *Sandžaklije* (people from Sandžak), with their associated "cultural mentalities and behaviors" (Stefansson 2007, 74). The massive scale of displacement taking place during and after the recent war, as I have suggested earlier in this chapter, has deepened, and brought new meaning to, the cultural stereotyping of rural newcomers. In addition to blaming them for bringing about cultural deterioration, Sarajlije also accuse them of having caused the war in the first place. Due to their alleged aggressiveness, backwardness, and cultural ignorance, those coming from the countryside are believed to be more inclined to take up arms against their neighbors of different ethnic backgrounds, and thus betray an ideal model of a civilized and

---

urbanites for rural newcomers. Combined with urbanity, longevity implied that the family in question predated socialism. "This conferred prestige not because of widespread disapproval of or resistance to communist rule but because longevity was seen to imply the containment and contextualization of socialism within an older and deeper moral tradition which, from the Bosniak perspective, also contained Islamic piety" (Sorabji 2006, 6).

"ethnically mixed [...] community of neighbors" (Maček 2001, 218). This idea is mirrored in the works of numerous western scholars who seem to uncritically adopt the Bosnian model of hierarchized cultural mentalities, portraying the urban locals, especially the eloquent, upper-middle-class intellectuals, in highly idealistic ways (see Donia and Fine 1994; Malcom 1994).[5]

The distinction between "cultured" urban locals and "non-cultured" rural newcomers is such a pervasive emotional issue that it seems to sideline the cleavages between numerous ethnic groups.[6] As anthropologist Andreas Stefansson notes, while criticism of other peoples' lack of culture is voiced with great emotion, remarks directed against other ethnic groups are rare and carefully expressed. This testifies both to a sense of political correctness and genuine, "surviving multiethnic attitudes" (Stefansson 2007, 65). In this regard, it is worth noting that rural newcomers are believed to nurture fundamentalist ethnic, religious, and political attitudes that threaten the fine and complex, even "fragile," pluralism of Sarajevo (Karahasan 1994, 16). They are seen as "easy prey" for manipulation by the nationalist parties due to their low levels of education (Stefansson 2007, 68). Furthermore, as I was told over and over, they are more prone to authoritarian policies in which mosques and other faith-based organizations impose their own version of Islam, and meaning of a Muslims identity, designed to curry favor with the political and economic elite, on the one hand, and some of the Arabs who took part in the war, on the other. Sometimes dubbed "Wahhabi," the latter version of Islam is experienced by many Muslims in Sarajevo, and especially those born and raised in the mahalas of Stari Grad, as an attack on Bosniak national identity, familiar practices, and their own sincerity as believers and legitimacy as religious authorities. It should come as no surprise, given the tensions and ambivalences I describe in this chapter, that its rejection is one of the most common markers of culturedness, cosmopolitanism, and belonging to "civilized" Europe.[7]

---

5 Such analyses tend to neglect the fact that "the ideology employed for stirring up ethno-religious antagonisms for political purposes largely emanated from the urban intellectuals based in major cities," such as Belgrade, Sarajevo, and Zagreb, as is usually the case with nationalist movements (Stefansson 2007, 64).

6 When Sarajlije describe other groups as "non-cultured," they are in fact not claiming that these people have no culture at all, "but that they have the 'wrong' kind of culture" (Stefansson 2007, 61).

7 To be clear, the rejection of "radical" attitudes imported from outside stems in part from their growing power in many spheres of daily life, threatening to uproot Sarajevo's multiethnic legacy. It is important, however, not to be seduced by the symbolic aspects of boundary-making, since piety, especially among younger generations, is an aspect that also plays a role in this process (see Bartulović 2015; Jevtić 2017; Mesarić 2013).

The importance attributed to urbanity, culturedness, and cosmopolitanism is rooted in a distinct project of constructing the Balkans in general, and what was Yugoslavia in particular, as the "other" in Europe, more a backward and primitive "self" than an alien "other" (Helms 2008, 89). In contrast to Edward W. Said's orientalism, which was bound to histories of direct colonization, Europe's political, economic, and cultural domination and subordination of what used to be Yugoslavia was more dispersed and indirect. Crucially then, as historian Katherine E. Fleming has argued, the borders between the two categories "begin to blur" (Fleming 2000, 1224). Other scholars have observed an intense Yugoslav longing for Europe, a desire to escape the stigmatization of the Balkan label, and to be considered a part of Europe (see Bakić-Hayden 1995; Gallagher 2001; Green 2005; Patterson 2003; Todorova 1997). On the perceived fringe of Europe, in other words, the idea of "Europe" carries an explosive, symbolic weight. That said, in light of the blurriness and ambiguity reported by Fleming, people in Bosnia and other parts of the former Yugoslavia have the arguments to challenge, invert, and transform negative depictions. Some, for example, strive to behave according to the standards of refined, educated, and knowledgeable Europeans in contrast to "non-cultured" rural newcomers, an opposition that was carried over from the socialist period but intensified by the war. A good case in point, as I hope I have made clear, are the Bosniaks.

Earlier in this chapter I suggested an increased pre-war emphasis on Muslim identity as European identity. And while many Bosniaks today maintain that they are European Muslims, and that they belong to Europe despite their cultural Muslim identity, the perception of Europe's failure to reciprocate has undermined the feeling of belonging to Europe, and has shattered the notion of Islam and Europe as joined by civility, rationality, and peace. The current de facto partition of Bosnia, the Bosniak enclosure into a small central area of it, and Europe's continued indifference have paved the way for Bosniaks, and particularly younger generations, to reconstrue "Europe," and the meaning of their own "Europeanness," in more critical terms. That said, disappointment with Europe, and its (mis)management of the war, does not suggest an abandonment of "Europeanness," and adoption of Middle Eastern fundamentalism and militancy, as has been suggested by several scholars from Serbia and Croatia (on this, see Sorabji 1993). Instead, it is one part of the modern political landscape shaped by the styles of Islamic argumentation and deliberation that are seen as essential to Europe's return to its forgotten, better self. I situate my analysis of BDS within this ideological struggle to establish a place for Islam in Europe. As will become evident to the reader, for young Bosniaks at the lower end of the social hierarchy, BDS is a means to fuse what are in effect two different projects—the deliberation of issues of public concern and the virtuous performance of one's duties in secularizing societies and spheres.

In the earlier chapters of this book, I touched on generational debates about Islam. In short, I argued that the challenges and difficulties of life in Europe have led young Muslims to embark on a project of Islamic reform through community participation, social responsibility, and greater activism. One effect of what was defined as "public Islam" has been to loosen the grip of more traditional sources of social and religious authority, such as parental authority and mosque-based imams. In what follows, I think about these generational changes and conflicts in the context of Tower Hamlets, and explore the ways in which they intertwine with BDS. Simply put, rather than describing Islam in all of its plurality, I turn to BDS to emphasize some of the cleavages that run through it, one the one hand, and the agency of ordinary Muslims who give life to it and take on themselves the moral guidance and improvement of the umma, on the other.

CHAPTER 4

Private Lives, Public Duties, and the Generational Gap

The sight of flowers, bulbs, and shrubs line this narrow Bethnal Green Street. The scent of jasmine, lilies, and daffodils linger as you wander down a gauntlet of blooms. The distinctive shouts of traders who have been manning stalls here for decades echo long after you leave. There is nothing quite like a visit to the Columbia Road Flower Market. Since its beginnings in the mid-nineteenth century, the market has become a popular destination for locals and tourists alike, elbowing their way to seasonal flowers at bargain prices. One of the men I met while visiting the market on a rainy Sunday morning was a sixty-eight-year-old trader named Asad. Before setting up a stall in the late 1980s, he worked for a dry-cleaning business owned by his brother. There were times when he was earning less than twenty pounds a week. "If I was back in Sylhet, my life would be better," Asad told me shortly after we met. "I cannot go back now. My sons study here. They will work here and start families here. I had a hard life, but they will have a better one." This conversation revealed to me a pioneering spirit of first-generation sojourns who intended to stay in England for a year or two, and return to villages in Sylhet after saving enough money. The increasing demands for remittances, and the inability to save as much as they would need to settle down to a comfortable life in Sylhet, however, meant that the temporary sojourners became settlers (on this, see Ahmed 2005; Begum and Eade 2005).

This kind of reflection on home and away characteristic of the first generation was illustrated in a conversation with Ashur, a sixty-two-year-old tailor from Whitechapel. "I belong to Sylhet with all my heart," he told me during one of my visits to his Leman Street home. "No one here sees me as an equal. It does not matter how long I have lived here. I am described as an 'outsider.'" It has been difficult for Ashur to come to terms with his status in England, and he spoke passionately about means of integration that stand in tension with cultural or national identity. "I do not want to give up who I am so that I am better integrated. I want to celebrate my Sylheti identity and go home a proud man someday." Ismail, a sixty-one-year-old who ran several corner shops thanks to what he called "years of hard work and hustle" expressed his identification with Sylhet in a similar manner. Sitting in his kitchen, with his daughter cooking and his grandchildren running about, Ismail told me, "Staying here is not what I want, but I have to do it for economic reasons. I want to go home and enjoy the rest of my life, but I have to stay here where I do not feel accepted." Men like Asad, Ashur, and Ismail who had remained in Tower Hamlets well into old age told me about their initial enthusiasm for, and subsequent disappointment with, living on council estates. Although they struggled with loneliness and isolation, these men and many others were actually grateful because they had experienced the hardships of Sylhet. But living on council estates also meant exposure to a claustrophobic and unpleasant environment with high rates of crime and vandalism—experiences that contributed to a nostalgic preservation of values and beliefs associated with Sylhet. These experiences have led to a mediation of "here" and "there" that should be seen as an attempt to uphold some kind of equilibrium in the lives of the first generation. In this light, it is not surprising that their activism and community participation have remained connected to, and inspired by, the political events surrounding Bangladesh and its 1971 liberation from Pakistan.

As I have discussed in previous chapters, most Bangladeshis of the first generation proclaimed their beliefs in democracy and socialism, and they sought a secular government that facilitated cultural norms tied to those of the greater Sylhet district. After most family reunification had taken place in the late 1970s and early 1980s, and ties with Sylhet faded with the memory of the Bangladesh Liberation War, the first generation's leadership was challenged by an Anglicized second generation that forged highly effective alliances with white Labour activists. By the end of the 1980s, these individuals had gained positions of responsibility in a range of government bodies, community organizations, and development agencies that remain relevant today, but they usually continued their elders' tradition of socialist secularism. They are now challenged by British-born activists who are inspired by the kind of "reformist" Islam that their elders had rejected in Sylhet. Many seek guidance from modern religious reformers like al-Qaradawi, Muzaffar, and Soroush who set moral boundaries for their engagement with a secularized and pluralized majority society. These British-born activists also challenge the more formal city hall politics of their elders that have failed to emancipate them from political and economic marginalization. What emerges from these generational changes and conflicts are different imaginaries of BDS centered upon questions of parental authority and dominant social mores. Not just who are "insiders" and "outsiders" in Tower Hamlets but also who are the most "authentic" among those who see themselves as "insiders." Differently put, BDS has provided an arena for Bangladeshis from a range of socioeconomic and age backgrounds to act out their claims to be the genuine voice of their community. In what follows, I want to explore how BDS is debated, interpreted, and adapted with these questions of authenticity, legitimacy, and representation at the forefront.

1   First-Generation Bangladeshis and the Individualization of Responsibility

"Hey, what have you done today," I would ask Ashur again and again during my visits to his Hackney Road home. "Nothing," he would respond, shrugging his shoulders. "Just some shopping." I had become accustomed to such an exchange. It was frustrating at first. What is there to write about if nothing seems to happen? Shopping creates what anthropologists Billy Ehn and Orvar Löfgren call "rhythms and temporalities in everyday life," which are rarely noticed or reflected upon (Ehn and Lofgren 2009, 99). Their apparent mundanity may hide questions of authenticity, legitimacy, and representation, but it is precisely mundanity that seems to characterize the BDS activities of first-generation Bangladeshis. In contrast to their children and grandchildren who consider BDS a spartan political movement, one that has the potential to transform majority views of Islam and Muslims through its energetic community participation, first-generation Bangladeshis participate in less public ways. Or to put it another way, their BDS activities are confined to the intimacy and invisibility of homes where they become intertwined with forms of communal solidarity in the face of hardship and anomic settlement experience. Abra, a sixty-one-year-old housewife from Bethnal Green, once told me, "I do not feel at home in Tower Hamlets. Sure, I am here with my husband and daughters, but I have experienced hardship since settling. I have been pushed and yelled at on the streets of Tower Hamlets." Over scones and lemon curd, Abra explained to me that she "remains patient in the face of hardship" and "never complains." The younger, British-born generation regards such an approach to life as defeatist and fatalist—as an acceptance of social injustice that allows no possibility for change. However, note that Abra does not dismiss the possibility for change. Rather, as she pointed out to me later, she believes that people choose how to deal with their difficulties and unjust circumstances. What we have here is a notion of agency defined in terms of "individual ethics whereby each person is responsible for their own actions" (Mahmood 2012, 173). In this conception, BDS is relegated to its own differentiated sphere, its influence limited to those aspects of life that are deemed "private."

During my stay in Tower Hamlets, I spent much of my time meeting with first-generation Bangladeshis for whom BDS implies entering into personal matters of religious faith. That said, even when confined to the private sphere of domesticity, family, and home, BDS often takes the form of argument and discussion about the moral health and fortitude of the community as a whole. Thus, it becomes particularly important for, what anthropologist Charles Hirschkind describes as, "perfecting and sustaining [...] practices upon which an Islamic society depends" (Hirschkind 2006, 8). For example, Abra went shopping on Friday, always to the same store on the corner of Hanbury Street where no Israeli products were sold. She described in detail how she used to take her daughters with her, instructing them about what to buy. "I taught them well," Abra said with a warm smile. "To do good and to forbid evil is an obligation and sacred duty made incumbent upon Muslims by God. By refusing to buy Israeli products, they avoid supporting the oppression of brothers and sisters in Palestine. They have children now, so they will pass on what I taught them. When I am grey and old, they will do my shopping too." In short, Abra's participation in BDS is about a variety of ambitions and goals, foremost among them the desire on the part of ordinary Muslims to live in accord with the demands of Islamic piety. I might add that this participation is also about the restoration and strengthening of the Muslim community, a sacred duty Abra is meant to be in charge of as the first teacher of the children. That said, BDS cannot simply be interpreted as a religious practice passed on from one generation to the next. On the one hand, although morally good or pleasing to God, it is not mandatory. On the other hand, as I hope to show, we can observe the emergence of a new generation of Muslims for whom BDS externalizes a discovery of a different kind of Islam, different from the images propagated in the majority society, and different from the versions transmitted by the first generation.

1.1 *Islamic Pedagogy in a Secular Society*

The desire on the part of ordinary Muslims to live in accord with the demands of Islamic piety that I mentioned above is met within a context of changing social, political, and technological conditions, and entails the creation of a new deliberative space for ordinary Muslims to argue about and act upon the conditions of their collective existence. Lama, a sixty-one-year-old seamstress from Mile End, for example, told me that watching television is a "family event." When I asked her what she meant by this, Lama explained that her family of five gathers in front of television night after night to talk about the Palestinian struggle for freedom, justice, and equality, thereby alluding to one of the ways in which distant political commitments filter into my informants' lives. The atmosphere of such practices as watching television is often bursting with energy and excitement. Lama gets upset and shouts at the newscaster, arguing with positions she regards as inaccurate and protesting when he moves onto news of current events in England. She reported later that her interest in BDS is fairly new, sparked by radio and television programs, as well as booklets and pamphlets widely distributed on the streets outside of mosques and bus stations, the primary purpose of which is to provide information on practical rules of pietistic conduct. They cover an array of expected topics, such as the performance of religious rituals and the manner of conducting oneself with kin and neighbors. More recently, they focused on the Muslim responsibility toward the Palestinian struggle for freedom, justice, and equality.

In Tower Hamlets, a huge market exists for Islamic ethical and pedagogical materials. The pedagogy of BDS is commonly understood to refer to these materials, as I hope I have made clear in chapter 2. What I want to emphasize here is that their proliferation has allowed women like Lama and Abra to think more productively about the demand to live piously. This in turn calls for the practice of certain virtues, such as compassion, sincerity, and fear of God, and the creation of certain conditions under which these virtues can be realized. During one of my visits with Lama, she told me that whenever she reads a pamphlet about the bloodshed, suffering, "and decades-old injustice that Israel has visited upon Palestinians," she remembers that one day she will come before God to be judged and that fills her with fear. "Fear does not paralyze me. It forces me to correct my behavior. If I buy Israeli goods, I condone occupation, dispossession, and apartheid. I will not have the blood of Palestinians on my hands." From this perspective, fear of God is a condition that undergirds a broad range of ethical actions in Tower Hamlets, notably BDS. At the same time, however, these actions must be understood as means by which such fear, as a condition for the "doing of good or right" and the "forbidding of evil or wrong," may become sedimented in one's character, "enabling one to live [...] piously" (Hirschkind 2006, 71).

As Lama's husband entered the room we were sitting in, the conversation briefly halted, just long enough for me to look at my notes. It then returned, with no sense that there had been a pause, but in a way that came as a complete surprise to me. "Everyone in Tower Hamlets is boycotting," Lama suddenly said. This shift from the broader moral project of an umma to a seemingly incongruous point of reference, the diverse local community, made it possible for Lama to describe her participation in BDS as "unproblematic" in relation to the British state. Over time I began to recognize this responsiveness among the first generation. Fatima, a sixty-two-year-old housewife from Blackwell, who began boycotting "long before the call for BDS had even been made," noted that it is a good thing that BDS has mass appeal. According to her, this makes the fact that Muslims participate "less suspicious." Noting the look of puzzlement on my face, Fatima explained, "We do not want anyone to call it an Islamic movement. That would cause problems for us." Here I want to suggest that BDS is not considered a collective responsibility but an individual one that is incumbent upon each and every Muslim to undertake precisely because Fatima and others had struggled to comprehend what it means to live as Muslims in a non-Muslim society. Delicately poised in relation to the state and society, and reluctant to leave the relative safety of Bangladeshi traditionalism, they participate in BDS from the intimacy and invisibility of their homes with an implicit claim for the resurrection of a vibrant and vigorous umma. Their homes, moreover, are the sites through which cultures of here and elsewhere are mediated and articulated in a vocabulary structured by the legacies of Bangladeshi nation-building, which translates the Palestinian struggle, as well as the events of September 11, the war in Afghanistan, and the invasion of Iraq, to create a distinctly Bangladeshi politics (Back et al. 2009, 17–18).

The link between Bangladesh and the organization of politics in Tower Hamlets is intimate but not static. Although there has been a move in recent years from alignment with secular nationalist politics as a means of representation toward faith-based organizing, a phenomenon the previous chapter explored at length, the first-generation Bangladeshis I met in Tower Hamlets invoked the memory of the Bangladesh Liberation War, and its emphasis on sovereignty, freedom, and democracy, in order to explain to me a feeling of responsibility one feels toward the Palestinian struggle. Ashur told me, "The monsters who engaged in coercion and cruelty during the nine-month-long Bangladesh Liberation War must be brought to justice. Even today, they continue with their savagery in a country they wish had not been born. Same as the monsters who murder Palestinians in pursuit of their Zionist agenda." We would sit in his kitchen, drinking green tea while reading booklets and pamphlets on BDS I picked up on the way. While reading, Ashur would often interject comments intended to help me understand the peculiar link between BDS and the legacies of Bangladeshi nation-building. "At the root of the Palestinian struggle are the principles of democracy and self-determination," Ashur would tell me. "The same principles guided the students and intelligentsia who rode the tide of civil disobedience in what was then East Pakistan. We too, like Palestinians long before us, were systematically abused, persecuted, and tortured. Thus, we understand their struggle. And we refuse to accept injustice as fate."

Similar mediation was conducted by Omar and Naaza, a couple in their late-sixties I met at a supermarket. I watched them read labels and ponder for nearly twenty minutes before I approached them at the counter. "We had a hard time today," Omar sighed. "We have never been to this supermarket, so we did not know what products it stocks. We usually go to a neighborhood one, but it was closed today." Most supermarkets and grocery stores in Tower Hamlets are deemed "BDS friendly zones," with stickers on doors and windows that let men and women like Omar and Naaz know that they do not stock products from Israel, or any companies implicated in its violations of international law. That said, the Commercial Road supermarket I approached Omar and Naaz in had no such sticker on its doors and windows. "Shopping took ages today, but that is fine," Naaz sighed, making a gesture of resignation with her hands. "I fled my home in March 1971. Did you know that women like me were murdered and raped by the Pakistani military? I had to escape from violence that still haunts me." Naaz then proceeded to link her own personal experience with that of the Palestinian people, saying, "I recognize their suffering. It is my duty to boycott, to do however much I can to save them from this suffering." This duty to do good, as I have suggested earlier, manifests in BDS, and is commonly understood to be important for upholding individual piety.

1.2 *Ethno-National Heritage and the Generational Twist*

The renewed concern with Islam and Islamic piety derives in part from the conditions of life in Tower Hamlets. When speaking about this predominantly working-class borough, it is hard to think of, much rather depict, activism that has ever been secular. According to Les Back et al., the conventional forms of "religious identification" have historically fed directly into an understanding of activism and community participation in Tower Hamlets (Back et al. 2009, 7).[1] In the case of first-generation Bangladeshis, more recent tensions with members of the white working-class, which I discussed in detail in chapter 3, provide important clues for understanding their particular take on Islam and its role in BDS activism. In contrast to Bengali Hindus, who show high levels of integration and social mobility, those I worked with, who migrated at the same time and from the same region, and settled in the same council estates, often reported their disappointment with England and wondered whether it would not have been better if they had remained in Sylhet. They also developed what Werner Schiffauer calls "defensive religiosity," meant to preserve and protect cultural values and life designs of "home" (Schiffauer 2007, 74). Unlike Lama and Abra, whose goal was to render all details of their lives in accord with

---

1 In the late nineteenth century, concerns over health and sanitation raised questions about the welfare of people in Tower Hamlets. At the turn of the twentieth century, this issue was taken up by the Salvation Army and a range of Christian missionaries. More recently, a number of reform movements concerned with alcohol and substance abuse were either run by the Church or had a faith-based core (see Gidley 2009; Kershen 2005). This does not imply that all reform movements that have emerged in the borough are religious. But it does imply that faith-based activism had always played an important role.

standards of Islamic piety, others I met during the period of my fieldwork in Tower Hamlets, who turned their backs on the majority society, practiced their religion in a ritualized and secluded manner, without much attention to how this contributed to the realization of a pious self.

Rahil, a sixty-two-year-old who runs a small café in Hackney, recalled coming out of a Bethnal Green Mosque after the Friday prayer and being handed a "Vote Respect" pamphlet by a white activist campaigning with a group from the East London Mosque. He recounted the experience saying, "Some white people bonded with our young people. They campaigned together for Galloway's Respect. I am also a Muslim, but they did not come to me. Why? Is it because I manage my relationship with God in private? I do not need to show it to anyone else. I do not need to keep saying 'I am a Muslim.' But it seems that I am not Muslim enough if I do not."[2] Rahil shook his head and went on, "This comradeship with white people poisons our community. It clouds our knowledge about who we are and what we stand for." Ismail similarly warned against practices that transform the political consciousness of Bangladeshis and their sense of agency. He was in his early sixties when I met him and, after the death of his wife, was the only breadwinner in a family of six. Despite the long hours he worked, Ismail found time to give informal lessons in Sylheti history and culture at a neighborhood mosque. He believed that young people had abandoned their Sylheti roots that had once worked seamlessly with Islam to set them apart in an all-Muslim region carved from a Hindu subcontinent. While Ismail and Rahil have maintained points of reference from their rural lives in Sylhet in urban Tower Hamlets, young people cannot make this connection. During one of our conversations, Ismail asked, "Whose standard is community cohesion based on? It is about accepting people, not changing them. Our young people are disowning the very culture they are from. They are changing their names, everything." As will become evident to the reader, young people tend to express a disconnection with Sylheti culture, which they perceive as somewhat "backward." Their vociferous opposition to "traditional elders" and "irrelevant secularists," we might add, points to the emergence of a new political landscape in which BDS is debated, interpreted, and adapted.

Asad, whom I cited at the beginning of this chapter, told me that generational changes and conflicts have long shaped Tower Hamlets' political

---

2 As we have already seen, the East London Mosque has been very successful in aliening with white Labour activists. Leaders of the IFE and YMO have also been increasingly involved in social and youth work across divisions through community campaigning against alcohol and substance abuse, anti-social behavior, and school truancy (on this, see Eade and Garbin 2006).

landscape. "Even after living here for decades, I hold onto my Sylheti roots. My worship leader is also from Sylhet. When I go to the mosque, I feel like I have a place of my own. Young people are finding a place of their own. But in doing so, they abandon their Sylheti roots. I think that is wrong." These and similar attitudes suggest that although the first generation has taken on BDS with enthusiasm, and may even see it as important for individual practices of piety, it has done so without any meaningful connections to the majority society and the younger, British-born generation. In short, the first-generation participants in BDS I knew in Tower Hamlets did not engage in rallies, protests, or any organized BDS activities. Rather, their participation was a private and intimate matter that centered around two points—the desire to live in accord with the demands of Islamic piety for some, and for others, the desire to uphold familiar traditions and customs in a post-migration context.

The first generation conveyed attitudes, beliefs, and experiences of life in Sylhet to the second generation. Those in the forties–fifties age band were thus familiarized with power dynamics in which cultural and national identity were recognized as a means of political and social mobilization. In addition, they identified with "being British" by virtue of national citizenship and the notions of civic responsibility implied in that status. In contrast to their elders, they were more willing to engage with and challenge what they saw as racialized configurations of "Britishness" by developing and maintaining ties with white Labour activists. In what follows, I will reflect further upon the relationship between a clear generational divide and BDS activism in Tower Hamlets.

2   Second-Generation Activists and the Anti-Racist Struggle

Many of the second-generation activists I came to know cut their political teeth in youth organizations of the late 1970s. In contrast to their elders who turned their backs on the majority society, they were able to build on their connections to escape the tailoring workshops, cafés, and restaurants, and get white-collar jobs with local administrative and political institutions. In doing so, they wanted to go beyond the reservations and negative experiences of their elders, and develop their own feeling of "Britishness" as national citizens. At the same time, their connections with local authority, and their incessant pursuit of government contracts and funds, has led to what anthropologist Pnina Werbner calls "ethnic absolutism," the term which implies that "it is not only western representations of the 'other' that essentialize." Rather, within the spaces of civil society, "the politics of ethnicity [...] are not so much imposed as grounded in essentialist self-imaginings of community" (Werbner 1997, 230).

Indeed, the second-generation activists in Tower Hamlets commonly narrated and argued over the conceptions and representations of their community, as well as the intertwined role that secular and religious institutions have played in this process. This relationship is best tracked, I want to suggest further, through attention to their lasting commitment to the Awami League.

Although they stressed their party's secularist heritage, the second-generation activists in Tower Hamlets explained to me that Sheikh Mujib Rahman, one of the leaders of the Awami League and the first President of Bangladesh, drew on his country's Muslim heritage before his death, and that the Awami League worked with religious institutions in order to remain in power since his death in 1975 (on this, see Begum and Eade 2005; Eade and Garbin 2006). Thus, although they espoused secular nationalist views, the second-generation activists in Tower Hamlets viewed Islam as an essential part of the cultural terrain upon which the Bangladeshi nation was developed. This in turn ushered in an acceptance of Islam's cultural requirements. Rabah, a fifty-one-year-old primary teacher from Mile End, remarked to me that when the Bow Central Mosque needed support for its renovation of the Islamic Center, he "chipped in." In contrast, Rabah was less eager to donate when "people from the mosque started using Islam for political aims." There is little doubt that Islam has long played an important role in mobilization and community participation of Bangladeshis in Tower Hamlets, as I have mentioned earlier in this chapter. At the same time, a number of scholars have shown that old networks of mobilization are challenged by networks that cut across Islamist, secularist, liberal, and leftist lines (on this, see Jevtić 2015; Peace 2013; Tatari 2014). The demands of those who are part of these dense social networks center around one point—the desire to be recognized as British in a way that is blind to the differences and contradictions of culture, religion, and ethnicity. These demands are also reflected in the biographical trajectories of the second-generation participants in BDS I came to know, many of whom got involved through the Palestine Solidarity Campaign (PSC).

2.1 *Racism, Zionism, and the Negotiation of Belonging*

The PSC is a nonprofit and nongovernmental organization with supporters from communities that span across England, and increasingly across the world. Established in 1982, during the build-up to Israel's invasion of Lebanon, the organization has since become one of the leading figures in the transnational struggle for Palestinian rights. In March 2011, during the "Celebrate Palestine" event held at the School of Oriental and African Studies (SOAS) in central London, I spoke to Sebastian. At the time of my fieldwork, Sebastian was the PSC's national organizer and longest-serving staff member. Sebastian spoke passionately and clearly about the PSC's goal to contribute to a large-scale movement that lets Palestinians know they are not forgotten, and that the justness of their cause is recognized. As he explained to me, "BDS sends a message that the world will not sit still as Israel blatantly disobeys international law, the Universal Declaration of Human Rights, and the Geneva Convention." Let me also draw the reader's attention to the way in which Sebastian linked between global political issues like the Israeli–Palestinian conflict and local grassroots organizations like the PSC, which send their members on visits across the country to mobilize for what is considered to be a more ethical foreign policy. In an interview with me, Sebastian noted that mobilizing for BDS is about stirring public debate. "People are urged to challenge their elected Members of Parliament on an important political issue and pressure them to take a stand for Palestinian rights, rather than remain silent as they had done in the past."

There is a specific series of steps essential for this type of public engagement. One, people are urged to display power and perseverance, and to hold Israel accountable to international law and universal principles of human rights. Two, they are urged to educate and mobilize support for ending Israel's impunity. Three, they are urged to keep informed through booklets, flyers, and pamphlets. Four, they are urged to build solidarity with Palestine through forms of public activism that include demonstrations, protests, marches, and sit-ins. The email I received in September 2011, having subscribed to the PSC's weekly communiqué, explained that the organization aims to run a targeted and nuanced campaign, which in turn allows it to "organically engage in a large-scale, emancipatory movement against Zionism."

The movement against Zionism is nothing new in England. However, before 1948 and during the early stages of the State of Israel, activists were often members of the establishment, notably former army officers, conservative politicians, Christian missionaries, and the Arab ulama from elite universities (on this, see Wistrich 2012). Today, it is more likely to discover alliances of peace activists, anti-globalists, radical left-wingers, and Islamic organizations leading the movement, many of whom clustered around the PSC. For example, in August 2005, the organization provided support to academics calling on the Association of University Teachers (AUT)—at the time one of the largest associations in England—to break ties with Israeli institutions of higher education and the vast majority of Israeli academics. In June 2018, the organization supported a conference on Nakba organized by the Friends of Sabeel Ecumenical Liberation Theology Center UK, "an expending network of individuals, organizations, and communities of all backgrounds [...] who stand in solidarity with the Palestinian people" (Sabeel-Kairos n.d.). The organization also developed and maintained ties with the Muslim Council of Britain (MCB) and the Muslim Public Affairs Committee (MPAC), both of whom encourage Muslims to partake in tactical voting against Members of Parliament who endorse policies regarded to be not in Muslims' interests, especially on the Israeli–Palestinian conflict. In short, the organization draws support from all sectors of contemporary British society, cutting across lines of difference to create a common political project whose goal is to reject all forms of racism, including Zionism, Islamophobia, and anti-Semitism. When I met Sebastian, he reported that the racist principles of Zionism treat the indigenous Palestinians as "lesser humans," and that this has also been the experience of "many non-whites in Britain," albeit in a non-institutionalized and non-legalized form. The desire to be recognized as British, not be discriminated against or treated as outsiders and outcasts, and the perceived failure of the majority society to reciprocate, have played an important role in the rising popularity of BDS among the second generation. In order to elaborate this point, let me turn to an ethnographic vignette that focuses on an ever-present memory of racism that undergirds the BDS activities of the second generation.

"I was born in small village in Sylhet. My father moved to Tower Hamlets in the early 1970s, and we joined him shortly after. I remember growing up poor, in a cramped council housing, with thin walls and no privacy. I remember being chased by racist gangs of British nationalists who would roam the streets of Tower Hamlets." Sitting in his cousin's restaurant in Mile End, Jeet, a forty-nine-year-old software engineer, opened up about the difficulties and challenges of growing up in a borough shaped by the discriminatory housing policies of the 1980s and persistent hostility of the white working-class. He told me, "Whites were abusive back then. They would spit and throw rocks at me. They would yell that I should go back to where I came from. I had to be left out of school early and walked home by my father who protected me from attacks." Racist gangs, mostly comprised of the National Front members, also passed out racist pamphlets and vandalized property. The experience of being harassed and threatened on the streets of Tower Hamlets meant that first and second migrants like Jeet formed tight-knit communities to rely on and protect themselves. As racist gangs receded in the mid-1980s, with much of the white working-class moving east toward Essex, greater numbers of Bangladeshis migrated, making Tower Hamlets the largest hub of twenty-five to thirty-five-year-olds of any local authority (Tower Hamlets Council's Corporate Research Unit 2013). Due to the greater safety in numbers, and despite the warnings of their elders, many second-generation Bangladeshis decided to challenge a mindset that limits them to their local "square mile." At the same time, community structures, cultural values, and forms of belonging and collectivity, which shaped their elders' lives in Sylhet, have remained and, one may argue, intensified given the feeling of rejection at the hands of the majority society and the apparent ineffectiveness of the British state and its institutions. Let me elaborate.

Dabir, a forty-six-year-old data analyst from Hackney, talked about growing up in a way similar to Jeet, concluding more pointedly, "When you take racism into account, you do have to wonder where your alliances lie." Dabir looked at me and explained that he identified as British when applying for government contracts and funds. However, when it came to his national belonging, Dabir identified as Bangladeshi. What I want to draw attention to here is a tendency among the second generation to describe national belonging in terms of origin, which was then relativized by references to a hybrid belonging, for example, "British/Bengali." Although "Britishness" was considered to be a flexible identity that embraces a spectrum of difference, Dabir and Jeet, as well as others I worked with, believed that its recognition was dispensed on a highly conditional basis, riddled with double standards and discrimination. Specifically, they showed a deep awareness of their rights to a responsive governance, and were sensitive to its failure to deliver. In contrast to the first generation that recognized such democratic flaws as features of an imperfect political system that nonetheless bestowed great benefits on those who had yet to contribute to it, the second generation believed that these flaws were reflective of a political system that was not interested in their welfare and equality.

While speaking with Dabir one day at the Bean and Leaf Café on White Horse Lane, he explained to me that he joined the PSC in order to challenge discriminatory and racialized constructions of "Britishness," and create possibilities for alterative expressions that utilize varied cultural and racial resources. Taking on BDS as part of his engagement with the PSC, instilled in Dabir pride and dignity in the context of local expressions of race and racism. It is interesting to note that although both the first and second generation intertwined BDS with the legacies of Bangladeshi nation-building, thereby emphasizing shared moral orientations and languages, in contrast to the first generation, for whom this played out in the intimacy and invisibility of homes, the second generation aspired to end this quietism and seclusion, and join contemporary British society as an accepted member. Often, for example, Dabir would account for his participation in, and support for, the BDS movement in terms of the realization of his "authentic self," one that preserves and protects traditions and customs of "home" without resorting to isolationism. My goal is not to provide a genealogy of ethnic mobilization in Tower Hamlets that, as I hope I have made clear, was organized principally in racialized terms through the Labour Party, but to ask how BDS has come to be perceived as a new form of democratic participation in a racialized context.

2.2 Pride, Dignity, and the New Dimension of Solidarity

Rabah got involved in the BDS movement in 2010. Like Dabir, he identified as British by virtue of national citizenship. "This," he was quick to tell me, "is different to English. I am not English." Rabah embraced the term "British" but rejected "English" because of its association with "whiteness" and notions of indigenous culture (on this, see Eade 1997; Wemyss 2008). According to him, BDS was an expression of solidarity inspired in part by the need to escape stigmatization that brings "race" into being. When I met Rabah, he spoke with enthusiasm about a conference he had attended at Birkbeck University in central London. "People from around the world talked about the situation in the West Bank. About what needs to be done to put an end to Israel's regime of institutionalized racial domination. I asked questions and raised serious issues. No one told me I have no right to do so because of my skin color or the shade of beard I keep." Amna, a forty-six-year-old project officer from Hackney, similarly reported that BDS helped her connect to other non-whites in Tower Hamlets, those who "struggle to be politically active" in an environment where they are constantly described as "outsiders." Those who "do not belong." People from different cultures, races, and ethnicities, according to Amna, "are most susceptible to such exclusion."

In many ways BDS is a function of local, contingent, and emplaced struggles between "insiders" and "outsiders." The exercise of power at local level, one may argue, has long reflected the lack of power at national level. Thus, despite the fact that Amna and Rabah, and many others like them, had entered local administrative and political institutions through their participation in youth organizations of the late 1970s, they found the acceptance of their "Britishness" absurd in light of the democratic system's failure to deliver on welfare and equality it promised. Amna asked, "What is British? Is it my passport? Or do I have to adopt the British culture? Britain is multicultural. But where is this multiculturalism if Britain treats people differently? I have experienced it. I have been told to go back to 'my country' more than I care to remember." I would argue that BDS provides Amna with a set of frames that elide difference through language of political and social mobilization. The fact that it cuts across cultural, religious, and ethnic lines, moreover, de facto poses impediments to double standards that Amna feels subjected to. As she once explained to me, "It would be hypocritical of whites to call for an end of Israel's racism but to accept racism at home."

I first met Amna in December 2012. "Crazy country," she shouted while entering the Ashby's Sandwich Bar in Aldgate an hour late for our meeting. "One snowflake and nothing works. State of emergency," Amna proclaimed, and I could not help but wonder if her barely concealed rage had less to do with snow that paralyzed the city's transport and more with racist pamphlets that have swapped the streets of Tower Hamlets in the last few days. "A national emergency today, in twenty years a catastrophe," warned one of the pamphlets I was handed earlier that day. Extortion for London, the organization responsible for these materials, urged all white East Enders who felt victimized by the "Islamification of Tower Hamlets" and the rapid "ethnic cleansing" to take a stand against Tower Hamlets becoming a mirror image of Bangladesh. "Their birth rate is the highest in the developed world, and quite possibly the highest in the whole world. Poverty, crime, and deprivation have become the norm in this new Islamic State of Tower Hamlets," the pamphlet warned. "Over the next two decades the population is predicted to rise exponentially. With nowhere for this community to expand, the chronic overcrowding, disease, and poverty will become a national disaster." To illustrate this supposed "migrant boom," Extortion for London used a sketch by a conservative cartoonist Derek T. Devareaux. His sketch of a pregnant veiled woman, with a ticking bomb in place of her belly, also appeared on the organization's website where claims were made that the "Blitz generation" has watched helplessly as their sons and daughters were forced to move out of their historic homeland. "From the early 1980s," the website stated, "housing resources have been diverted to Bangladeshi Muslim families. This policy has practically eradicated the indigenous white population, and has continued for decades without comment or constraint." It is worth recalling that Margaret Thatcher's "right to buy" scheme has resulted in a highly racialized issue of housing in Tower Hamlets, and that it has opened the door for right-wing organizations like Extortion for London to suggest that only a few "isolated and ageing pockets of the indigenous white population survive" (Extortion for London 2012).

To counter the claims that equate her community with crime and deprivation, Amna was quick to point out that she has long played an active role in public, social, and political life of Tower Hamlets. "I go to neighborhood meetings, and when I encounter someone who does not know about Bangladeshis, I have to educate them that it is not enough to oppose the biases and intolerances of contemporary British society. What we must do is bridge the differences between us." This task, according to Amna, gives direction and form to the BDS movement. Beyond a common idealistic trope, however, there is a stock of stories about the lives of Bangladeshis in Tower Hamlets geared to this task that I want to draw attention to. Again and again in interview data, the story of Altab Ali, a twenty-five-year-old textile worker who was stabbed to death by three teenagers as he walked home from work along Adler Street, came up. I was told that this racist killing pointed to decades of violence against Bangladeshis. During an interview, Jeet explained it in these terms, "I believe that whites need to be more aware of the implications of racism. Migration laws introduced in the mid-1960s legitimized the idea that Bangladeshis were 'outsiders' in Tower Hamlets. We were blamed for everything, and we became targets of racism. At the same time, we were charged with carrying weapons meant to protect us and subjected to migration checks. On May 4, 1978, blood was spilled because of the system's failure to investigate attacks and protect victims." According to Jeet, the story of Altab Ali, infused with the fitting emotions of fear and sadness, was one of the steppingstones to an effective alliance between "progressive, secular Bangladeshis" and radical left-wingers to reject all forms of racism. The British-born generation, as I will show in the second half of this chapter, is sympathetic to these discussions about the lasting experience of racism in Tower Hamlets, but it is also interested in events affecting Muslims everywhere. Thus, Bangladeshi secularists of the second generation have to tread carefully, since they do not want to appear as "anti-Muslim," uncritical servants of local interests and agendas.

The approach to polarized positions of BDS activists in Tower Hamlets I outline here recognizes that those espousing secular nationalist views still regarded themselves as Muslims. They observed public rituals with their fellow Muslims and expressed their religious identity through various observances at home, but this was not instrumental in organizing or promoting BDS. Jeet and Amna, and many others like them, told me that although religion played an important role in debates about Bangladeshi national identity, their decision to participate in BDS was not grounded in it. Rather, what I observed where moments of ambiguity where affiliations of religion, ethnicity, and race overlapped and complexly intertwined to provide the bedrock of the second generation's participation in BDS. As Jeet once remarked to me, "I boycott as a Bangladeshi Muslim. Because as a Bangladeshi Muslim, I was attacked, discriminated against, and made to feel worthless. As a Bangladeshi Muslim, I have a sense of closeness to the Palestinian people." Jeet continued, "In discriminatory public discourses, I am described as a Muslim first and foremost. Maybe this makes it easier to rationalize endemic racism in Tower Hamlets? Like, it is all to do with Islam and the idea that it has no place in Tower Hamlets. But Gujarati Muslims have done well, so it is not a Muslim thing. It is not a Bengali thing either. Look at Bengali Hindus and how well they have done. I think it is a mix of our Sylheti roots, skin color, and Islam that makes us susceptible to racism." What I want to emphasize here are fine-grained modes of identity expression that organize themselves in part through the dynamic and interactive field of BDS. In contrast to the first generation, for whom BDS was one part of the larger project of realizing piety, generally relegated to the sphere of private life, Jeet and other members of the second generation I knew in Tower Hamlets, who did not find their demands for recognition, distributive justice, and political representation to be incongruent with the demands of pious living, positioned BDS within the larger project organized by the political left to reject all forms of racism. It was precisely this secular, left of center, municipalist politics that was opposed by a new generation of idealistic activists that were much younger and got involved in BDS through Islamic organizations of the kind I describe below.

3   British-Born Pietists and the Ideal of Ummatic Collectivity

Participation within the conventional structures of local politics confirmed the success of ethnic mobilization in seizing power, as well as the limits within which such mobilization was constrained (see Back et al. 2009; Eade and Garbin 2006). Indeed, many of my British-born informants claimed that Tower Hamlets' councilors were illiterate in English and elected through "village politics." They seemed at best detached from day-to-day struggles in Tower Hamlets and at worst irrelevant. Jalal, a twenty-three-year-old student of politics at the University of Westminster, would tell me on occasion that the Tower Hamlets Council had "more Bangladeshi councilors than any other," but that issues like unemployment, lack of public services, and poor housing conditions went untackled. Others, at the same time, claimed that the Tower Hamlets Council was managed by career bureaucrats of the second generation, unaccountable and unreflective of Tower Hamlets. At the same time, levels of activism among the British-born generation were high, especially when compared to white Britons of roughly the same age (see Gest 2010; Glynn 2008). Like many Bangladeshis of this generation, my informants tended to associate themselves with organizations that were nonprofit and nongovernmental precisely because they were seen as less complicit with city hall politics and the more formal democratic institutions of the British state.

A number of scholars have observed that after the Labour Party's defeat in the 1986 Tower Hamlets Council elections, driven by a powerful mix of right-wing populism, racism, and the degree of ethnic segregation I discussed in chapter 3, there was more room within the borough's political arena for the emergence of recognizably Islamic organizations, unencumbered by the patronage of the British state (see Anwar 1998; Eade 1997; Gardner and Shakur 1994; Glynn 2002). As Tower Hamlets over the last thirty years became the site for new kinds of social and political organization and expression, questions that took a global Muslim community as their primary reference, as the category of belonging and commitment understood to underlie the moral and political project that I explore in this book, were gradually connected to local concerns about unemployment, lack of public services, and poor housing conditions. The ways in which the British-born generation engaged in this process, and an incisive political critique of the British state it engendered, can be gleaned from my ethnographic vignettes of Friends of al-Aqsa (FOA).

3.1   Shifting Sources of Knowledge and Authority

FOA is a nonprofit and nongovernmental organization founded in 1997 by Ismail Patel, a Malawian-born Muslim who grew up in England. During my stay in Tower Hamlets, Patel participated in the affairs of the British Muslim Initiative (BMI), an organization that seeks to "fight racism and Islamophobia, combat the challenges Muslims face around the world, and encourage Muslim participation in British public life" (British Muslim Initiative 2006). Patel was able to build on his connections in the BMI, as well as his involvement in the Stop the War Coalition, to campaign for justice, freedom, and equality in Palestine. To this end, he organized demonstrations, marches, and rallies that were supported by, among others, George Galloway, Jeremy Corbyn, and Ken Livingstone. He was also on board the Mavi Marmara during the Gaza flotilla raid together with Sarah Colborne of the PSC, an organization I discussed earlier in this chapter. Patel founded FOA in order to "raise awareness, build support, and implement change for Palestine," and manifest it through a boycott of Israel's products and manufactured goods (Friends of al-Aqsa n.d.). It is worth noting that the organization, which takes its name from the significance and centrality of the al-Aqsa Mosque to the Islamic faith and Muslim identity, publishes a weekly communiqué on its website to bring the Palestinian struggle to the attention of those concerned with international law and human rights. It organizes conferences and lectures, publishes papers, and works with a number of cultural, heritage, and humanitarian organizations around the world on ventures like the BDS movement, as well as the "Red Card Israel," which aims to suspend Israel from FIFA and other international forums until it ends its attacks against Palestinian football, and the "Keffiyeh Project," which aims to ensure that Palestine's only keffiyeh (traditional Arab headdress) factory stays in business.

FOA is also active locally, and finds wide support among young Bangladeshis of Tower Hamlets' lower classes who seek to oppose a political machine that evolved out of communal resistance to racist attacks and murders in the 1970s. Although very successful for a particular generation in penetrating local administrative and political institutions, this machine that could mobilize villages from the diasporic divisions of Sylhet did not find success at national level, and has generally failed to address issues that all of my young informants found relevant to the community as a whole. It is not necessary here to rehearse the details of a clear generational divide in Tower Hamlets, but I do want to point to the ways in which they have contributed to reshaping the discourses of Muslim solidarity and community in a political context structured by the discourses of citizenship and nation.

In June 2009, I attended the launch of "Kafa," a movement backed by the Stop the War Coalition that emerged from within the social fabric of Tower Hamlets in order to defend the interests of Muslims everywhere. In front of some 150 attendees between the ages of twenty and thirty, I watched Vimesh, an officer of the Stop the War Coalition and Head of Public Affairs of FOA, speak passionately about sentiments, loyalties, and styles of public conduct understood to be in tension with the political demands of citizenship and nation. He explained that although he was not a great speaker, "nor he enjoyed giving public talks," he felt obliged to step up. "I have been going to universities to speak about the Israeli–Palestinian conflict, and students have been telling me, 'Oh, I do not want to come to certain conferences.' [...] And I asked, 'Why?' Oh, they do not want to be targeted. They do not want the police to look at them. They do not want to be associated with political activity." Vimesh continued, "Now, that is really sad. [...] When you are at the prime of your political activity, [...] you are being made to feel as though you cannot think, as though you cannot engage in your society. But it is through political activity that you become a part of society. And that is why I am here. Not because I am a great speaker. I want Muslims in universities to see that I stepped up. That I will not be silenced by the government, trying to make me feel like I am not a part of society. Or that I am radical because I oppose a certain foreign policy. It is my government. If I oppose it, I will say that I oppose it. [...] I refuse to be complicit through silence. I want students to do the same. To step up and not be afraid to be political." The point of Vimesh's commentary is to give direction to a moral project that is centered upon questions of social responsibility and pious behavior. While I return to this discussion later in the chapter, what I want to point out here is that his discourse, delineated and organized under the rubric of BDS, points to moments of opposition to several structures of authority, some grounded in the authority of parents, and others in state institutions.

Jalal told me, "My parents came to England because they saw an opportunity for a better life. They were migrants. They knew that if they 'messed' with the government, there would be problems. Why should I conform like my parents? I was born here. I have the right to criticize government policies and officials." Because they had experienced the hardships of Sylhet, Bangladeshis of the first generation often viewed the British state as a provider. As I have suggested earlier, this shaped the conditions of their participation in, and support for, the BDS movement. The British-born generation, however, has an entirely different relationship with the British state. "I do not feel indebted at all," Gajal, a twenty-one-year-old student of politics at Birkbeck University told me shortly after we met. "My parents might because they fled here for a better life. They fear that the day will come when migrants will get booted out. But not me. Not my generation." It is in keeping with this logic, that I was told that the BDS movement points to a new disposition toward community participation, social responsibility, and greater activism among the British-born generation. In contrast to quietism and seclusion of the first generation, these styles of conduct are understood to be the hallmark characteristics of a different kind of Islam, one that inclines the British-born generation to render public issues that the first generation relegates to the private sphere of individual choice, notably the clearly political issues like the Israeli–Palestinian conflict.

In April 2009, few months prior to the launch of "Kafa," I met up with Vimesh for an interview. Sat in a small café next to the Caledonian Road metro station, he expressed his concern with those Muslims who have lost the ability to shape their attitudes and orientations in accord with what he considered to be standards of pious behavior. Vimesh, as well as others who sought to oppose the way their elders have treated Islam as a set of rites and rituals to perform, looked to BDS to provide them with a global source of community that supplements the problematic local, and facilitates claims to collective honor and loyalty, but also injury and disrespect, that have been effective in encouraging pious behavior. Fardeen, a twenty-three-year-old sociology student at London Metropolitan University, explored the theme of Muslim solidarity in a series of conversations we had during my stay in Tower Hamlets. He spoke about Afghanistan, Iraq, and Palestine, his voice strained with grief, and the duty of Muslims to do good, "to refuse to be silent in light of social and political injustice." This discourse on moral action was mediated by local histories and social and political circumstances. For example, Fardeen demonstrated awareness of career prospects that seemed extremely dire for Muslims who, although well-educated, were twice as likely to be unemployed, compared to the national average. In his view, Muslims were not given the opportunity to advance in Tower Hamlets, "which is their only home."

The success of organizations like FOA among the young men and women of my study resided in their employment of a gripping moral paradigm that countered that of the state and desi politicians who, in spite of their access to power, had failed to address a set of welfare needs in Tower Hamlets. During one of our conversations, I asked Fardeen what he thought about traditional leaders of the first generation, who drew on kinship and village networks, and community representatives of the second generation, who pursued careers in state institutions and local organizations that received public funds. In responding, he returned again to the theme of Muslim solidarity. "We have a mentality of being victims. 'Why,' you might ask. It is because those in power do not care that one million people marched against the war in Iraq. This is a moral issue, a sign of sickness and decay in Tower Hamlets, where interests are represented in hypocrisy and bigotry." As politics, both global and local, impose on the structures of moral life, the discourse I mention above extends to political topics. Indeed, as a type of activity aimed at realizing Islamic ideals of moral life through debate and deliberation, BDS emerges not at a point of commonality but at one of difference, "where a discrepancy in practice makes argument necessary" (Hirschkind 2006, 117).[3]

In order to elaborate, let me draw the reader's attention to an exchange with Hamza, a twenty-five-year-old administrative assistant from Whitechapel, who told me shortly after we met, "If I am a Muslim, then I must ask myself every day, what have I done for Islam? If I stay silent, I do nothing. Thus, I must speak and act with decorum. For the sake of Islam. For the sake of Muslims everywhere. It is not a choice. This is something that many Bangladeshis do not understand." This exchange is instructive because it reveals the contentious relationship that Hamza has had with older Bangladeshis for whom Islam was a set of rites and rituals to perform, without any regard for how this contributed to the realization of piety. Like many of the young Bangladeshis who make up the backbone of BDS in Tower Hamlets, Hamza had attended mosque lessons but decided to stop because he believed that imams were "twisting the teachings of Islam." He told me that they "overstressed the role rituals play in Muslim's life." As should be clear from the discussion in this chapter, this was an issue not because these rituals were irrelevant but because the mosque attendees believed that the "mere performance of [...] rituals would make them pious" (Mahmood 2012, 146).

Calim, a twenty-one-year-old student of law at Birkbeck University, weighed in on the issue of guidance during one of my visits to his Penang Street home. "Imams cannot speak English. Only Arabic. Angry old men, 'imported' from Bangladesh." He was visibly irritated at this point but went on to recount how, when he was younger, he wanted to get rid of the mosque and start one in the basement. "Imams are supposed to share knowledge, but they have forsaken their duty. Questions and challenges in the mosque are not tolerated.

---

3   There is a growing body of literature that focuses on the question: "What makes moral action within one's life possible?" Among the scholars whose insights have most shaped my own thinking, see Asad 2003; Hirschkind 2006; Mahmood 2012.

You go, you pray, you leave." Similarly, Fardeen told me that, when the war in Iraq started, he went to the East London Mosque for a response. "Imams did a talk on the importance of salat or prayer. It seemed to me that the mosque was not a place to discuss political topics relevant to each and every Muslim. But if you wanted to know about prayer, imams were there for you." In short, the young men and women of my study found this religious leadership to be very dogmatic and narrow minded in its understanding of Islam. They also commented on its partnership with national and local governments, a phenomenon I explored at length in chapter 3. "Because so much is government funded, imams have to play ball," Fardeen explained to me. "They teach Islam the 'wrong' way and make it look like a bunch of rituals, rather than a complete way of life. There are countless issues that Islam can help with. Do not tell me it is all about prayer."

Such a gaping void in guidance was filled by other sources of information, notably organizations like FOA that, unencumbered by the patronage of the state, could claim to act and speak in the name of pious commitment. It is not a coincidence that, at the time of my fieldwork, the organization's website was watermarked with Islamic calligraphy and Qur'anic quotations. The stock of texts on how to conduct oneself in accord with Islamic principles in everyday life focused on the Muslim responsibility toward the Palestinian struggle for freedom, justice, and equality. I want to highlight the place and significance of the al-Aqsa Mosque in these texts. When I met Upal, a twenty-three-year-old administrative assistant from Blackwall, she reported that one of the reasons she joined FOA was because she had read a text about Israel's continuous attempts to impose sovereignty over the al-Aqsa Mosque. "To perform Talmudic rituals in and around the mosque is to monopolize it, and send a message that Israel is keeping tight control over a sacred site in Islam. The lack of ummatic response is a problem. We simply do not know about the meaning of the mosque for Muslims. It was the first direction of prayer. But we let Israel continue its conspiracy against it." Upal went on to recount how she reached out to FOA via social media, and found out that one of its goals was to advocate for a targeted boycott of Israel as a tactic to "reaffirm the Muslim historic and religious rights to the mosque."

Upal got involved in BDS as a student during her years at SOAS, from which she had graduated the year before I met her. She had joined a small group of students that met every Friday in a mosque not far from her home, where they exchanged the kind of Islamic ethical and pedagogical materials I addressed at some length in chapter 2. BDS, I would suggest, is an important site where these materials are cited and used by Upal today. The age hierarchy, which emerged in conversations I had with Lama and Abra, is reversed when the younger, British-born generation invoke greater religious knowledge and moral authority than the elders to criticize them for ritualized performance of religious duties, "and lax religious lifestyles" (Mahmood 2012, 116). In this sense, Upal's defiance of established authority is best explored through an analysis of the ends toward which it was aimed, "and the terms of [...] responsibility that made up the grammar of her actions" (Mahmood 2012, 180).

3.2 *Public Activism and Moral Reform*

In conversations I had with Upal during my stay in Tower Hamlets, she catalogued religious duties related to her kin and neighbors but also to Muslims everywhere. As with other young Bangladeshis I met, she stressed here the importance of religious knowledge and instruction, which she considered to be the only proper path to a "rediscovery" of Islam's transformative potential as a medium of political contestation and debate. One effect of a clear generational divide in Tower Hamlets, in other words, has been to articulate the links between global political issues and practices of moral reform. I make use of Hirschkind's work on the da'wa movement in Cairo to argue that the stakes here include "both one's own salvation and the moral health and fortitude of the community as a whole" (Hirschkind 2006, 120). This concern for Muslims everywhere has also inspired new practices of moral reflection. As Calim told me after hearing about thousands who marched in solidarity with Palestine on the streets of Sarajevo, "When I hear that brothers and sisters in Sarajevo are becoming more meticulous in the performance of their divinely mandated duties, I am moved toward reforming my practice." It can be said in this sense that newly emergent forms of Islamic public engagement, of which BDS is an integral part, have created the conditions for the development and practice of virtues like compassion, sincerity, and fear of God, providing them with a noticeably transnational dimension. This trend has been reinforced by the fact that scholars whose boycott fatwas are used and cited in Tower Hamlets are often from abroad, as I discussed in chapter 2.

For the British-born generation, the development and practice of these virtues is seen "both as an end in itself and as a means internal to the dialogic process by which the reform of society is secured" (Hirschkind 2006, 130). In other words, while individual salvation remains important to many of those I met in Tower Hamlets who participated in BDS, it is now coupled with a goal of upholding and reinvigorating the forms of sociability, public speech, and political critique by which moral reform is to be brought about. I might also note that this way of linking public activism with moral reform helps the

British-born generation unsettle fixed conceptions of Islam held by the first generation, as well as more radical organizations that have been active in Tower Hamlets and other Bangladeshi enclaves.

When I met Faraz, a twenty-one-year-old student of politics at SOAS, and Calim's close friend, he remarked to me that he was often confronted by Hizb ut-Tahrir (Islamic Liberation Party) on campus. In the BBC Newsnight special, which aired on August 27, 2003, the organization called on "all Muslims in Britain to take a long, hard look at themselves" and decide what is their identity, suggesting that there is "no such thing as a British Muslim." In other words, Hizb ut-Tahrir's activists have recognized and exploited the fact that Bangladeshis from a range of socioeconomic and age backgrounds have at times retreated into a defensive embrace of Islam. "Radicalization," of course, should not be laid decisively at the door of Hizb ut-Tahrir, but it is important to recognize that those I worked with who described themselves as "more reformed" believed that Islam itself was wronged by the organization.

While speaking with Faraz one day at the Bean and Leaf Café, the same place in the lower-class neighborhood of Stepney where Dabir had talked about pride and dignity associated with BDS on a previous visit, he recapped his frustration with being compared to Hizb ut-Tahrir's activists. "We work on the same political issues, notably Afghanistan, Iraq, and Palestine. But this is where the similarities end. They have no actual ideology, no scholars. [...] If you want to attract younger generations, you need to address the problem of how to make Islamic principles relevant to the practical organization of everyday life. Hizb ut-Tahrir does not do that. Some of them, who are very radical in their practice, still live in a cave. They need to come out and realize that younger generations want to live piously but that this sits in some tension with the secular-liberal and technocratic discourses central to the state's own legitimacy." Drinking his green tea, Faraz continued, "If we neglect our Muslim identity, this is like assimilation. Although we participate in the majority society, this does not benefit the umma, because we do not see ourselves as 'good' Muslims. But we cannot survive here in isolation." Similarly, during the launch of "Kafa," Vimesh commented that most Muslims do not want to be suspended between different identities and belongings. "I am British. I was born on this great island. I am also Muslim, and I am proud. [...] This is my identity." Vimesh proceeded to call for the development of a more critical thinking in Islam that is capable of external disagreements and internal interventions. What is significant here is that newly emergent forms of Islamic public engagement that I examine throughout this book intertwine moments of dialogue and dispute as practices necessary for the moral guidance of the collective. They also place upon the young men and women of my study a task of having to explain themselves in order to say who they are not. This is quite clear in the conversation with Faraz I described earlier.

To make his case, and to distance himself somewhat from Tower Hamlets' more radical organizations, Faraz referred to an expending network of BDS organizations that includes FOA, as well as Jewish Voice for Peace (JVP) and Jews for Israeli–Palestinian Peace (JIPF). In general, the young men and women of my study claimed that BDS externalizes a uniquely Islamic call for inclusion and diversity. Faraz relied on an edificatory story about the Prophet to support this claim by saying, "Tolerance and friendship were affairs of high importance for the Prophet. God had ordered him to allow even polytheists and pagans to come to him safely. This led to a reformation of the society, social relations, and affairs. If it was not like that, the ground would not have been paved for guidance and promotion of Islam." Thus, Faraz steered clear from the positions and attitudes of more radical organizations and familiarized himself instead with the BDS activities of the abovementioned JVP and JIPF, as well as the International Women's Strike with whom he often exchanged emails. Similarly, when I met Vimesh, he told me that his boss had recently returned from Johannesburg, where he met with South African activists to "learn about their struggle against apartheid and how to draw from it." This informal exchange makes clear that the vocabularies of religious tolerance and friendship have been used productively by the British-born participants in BDS in order to expand their political horizon and contribute to the morally inflected cosmopolitanism evident in the comments of Vimesh and Faraz, as well as Calim earlier in this chapter. In the section that follows, I want to expand a little more on the idea of binding together of Muslims with cooperative ties by turning to an ethnographic example of BDS activism during the month of Ramadan.

In October 2009, I attended a BDS conference organized by the PSC's branch in Tower Hamlets. Some of the attendees were the men and women I came to know, others resided in Tower Hamlets but were not attached to the organizations I describe in this chapter. Attendees frequently interrupted the speakers, including Vimesh and George Galloway, to ask questions or to put forward opinions, and a steady stream of conversation filled the air. For example, a young woman in her early twenties expressed the difficulty she encountered in identifying Israeli products in a supermarket and asked the speakers what she should do about it. The answer Vimesh gave was one that enjoyed currency among many of the young Bangladeshis who make up the backbone of BDS in Tower Hamlets. Seated on a podium facing the attendees, Vimesh answered, "As I am sure you are aware, we recently had Ramadan, the blessed month of fasting, when we launched, along with Easy Talk, a community-based organization from Leicester, 'Check the Label' campaign. You check the label so dates that you break your fast with are not from Israel, the West Bank, and Jordan Valley." Looking puzzled, the young women asked, "What do you mean? What does Ramadan have to do with daily shopping?" Vimesh smiled for a moment, and then responded, "The first *jumu'ah* [Friday prayer] of Ramadan, we were outside the London Muslim Centre. There was six or seven of us handing out leaflets. People were wondering why are these guys standing here with the Israeli flag. As we were handing out leaflets, we would say, 'Do not break your fast with a blood date.' 'Make sure you check the label.' There was support there. 'We do not want to buy dates that support oppression.' It was from there that we went to supermarkets, to cash and carries." Lowering his voice, and adopting a stern-but-concerned expression, Vimesh said, "Unfortunately, we found out that although some supermarkets, some cash and carries, had collection boxes for the mosque, they supplied Israeli dates. We asked, 'What are you guys doing?' They said, 'Oh, profit margin. Profit margin.' Obviously, we went back to the community, and this is why Tower Hamlets is important. Soon, maybe two weeks later, some supermarkets, some cash and carries, took Israeli dates off the shelves. No one in Tower Hamlets wanted to buy from them otherwise."

After the applause died down, Vimesh turned to the young women. "Palestinians look to London, what we are doing for them, that they are not forgotten. But London is looking to Tower Hamlets. The global movement for Palestinian rights is being led here by you." At this point, Upal entered the debate, "Sister, day-to-day deeds like running an errand and shopping, these are the marks of your dedication to be a 'good' Muslim. I know you have a conscience, but do you have the time to read everything and see where all the products are coming from? The month of Ramadan propels you to do good. It would be an affront if at such a time you helped support oppression. But I ask you, sister, whenever you go shopping, to check the label." The exchange was interrupted as Vimesh added his own instruction, "Here in Tower Hamlets, we can boycott, we can divest, and we can sanction. You can find information about BDS on our website, about what products to avoid. Obviously, I talked about dates. Also look out for oranges, limes, and potatoes from Israel, the West Bank, and Jordan Valley. In the following weeks, FOA will launch a boycott campaign. I hope and pray inshallah that the whole community will come together to boycott anyone and anything tied to Israel's occupation, colonization, and system of apartheid. It shall start very strong here in Tower Hamlets, and Palestine will be free" (on this, see Friends of al-Aqsa 2009).

Finally, it is worth to recall that Vimesh and Upal, and many others like them, sought to educate ordinary Muslims in those virtues and ethical capacities that they believed have become either "unavailable or irrelevant to their lives" (Mahmood 2012, 4). Practically, as is obvious from the example I give above, this meant instructing ordinary Muslims in how to organize their daily conduct in accord with principles of Islamic piety and virtuous behavior. "There are varieties of dates from other countries to source from," Upal told me after the conference. "Medjoul dates from Palestine that help the Palestinian farmers are available from Yaffa. Another provider is Zaytoun. [...] You see, supermarkets will claim that the affordability of Israeli dates means that customers are not complaining. The goal is not to compare different prices but to question why something is more affordable. Israel tricks us into thinking that dates are legitimately farmed in Israel, instead of illegitimately farmed on stolen Palestinian land, exploiting cheap Palestinian labor. Dates offered by Zaytoun might be more expensive, but it is we who benefit. We attest to our faith by doing good deeds constantly." Notably, Upal's remarks reveal that she is concerned with inciting those virtues that enable ordinary Muslims to live in accord with what is considered to be God's will. Suffice it to say, these concerns with an Islamic ethos make FOA very different from secular organizations mobilizing for BDS elsewhere. Although BDS is directed at Muslims and non-Muslims alike, Vimesh and Upal, and many others like them, consider it to be a religious obligation that requires all members of the Muslim community to urge fellow Muslims to greater piety. This inculcation and realization of piety, as I hope I have made clear, is predicated on, and transformative of, different arrangements of power and authority, which in turn enfold different ideas about what it means to act politically in Tower Hamlets. It is worth keeping this in mind as we move onto the next chapter that focuses on BDS activism in Stari Grad.

CHAPTER 5

European Hopes, Nationalist Desires, and the Urban–Rural Divide

> History had never made such a joke with anyone as it did with us [Bosniaks]. We had been torn away and disconnected and were not accepted. Like a branch of the river which had […] neither a stream nor its mouth of the river, too small to be a lake and too big for a soil to absorb it within itself. We live at the crossroads of two worlds, on the border of nations. We bear the brunt of everybody, and we have always been guilty in the eyes of someone. The waves of history break themselves over our backs, as on a reef.
> SELIMOVIĆ 1966, 8, cited in KARIĆ 1997, 88

∴

The images of BDS I have sketched so far show that Bangladeshis, across a broad range of the age and political spectrum, debate about the proper Muslim response to the Israeli–Palestinian conflict in the bustling lower-class neighborhood of Tower Hamlets, where the elaboration and practice of concerns, responsibilities, and virtues of the Muslim community are fused together in a unique manner. BDS has provided the vehicle wherein this interdependency is effectively worked out. In this chapter, I turn to an analysis of these discussions in Stari Grad. As in the case of Tower Hamlets, I argue that the cultivation of virtues like fear of God appears to be the necessary condition for the development of political projects like BDS. This process by which virtues manifest in political projects is structured by, and embedded in, ongoing social and political tensions in Stari Grad that are heavily based on claims to victimhood at the hands of rural and supposedly primitive newcomers. It is important to point out, in this regard, that a number of scholars have suggested that class and urban–rural distinctions, which were common before the war, lost considerable stature after the war began and Sarajlije, especially those of Islamic faith, "played down status divisions […] in the interest of unity" (Sorabji 2006, 4, see also Maček 2007; Markowitz 2010). In this view, staying behind, as opposed to taking refuge elsewhere, was understood to delineate and sustain the boundaries of inclusion and exclusion in Stari Grad. It would be wrong, however, to conclude that distinctions between "insiders" and "outsiders," those who "belong" and those who do not "belong," are nowadays less those of class and territorial origin and more those lodged in war memory. Indeed, the manner of reflecting on BDS practiced by those I worked with reveals that the memory argument may only stretch so far and not as far as to inspire a locally cohesive movement for Palestinian rights. It follows that BDS cannot be comprehended only as an expression of Muslim solidarity. Rather, it is an important site of inquiry into how Muslims from a variety of class and social backgrounds deal with an issue demanded by and integral to the umma. In this chapter, I look at different categories of BDS participants, from unemployed to those who earn well above the national average, from internally displaced to those born in Stari Grad, to explore how BDS is shaped by patterns of experience, memory, and affect cultivated within everyday life.

In short, I extend the line of inquiry opened up earlier, that is, I situate my discussion of BDS within the context of recent historical and sociopolitical currents in Stari Grad. I show that from the Sarajlije's point of view, the principal source of cultural disorder is the influx or "invasion," as it is often called, of displaced persons and other newcomers who came during and after the recent war, and are all seen as having come from rural and "non-cultured" territories. That said, the distinction between locals and newcomers is not only a matter of different territorial origin or cultural mannerism. It also relates to other cleavages between urban and rural, "cultured" and "non-cultured." In other words, the deep-rooted belief in a cultural hierarchy includes a range of dichotomies, such as rich versus poor, educated versus uneducated, European versus Balkan, and "modern versus backward" (Bringa 1995, 58; see also Bougarel 1999; Sorabji 1993). Furthermore, in the popular imagination, locals are characterized by secular-liberal and progressive sensibilities. In contrast, newcomers have come to be understood as "primitive, traditional, and religiously-radical" (Stefansson 2007, 61; see also Jansen 2009; Maček 2001).

The intertwining of these dichotomies is not unique to Stari Grad but rather widespread throughout neighborhoods of the former Yugoslavia. Nor is ostracizing and stigmatizing newcomers a recent practice caused by the massive population displacement and migration. I want to communicate, however, that both practices have been revitalized during and after the recent war. BDS is debated amid the Sarajlije's sense of a major post-war upheaval. To begin with, contrary to the transnational capitalist class and the truly deprived, whom I discuss later in the chapter, Sarajevo's middle and upper-middle classes have been left without an ideological project of their own following the independence of Bosnia and its violent partition.[1] This ideological vacuum has been filled by various nonprofit and nongovernmental organizations committed to the ideals of human rights, tolerance, and equality, which I address in the section that follows.

1 Middle-Aged Urbanites and the Invocation of Europe

Bosnia is a country with a high concentration of nonprofit and nongovernmental organizations. By my own rough estimate, based on data collected in interviews, 300 were active in Bosnia right after the war, in comparison to forty organizations that were active during the war (see Coles 2007; Sarajlić 2011). Importantly, a number of these organizations had headquarters in the Muslim world or among the Muslim migrant population in Europe. Most had left with the stabilization of Bosnia, but a few stayed on. Turkish organizations, for example, continued their grassroots efforts to revitalize Islamic forms of knowledge, pedagogy, and sociability against a traditionally secular backdrop (see Rucker-Chang 2014; Solberg 2007). In addition to Turkish organizations that received less attention than the Iranian and the Saudi ones (see Merdjanova 2013; Pargeter 2008), Bosnia hosts other smaller organizations. Not very influential on their own, these organizations serve as de facto links between Bosniaks and the umma. The Medjunarodni Forum Solidarnosti (MFS-Emmaus) is one such organization.

The MFS-Emmaus was founded in 1999 as part of the Emmaus International Network, made up of organizations in forty-one countries around the world. "These organizations run activities at local level with people who have experienced social exclusion to access their [...] rights and, through collective action, demonstrate credible alternatives to injustice" (Emmaus International n.d.). Specifically, the MFS-Emmaus's goal is to create and direct resources in consensus with the agendas and interests of "vulnerable population groups," a broad category that includes refugees, migrants, and victims of human trafficking (Medjunarodni Forum Solidarnosti-Emmaus n.d.). The MFS-Emmaus extended its program of action in 2008, when it joined a fast-growing movement for Palestinian rights. Five years later, in the course of conducting fieldwork, I met up with one of the MFS-Emmaus leaders in his office on Čekaluša Street

---

[1] In stating this, I am not suggesting that Sarajevo's middle and upper-middle classes were nostalgic about the old regime—often they were very critical of it—but rather that they were resistant to the new one.

to talk about the MFS-Emmaus, organizing and mobilizing in Stari Grad, and the role of grassroots advocacy networks in educating, and raising awareness, about the Palestinian struggle for freedom, justice, and equality.

Azim arrived to Bosnia decades ago as a political exile from Syria. "I had to stand up to the Assad regime," he told me shortly after we met. "I was being a 'smartass.' I voiced my anger, but this had dire consequences. I was seventeen. I had just finished high school, but I found myself at odds with the Assad regime. My options were very limited—being locked up or leaving Syria. I decided to leave, and I came to what was then Yugoslavia in 1981." Azim went on to recount how he took up a job as a translator and, at the onset of war, worked for a slew of nonprofit and nongovernmental Islamic organizations, including the Iranian Cultural Center and the Kuwaiti Islamic World Committee. In 2002, Azim joined the MFS-Emmaus. I would argue that, pushed out by the government repression, and frustrated by the absence of legitimate channels for social protest at "home," Azim sought to establish himself as a prominent public figure in the vast proliferation of nonprofit and nongovernmental organizations whose focus has typically been on providing welfare and charitable services to the poor, doing good deeds for the elderly, and so on.

In 2008, when the MFS-Emmaus joined BDS, Azim took charge. During an interview, Azim explained that after his initial attempt to enter the Gaza Strip through Egypt fell through, he sought help from other BDS organizations, hoping that they would distribute canned foods and blankets donated by well-to-do supporters of the MFS-Emmaus. "I reached out to BDS organizations around the world, and they stepped up. I ended up in Cairo for the second time, joined by 1,300 activists." History repeated itself, however, as the Egyptian government prevented Azim and other activists from entering the Gaza Strip. This time, they refused to back down. They protested on the streets of Cairo and in front of the embassies. They organized sit-ins and went on hunger strikes. The Egyptian government finally caved in and allowed one hundred activists to enter the Gaza Strip in December 2009. One might view this concession as a major victory. According to Azim, this was not enough. "This was not about getting some or even all [activists] into the Gaza Strip," he said in a low voice. "Rather, this was about building international support and pressure to end Israeli siege on the Gaza Strip." While it is not my intention here to elaborate the architecture of BDS, what I want to point out is that Azim was the only activist from Bosnia protesting on the streets of Cairo. What is also analytically interesting is that, five months later, he was the only activist from Bosnia on board the Mavi Marmara, joining Sarah Colborne from the PSC and Ismail Patel from FOA, two of the BDS organizations discussed in chapter 4.

"It is the policy of local organizations to strive toward prominence. They want their name out there as the only organization from Bosnia working on the Palestinian issue," Azim told me, in obvious frustration. "This has its benefits. When you join a movement like BDS, you discover that many organizations not only share information and knowledge but also help each other financially. But when the MFS-Emmaus asked for assistance from local organizations in collecting donations for the Gaza Strip, hardly anyone responded." According to Azim, the local BDS community is focused on "micro operations," where everyone is fighting their own battle, therefore, "diluting the common goal of helping Palestinians." To illustrate his point, Azim mentioned Solidarnost (Solidarity), a network of BDS activists from Bihać, a small city in northwestern Bosnia. "They will organize an event that only twenty people will attend. Or they will ask for donations and collect 10,000 BAM [roughly 5,000 USD]. Sure, there is effort behind this, but their strategies are poorly formulated, and they address the wrong folks." While I return to many of these points shortly, what I want to point out here is that I tried to arrange a meeting with Zemira Gorinjac, a co-founder of Solidarnost, during the writing phase of this book. I was asked to send my questions via email. Most revolved around tactics and the choice of BDS targets at the local level that, as suggested by Barghouti, must be "governed by the context particularities [...] of the BDS activists" (Barghouti 2011, 60). Two weeks later, I received an unexpected response. My questions, Zemira's email noted, "had nothing to do with BDS." I was told that those who want to support the Palestinian struggle should look instead at how the movement is organized abroad, "in the west." This impression that BDS is a "one-size-fits-all" type of movement, evident in Zemira's response above, leads to inconsistencies of action and a lack of coherence with local situations and conditions. I want to focus here on how the issue was addressed by those I worked with.

During my visit to his Čekaluša Street office, Azim criticized organizations that copy or recycle BDS calls from abroad. "This strategy will not work. To call for boycott on websites visited by the unemployed is ridiculous. The same can be said for organizations like Solidarnost that mobilize among the displaced persons barely getting by. At the same time, Solidarnost calls for boycott of hundreds of products, some not even available to us. This is a small country. For this reason, it needs an effective campaign that is targeted and nuanced, concentrating on companies clearly implicated in Israel's occupation, colonization, and system of apartheid. Our focus in terms of the audience are those who can 'afford to boycott,' and we only focus on two companies at a time. Right now, those are Coca-Cola and Nestlé. Both have a huge market, and our goal is to mobilize the audience against them." When I asked him to elaborate in more detail, Azim responded, "Israel's military in the Gaza Strip imposes a strict regime of 'counting calories' on Palestinians. Some receive 850 calories a day, less than half the recommended daily intake. This happened in Sarajevo. You remember food aid packages and bread queues? When I think about a targeted and nuanced campaign, I think about what Sarajevans can relate to. They can relate to living under siege, being deprived of food, medicine, and clean water." The inherent connection between the siege of Sarajevo and the Palestinian struggle was revealed to me in conversations with the middle- and upper-middle-class participants in the BDS movement, all of whom were affected by the siege and the hardship of everyday life it had engendered.

1.1 *Practicing Decency in the Post-war Disorder*

Dženana, a fifty-one-year-old from Kovači, a small neighborhood in the heart of Stari Grad, had been working as a migration lawyer for over ten years when I first met her in June 2013. Her husband was a government employee. Both of her daughters lived in Vienna. Speaking in gentle and soft tones, Dženana recounted how she decided to stay in Kovači during the siege, a decision that has instilled a sense of pride in Dženana. "You have to be strong to experience hardship and loss, and for all of this not to defeat you. To be strong in difficult times is a quality that not many have. Sarajevans joke about 'outsiders' who think that having no access to the Internet is the worst. Try living under siege for years, without electricity and water. Sarajevans feel solidarity with Palestinians that 'outsiders' simply do not understand." Dženana was aware that her situation was better than that of her neighbors, many of whom have come to Kovači from ethnically cleansed villages in central and eastern Bosnia. That said, in talking to her, it was obvious that she was more conscious of what she has lost than of what she now has. Broken relationships, lost ambitions, and feelings of entrapment in a country that anthropologist Stef Jansen calls the European Union's "immediate outside" are some of the lasting sorrows that shape a political terrain upon which BDS is now carried out (Jansen 2009, 815).

The argument I am making here resonated with Elma, a forty-nine-year-old born to a family of architects. When I met Elma, she reported that she had travelled the world before coming to Kovači in the late 1980s with her husband. Elma held a job in the public sector and her salary was well above the national average. Her daughter, born at the tail end of the war, had just started university in Oslo. In short, Elma lived a comfortable life in the house she inherited from her parents. She explained to me that, with her educational qualifications and language skills, she could have "secured a much-coveted job with the United Nations' forces during the war." But she decided to stay in the public sector and work toward a professional role and stake in the post-war Sarajevo. Elma succeeded but, like many others I worked with, felt that the city she loved and decided to stay for did not exist anymore. This was made clear in the following remark, "This is not the city I want my daughter to live in. She is abroad, studying. I keep telling her that she should not come back." This shift in loyalties constantly reappeared in the comments of those I worked with. Again, in Elma's words, "It was easier during the war. You knew who was your friend. You knew who was your enemy. There is no neighborly trust today. I do not know my neighbors. I feel like a foreigner in my own city. If ever another shell falls on the city, I will be the first to leave." What this draws attention to is a clear distinction between the early days of the siege, when staying was understood as the brave and patriotic choice, and two decades later, when few of those I worked with claimed that, given the choice again, they would stay in the besieged Sarajevo. "Staying is seen as having been pointless" (Sorabji 2006, 5).

The shift from initial local patriotism to disappointment and emotional exhaustion can be further illustrated through a conversation with Sabina. This forty-six-year-old from Vratnik, one of the oldest neighborhoods in Sarajevo, worked as a newly qualified physician in the General Hospital during the siege. Although she aspired to become a resident, and therefore continue her father's legacy, Sabina left the hospital in April 2013, after what she described as a blatant "political firing" of the then-manager Bakir Nakaš.[2] "It was difficult to leave given the catastrophic economic conditions, but I no longer felt appreciated and welcomed," Sabina once remarked, echoing a widely held belief. "I worked there during the siege. Can you imagine how challenging that was? But everything I had ever done, all my qualities and qualifications, mattered less than my political contacts. I did not have friends in the main nationalist parties backing me up. I never even voted." Sabina continued, "The main nationalist parties exercise control over all aspects of life. There is a glaring 'ethnicization' of life, a call for ethno-national groups to come *zajedno* [together] under the patronage of their own nationalist parties." Sabina was made aware of this sociopolitical reality almost everywhere—when looking for a job, receiving a medical treatment, and enrolling a child in school.

To clarify these points, one might say that what has led many of the men and women I knew in Stari Grad to condemn nationalist ideologies, and

---

2 Bakir Nakaš was replaced by the wife of Bakir Izetbegović, the leader of the main Bosniak party—the Party of Democratic Action (Stranka Demokratske Akcije, SDA)—that took power in 1990 as socialist Yugoslavia was disintegrating. The other nationalist parties in power are the Croatian Democratic Union of Bosnia and Herzegovina (Hrvatska Demokratska Zajednica Bosne i Herzegovine, HDZ BiH) and the Alliance of Independent Social Democrats (Savez Nezavisnih Socijaldemokrata, SNSD).

nationalists' control over their lives, was the appearance of *bogataši* ("nouveaux riches") and *ratni profiteri* ("war profiteers"), who became rich through criminality and corruption, and *foteljaši* ("armchair politicians"), who set in positions of power in spite of their lack of qualifications, and ascended party hierarchy with the help of influential patrons, enriching themselves while the majority of population struggled to make ends meet. Some used the terms "nouveaux riches," "war profiteers," and "armchair politicians" to refer to particular events in recent Bosnian history. Others employed them to describe a transformative force beyond their control. For example, fifty-two-year-old Irfan started a catering business in the early 1980s, a phenomenon quite rare in socialist Bosnia. During one of my visits to his Logavina Street home, Irfan recounted how he had enough money to buy a car and take his family of four to the seaside. "I was able to put food on the table. But I was not rich. You do not get rich through decent and honest work." By referring to decency and honesty, Irfan was condemning the war-related behavior of new economic elites and inept, corrupt politicians, and everything they represented.

It is not the legitimacy of such attitudes and judgments that interests me but rather the modes of being and acting they require, and in some sense make possible. For one thing, it is worth recalling that virtues of decency and honesty, together with compassion, sincerity, and fear of God, are deemed germane to BDS. As with other practices that are incumbent upon Muslims, BDS is understood to be predicated on a prior cultivation of these virtues. They do not only inhibit wrong behavior. According to many of the men and women I knew in Stari Grad, they also encompass a manner of being and acting that pervades all of one's acts. It is no surprise, therefore, that the debate about these virtues, and their role in everyday life, is part of a much larger discussion about the correct or incorrect nature of an Islamic practice. As I have noted in previous chapters, one's participation in BDS needs to be viewed in light of this discrepancy in practice, which makes argument necessary.

1.2   *Sacralized Europe and Secularized Islam*

While speaking with Irfan one day at his Logavina Street home, he explained to me that his catering business was alive and kicking. His marriage, however, was over. "The city has been invaded by peasants who became rich through criminality and corruption. I do not blame my ex for staying in Malmö. She has made a good life for herself. I do better than most, but I should have left when my ex did." In other words, those described as "peasants" are not only accused of starting the war and invading the city, a phenomenon I addressed at some length in chapter 3, they are now said to be profiting from the post-war disorder. Irfan believed that many problems in the city would be solved if these newcomers would return to their villages, concluding pointedly, "They [peasants] came to the city, but here [pointing at his head], they remained primitive. They have a different kind of mentality, a different kind of life, that they import to the city. The biggest shift I see is within Islam."

To be clear, the discomfort Irfan felt had little to do with Islam as such. In fact, those like Irfan, born and raised in the mahalas of Stari Grad, were used to Islam's palpable presence. What caused the discomfort above all was the state's intervention into the religious practices of the population it governed.[3] This was readily visible in the policies undertaken by the SDA to "turn Islam into the new ideological criterion for the selection of political elites," whether they had the right qualifications or not (Bougarel 2007a, 170). In an interview with me, Irfan voiced his concerns about such a nationalist-identitarian understanding of Islam, "Fear of God is a requirement of Islam. *Ovdje se niko ne boji Boga* [here, no one fears God]. As I told you before, the city is full of criminality and corruption. Religious observance has become a sham designed to curry favor with the SDA." The issue, I would suggest, is not whether people carry out their religious duties out of pious fear or the desire to show off in front of others. Rather, it is the process by which practices that are meant to be part of a larger program for shaping the pious self lose this function and become "little more than markers of identity," such as when people pray and fast to signal an identity that makes them fit for political office (Mahmood 2012, 51).

Debates about how to interpret and enact religious duties permeate post-war Bosnian realities. They resonate not only with the religiously devout, but also, surprisingly, with the secular-oriented people I met in Stari Grad, those who experienced various post-war manifestations of Islam as an attack on familiar practices, as well as their own sincerity as believers and legitimacy as religious authorities. For example, Mirsad, a sixty-one-year-old geography teacher from Vratnik, reported that he was disappointed with the *licemjerstvo* (hypocrisy) of "neo-Muslims" who claimed to be sincere. "They lie, cheat, and steal. They act immorally. But they attend the Friday prayer, for everyone to see, and for them this is enough." If the proper locus of religion is the inner life of the individual, as Mirsad suggested, then it follows that one's sincerity in this domain cannot be measured in one's outer performance. Irfan's conception of religiosity, however, contrasts sharply with the one captured in Mirsad's discussion above. Irfan once said, "I was brought up in a pious family that settled on Logavina Street 400 years ago. I am proud to be *mahalac* [a person from mahala]. Our home was clean. We were nice to the neighbors. We gave charity and helped

---

3 I use the term "state" to denote the governing party, as was the case with many of the men and women I knew in Stari Grad. The term they used was *država*.

the needy. These, together with praying five times a day, fasting, and the like, were the signs of a 'genuine' Muslim, one who acts with sincerity of intent. For the purpose of pleasing God rather than for personal gain." In Irfan's understanding, outer performance is not just an expression of inner religiosity but also a necessary means of acquiring it. This form of religiosity, I argue, treats Islam as a set of values and ethics that are to be cherished, but that are also relevant to the practical organization of everyday life.

The discussion about the proper locus of Islam constructs a new aura of distinction and difference, and ultimately has important implications for exclusion of Bosniaks from a "self-essentialized Europeanness" (Coles 2007, 265). Note that Irfan, like many Bosniaks from the same social class and background, defined himself through the idiom of the "good, old family." Part of its prestige resided in longevity, hinting that the family in question preceded socialism, and was able to contextualize it within a long and continuing Islamic tradition. In other words, working hard, giving charity, and doing good deeds for the elderly, were all understood to be the outward markers of religiosity in line with socialism. The disputes about religiosity and its assigned locus I mention above, therefore, reflect not only social and political conflicts in Stari Grad today but also a range of historically grounded assumptions.

In addition to longevity, a family gained considerable prestige from urbanity, which in turn was associated with sophistication, cosmopolitanism, and "Europeanness." These terms are now used to counter the cultural and moral deterioration of Sarajevo, supposedly caused by rural newcomers. Specifically, the invocations of "Europeanness" call for the middle-aged and middle-class Bosniaks I worked with to restore the standards of life in which Europe takes on a superlative essence. It is something to be attained, to be deserved. It is a symbol of "ultimate good" (Sarajlić 2009, 56). Europe, moreover, represents freedom that is considered germane to democracy, such as freedom of choice and expression. With its emphasis on deliberation and debate, "consumers' rights for transparency and freedom of choice" (Micheletti and Oral 2019, 711), BDS provides a de facto window to Europe. Consider, for example, how Elma commented on a series of protests on the streets of Sarajevo, aimed at addressing the suffering of Palestinians. "What jarred me was the burning of Israeli flags at these protests. This was not an image of Sarajevo, clearly a European city, but rather an image of barbarity." The young protesters who burned Israeli flags were said to be peasants, displaced from rural territories and thus uneducated, backward, and primitive. "Definitely not from the city," as Elma insisted. Such dismissal is marshaled to support cosmopolitan attitudes, consumption patterns, and lifestyles of the middle-aged and middle-class Bosniaks I worked with. "What good is it to burn flags? This changes nothing. What is needed instead is a focused boycott," Elma remarked to me. "For every dollar of household spending, forty-nine cents are spent in a supermarket. Thus, the choice of products in a supermarket is important. BDS targets fifty to sixty products at any time. I boycott those available to us. This takes time and energy. Today, it is easy to focus one's energy on feeling good rather than on doing good."

Elma questioned the young protesters' sincerity because they placed undue weight on the public display of emotions as a measure of religiosity. She supported this claim by saying, "I cannot stand to go to protests. It is all for *furka* [a way of life that lacks in depth]. There is no sincerity of intent. Islam is about extending a hand to others, free from egoism. It is about self-reflection. What is done for Islam by burning flags? Nothing, but these new religious types believe it is enough."[4] I return to many of these points later, in the second half of this chapter, but what I want to reemphasize here is that Elma's comments serve to separate urban locals from rural newcomers who, due to their believed backwardness and primitiveness, are seen as more receptive to "extreme" Islamic attitudes imposed by *mujahideen* (those engaged in jihad) and humanitarian workers from the Middle East and South Asia who came during the war. They also convey a clear gendered warning about a kind of Islam that has "nothing to do with Bosnia." I was often told that Islam is what makes Bosniaks modern and European, as a religion that supports women's pursuit of professional careers, as opposed to their subjugation to realms of family and home. Those who lauded professionalization did not believe that this interfered with women's duties to family and home. In fact, as Helms observes in her study of the shifting balkanist and orientalist rhetoric in Bosnia, "The logic was that Bosnia's unique character of being simultaneously Muslim and European was what allowed women to do both" (Helms 2013, 104; see also Bartulović 2015; Jevtić 2017; Mesarić 2013).

---

4   In *The Use of Pleasure*, Foucault traces a set of specific discourses, procedures, and techniques through which a specific ethical-moral subject comes to be formed. Notably, as Mahmood succinctly explains, although he focuses on an individual's effort at forming oneself, "the subject of Foucault's analysis is formed within the limits of a historically specific set of formative practices and moral injunctions that are delimited in advance" (Mahmood 2012, 28). "Moral subjectivation," in turn, refers to techniques available "for setting up and developing relationships with the self, [...] for the decipherment of the self by oneself, for the transformation that one seeks to accomplish with oneself" (Foucault 1986, 29). This, I believe, is a central aspect of the BDS activities of Elma, and many others like her, who see in them an opportunity for self-reflection.

These "bridging" metaphors, well established among the middle-aged and middle-class Bosniaks I worked with, enfold the assumption that women need to have a "strong personality" in order to deal with an array of personal and political tensions produced or transformed by the war. For Elma, this meant acquiring self-confidence, notably through work. "I take pride in my work, and that I do it well. It is not the most important part of life, but it allows me to reaffirm my values in the city overrun by criminals, primitives, and profiteers," Elma once remarked, thereby evoking the sentiments of decency and honesty, captured so well in Irfan's discussion earlier in this chapter. Furthermore, I would argue that self-confidence is beneficial because it helps Elma realize self-directed choices and goals, as expressed in styles of consumption and culture linked to the BDS movement.

The younger participants of the BDS movement, born and raised in the mahalas of Stari Grad, who also worked, and may be best described as lower-middle-class, did not regard their professional careers and experiences in the same way. Although they shared a concern about the suffering of Palestinians with their parents, they differed markedly in their engagement with this suffering. BDS, in their view, was an instrument of Islamic activism and reformism. In other words, rather than defining it in terms of self-directed action, generally relegated to the sphere of private life, they considered BDS to be an action aimed at improving the moral conduct and reasoning of the community as a whole.

2 Educated Youth and the Cultivation of Piety

Ajla, a young woman in her early twenties, worked as a tour guide when I first met her in April 2013. A few months earlier, she founded Stand for Justice, an action network dedicated to raising awareness about the suffering of Palestinians. During one of my visits with Ajla, she recounted how Stand for Justice was founded after a confrontation with a former friend. "One *novopečeni* [new] believer, who was previously stealing cassette players out of cars," accused Ajla of being a "bad" Muslim when she posted Rihanna songs on her Facebook wall on the anniversary of the Khan Yunis massacre.[5] She explained to me that, had she known about the massacre, she would not have posted songs online. "I was annoyed. I could not believe that he judged the correctness of my conduct when he was once a petty thief." Ajla went on to recount how,

---

5 The Khan Yunis massacre took place in November 1956 in the Palestinian city of Khan Yunis and the refugee camp of the same name in the Gaza Strip.

after she watched YouTube clips describing the massacre, she began to cry profusely, thereby alluding to the affective resonances among Muslims around the world that the Israeli–Palestinian conflict elicits. "I remembered my childhood in Vratnik. Four years of horror. Four years of fear. This was no life for a young child." Ajla explained that children in Bosnia had to wait four years before the world, notably the United States, intervened. "As I watched those clips, childhood traumas came back. The world hesitated in Bosnia, making intervention difficult. It hesitated in Palestine, failing to protect children from the suffering and threat of violence. I thought about who to call, who can help. Then it hit me. Is there a more powerful force than the help of God? I prayed to God to make me a part of his plan for Palestine."

In contrast to the middle-aged and middle-class Bosniaks I worked with, who dealt with other people's opinions, differences, and conflicts through the cultivation of self-confidence, which in turn opened the space for self-directed choices and goals, Ajla told me that one of the things gained from watching YouTube clips was that she remembered what Islam really entails. "I posted Rihanna songs on the anniversary of the Khan Yunis massacre. This made me think about the afterlife. I felt remorse. But after I watched those clips, I gained enthusiasm for doing what is right, for correcting my behavior." In this view, a seemingly trivial act of watching YouTube clips sets in motion a progression from fear, to remorse, to repentance, and eventually to greater piety and closeness to God. It is understood to evoke in Ajla an attitude or emotional disposition that underlies correct conduct. It follows that Ajla's agency is founded on emotions of fear, remorse, and so on, by which "excellence and virtuosity at piety are measured and marked" (Mahmood 2012, 123; see also Hirschkind 2006; Lambek 2000; Starrett 2010). These ethical concepts appeared continuously in conversations I had with the younger participants of the BDS movement, born and raised in the mahalas of Stari Grad.

Motivated by emotions mentioned above, Ajla messaged friends on Facebook, and told them that she was organizing a protest in Sarajevo to raise awareness about the suffering of Palestinians. "Two friends responded. One told me to start a Facebook group, and get people to post and comment." Ajla called it Stand for Justice because, as she pointed out to me later, she wanted to be "on the right side of history." She wanted the voices from war-ravaged Sarajevo, "authentic voices that had not been heard before," to echo around the world, and expose a long history of international favoritism, hypocrisy, and double standards on human rights. "I suggested we gather at the Children's Square because children were the main concern. When I was a child, I relied on the help of others. I could not help, but I wanted to. I was now in a position to help with wisdom and sincerity of the heart, while others hesitated. In doing so, I could relieve my conscience." What I want to emphasize here is that when Ajla speaks about the ethical sensibilities or virtues cultivated by activists like herself, for example, a rightly disposed heart, she evokes a nostalgic desire to correct the horrors of a bygone past.

Muhammad, a thirty-one-year-old exile from Palestine who runs a small travel agency in Sarajevo, was one of the first people to get involved in Stand for Justice. Drinking green tea in the cafeteria of Sarajevo School of Science and Technology, where I worked at the time, he explained to me that getting people involved was easy. "They no longer wanted to be silent. They were silent for decades. When I started posting in the Stand for Justice group, I did not need to plea with people. They were ready." When I met Ajla, she reported that, as the number of supporters rose to 2,000, her enthusiasm was replaced with anxiety. "I was told that I needed to obtain a permission from the police to hold the protest. It was two days away. I messaged Džemila, an activist friend of mine, who suggested to push back the protest to avoid trouble. 'Too late,' I responded. 2,000 supporters were coming from all over Bosnia." Ajla continued, "Džemila warned me that protestors burned Israeli flags on the streets of Sarajevo, and that I would be held personally responsible if this happens because I organized the whole thing. Džemila suggested that I submit a formal request to the police, and make a list of twenty *redars* [monitors] who would make sure that the protest is orderly."

Ajla messaged friends on Facebook once again. "I saw that 'Mr. Believer' was online. The one who told me that I was a 'bad' Muslim a few days earlier. I asked if he would help as a monitor. I needed his national identity number and signature, but he fed me some *šuplju* [nonsense] about how he worked for the government and did not want to be associated with political activity. He sounded incredibly pathetic, so I cut him off and began messaging other friends instead." Ajla was met with similar resistance in her inner circles. "Everyone had an excuse for why they could not help." *Fina gradska raja* (decent urban folks, as opposed to scheming and untrustworthy rural newcomers), in her view, are passive victims of nationalist ideologies, "who let their lives be dictated by politicians and new businessmen," despised for their inherent cultural primitiveness, and criticized for their war profiteering and nepotism. Ajla continued, "I realized that I have no real friends *kad zagusti* [when times get hard]. I relied on the Stand for Justice group as one medium through which I could interact with like-minded peers, those who, with love, fear, and humility, turn to God for assistance in the struggle for Palestine." Let me expand a little more on the ideas of public sociability and political critique engendered by BDS.

2.1 *Religious Participation in the Public Realm*

Ajla's interpretation of activism is quite distinct from the one that Elma espoused. Recall, for example, that Elma imbues her views on activism with the language of free will, and other kinds of secular-liberal and progressive sensibilities. But, when it comes to Ajla, this language is best understood in terms of desire to secure God's forgiveness and satisfaction. What this illustrates is that the main challenge to older generations' sincerity as believers and legitimacy as religious authorities does not come from easily identifiable others like "Wahhabis," nor does it come from "neo-Muslims" vying for political office. Rather, it comes from activists like Ajla, who stepped in to fill the void in what they consider to be the lack of information on how to conduct oneself in accord with Islamic principles in everyday life. These generational debates about proper Islamic conduct, as I have mentioned in previous chapters, have profound implications for the organization of political life within private and public spheres.

For example, Ajla's call for monitors in the Stand for Justice group incited younger generations to "recognize their moral responsibility," and "realize a divine plan for Palestine," against the weight of custom, tradition, and social coercion. "Our parents hide like *miševi* (mice) in public," Ajla wrote, thereby expanding her criticism of passive Bosniaks beyond the simplistic registers of fina gradska raja. "Unable and unwilling to render to God, they accept Israel's strategy of dispossessing Palestinians." Such a judgment failed to recognize that older generations have taken on BDS with enthusiasm. But because they have done so in ways generally relegated to the sphere of private life, Ajla criticized them for upholding a form of religiosity devoid of sociopolitical consequences. By involving younger generations in BDS, and other activities she considered "Islamically-oriented," her objective was to provide an alternative source of information and socialization, different from what they were exposed to in their homes and mosques. In this light, it is not surprising that Aida, a twenty-five-year-old teaching assistant from Kovači, explained her decision to take on BDS in the following terms, "If you want to learn about Islam, do not talk to your parents. They have lost the ability to know what it means to live as Muslims in today's world. Do not go to the mosque, either. The imam only speaks to you during Ramadan, and he repeats the same thing year after year. As Muslims, we know the basics of religion, such as praying and fasting. But the hard question that confronts us is how to act and speak for the sake of the umma." Sociability, I would contend, is important in this respect. Simply put, what appeals to Aida is the opportunity to socialize with like-minded peers in a place of guidance that arguably moves Muslims toward correct forms of conduct and moral responsibility.

Notably, Aida's statement above suggests that younger generations reject the profound individualization of moral responsibility characteristic of older generations. This is supported by the comparatively high degrees of social power and competence, as manifest in their social networking, familiarity with political tools, and media knowledge. In order to enhance and extend Islamic forms of sociability, such as those created by the BDS movement, younger generations make use of this knowledge. For example, after she had failed to get her friends involved in the Stand for Justice protest, Ajla reached out to politicians representing ostensibly rival ethno-national groups. "The issue of Palestine came up," she remarked to me, "and all of a sudden, they were reluctant to get involved. Much like our parents, politicians are passive due to contradictory loyalties of the main nationalist parties. Izetbegović is pro-Palestine. [Milorad] Dodik, the leader of the main Serb party, is pro-Israel. It is political posturing, and nothing is done."[6]

In an interview with me, Muhammad honed in on the topic of political leadership. "Bosniaks feel like they cannot go to their own politicians. They are seen as nationalists who stir up divisions in order to maintain power. The contested discourse on the Israeli–Palestinian conflict is part of this post-war manipulation." What Bosniaks can do, he explained, is express frustration through public activism. "Through acts of social protest, Bosniaks say, 'We do not accept injustice for Palestinians, and we do not accept it for ourselves.' When Bosniaks protest on the streets of Sarajevo in solidarity with Palestinians, they also protest for their own political rights." As I suggested earlier, it is possible to read many of the BDS activities as having the effect of undermining the authority of a range of dominant norms, institutions, and structures. Indeed, talking about her interview with TV Sarajevo in November 2012, Ajla conveyed the fuller meaning of the Stand for Justice protest in the following terms, "One of the questions was whether Stand for Justice can grow. I answered, 'Absolutely.' The suffering of Palestinians has to end. This is our main concern. But Stand for Justice is also opposed to politicians and ethno-national clans that have been destroying Bosnia for decades." Ajla continued, "There is a sense of frustration

---

6 In January 2009, Dodik sent a letter to the then-President of Israel, Shimon Peres. He expressed solidarity with "Israel and its citizens," and explained that the Republic of Srpska, one of the two entities of Bosnia, the other being the Federation, "is opposed to anti-Israeli protests organized in the Federation." Izetbegović responded, calling Dodik's letter a disgrace at a time when "civilian victims are still being counted in Gaza" (see Gorin 2009).

EUROPEAN HOPES, NATIONALIST DESIRES, AND THE URBAN–RURAL DIVIDE   103

among younger generations. Politicians refuse to act in our best interest. For this reason, we support an international movement that draws attention to the real issues of today, such as equality, political rights, and distributive justice. It starts with Palestine, but it also affects our lives here. This is what Stand for Justice is all about." As I have shown, this way of connecting a particular struggle to broader ones is often invoked by the leading BDS figures like Barghouti.

2.2 *Islamic Mores and European Errors*
Dino, who was born in Kovači and studied Management at the Faculty of Economics, University of Sarajevo, when I first met him in June 2013, expanded on the implications of bitterness and distrust of politicians that seem to prevail in Sarajevo, "To be honest, we are so jaded that we distrust anyone who is local. It is not surprising, therefore, that those who lead the struggle for Palestine are from abroad." This resonated with my experience in Stari Grad. Azim was from Syria. Muhammad was from Palestine. In an interview with me, Muhammad recounted how worried he was after Ajla had asked him to help organize the Stand for Justice protest. "How am I to do this? I am a foreigner." Muhammad paused reflectively for a moment and then continued, "I realized that Bosniaks trust me. Because I speak from the heart. Free from selfish and greedy desires." From this perspective, Muhammad's ability to gain the trust of younger generations depends crucially upon a prior cultivation of a sincere and open heart—a figure for something like "the right attitude." This helps him embody in practice the ethical sensibilities or virtues that not only undergird the BDS activities I explore in this chapter but also serve as a disincentive to immoral conduct attributed to politicians, such as criminality and corruption. It is worth noting that this separation between *pošteni ljudi* ("decent people") and politicians was negotiated by many of those I met in Stari Grad during the course of my fieldwork, cutting across divisions of class, gender, and generation.

The instrumentality of virtues in relation to many of the BDS activities, especially those of social protest, is evident in the following comment, "How one acts in this life reflects upon in the afterlife, and life in the afterlife is better for those who fear God. Those who protest on the streets of Sarajevo in solidarity with Palestinians have fear embedded in their hearts, and this strengthens their resolve to do good." Muhammad's assertion here is that pious fear is one of the main conditions of moral conduct. It moves one to do good, to protest on the streets of Sarajevo in solidarity with Palestinians. One can say, in other words, that the BDS activities, especially those of social protest, have conditions of enactment that include certain virtues, such as pious fear. In this sense, they are both a means to moral conduct and an end. Muhammad's thank-you note posted in the Stand for Justice group following the protest is telling in this regard.

> Thank you, God, for enlightening brothers and sisters in Bosnia. For showing them the path to becoming better Muslims. Here in the heart of Europe, brothers and sisters are setting an example for others. To sober up to current realities and social needs. To rise above moral apathy and indifference. To act in solidarity with Muslims who suffer injustice everywhere, from Srebrenica and its nearby villages, to 'ethnic ghettos' in London and Paris, to refugee camps in the West Bank and Gaza Strip.
> STAND FOR JUSTICE 2012

What I want to emphasize here are two interrelated points. The first concerns the current plight of the umma, as a community riven with moral apathy and indifference, "and profoundly suffering all forms of injustice, disrespect, and insult" (Hirschkind 2006, 123). During an interview, Muhammad explained to me the meaning of his thank-you note in following terms, "Muslims are weak. They emulate western habits and lifestyles. They spend money on cars, but not on the needy. They sit at home, doing nothing, while Muslims are being killed and mosques are being burned. But those who act and speak for the sake of the umma, and therefore live a more enlightened existence, have taken the prescribed path to becoming better Muslims." From this perspective, the choice to take on BDS, and to act in solidarity with Muslims who suffer injustice everywhere, as Muhammad understands it, is not an expression of one's free will, as suggested by Elma earlier in this chapter. Rather, it is a central aspect of the struggle in the path of God. In addition, those who have taken the "straight" path—the principle around which the BDS activities of younger generations have been elaborated—are urged to guide others from being astray.

The second noteworthy aspect of Muhammad's thank-you note is his constative claim that the guidance I mention above originates from the heart of Europe and "genuine" European Muslims. For this reason, we might say that it represents both a call to greater piety and a call upon Europe from Europe itself to correct its moral errors. As we saw earlier in this chapter, older generations consider Europe a symbol of the ultimate good that transcends historical experience. Although its ontological values remain intact, younger generations describe Europe as flawed from the current, "historically relative perspective" (Sarajlić 2009, 72). This is best understood in terms of certain disappointment with Europe—its failure to prevent the Srebrenica genocide and recognize it as a European tragedy. In short, Europe's failure to enact civility, understood to be a European virtue, opens the space for younger generations to claim that Islam is essential to Europe's return to its forgotten, better self. To clarify this point, we might consider the following statement made by Dino. "Muslims pray for peace and tolerance in packed mosques at a time of fear and loathing of Muslims. But churches stay empty. Islam has 'shaken' Europe. Not in the sense of its recent clashes with Europe, such as those over same-sex marriage. But rather in the sense of showing Europeans how to 'return' to God. How to distance themselves from 'worship' of the state. How to rediscover [Christian] values that precede and outlast the state."

The BDS activities that I mentioned above, notably the Stand for Justice protest, are articulated against many of the concepts, sensibilities, practices, and forms of life associated with Europe and a secular-liberal understanding of religion as a privatized and individualized system of belief. It would be a mistake, however, to understand these activities in oppositional terms alone. In short, for Dino and others, these activities are grounded in what they consider to be Islamic values and ethics. But they also presuppose a distinctively European project of modernization and urbanization, one that I discussed in detail in chapter 3. In other words, the tensions that inform the BDS activities I explore in this chapter reflect the anxieties urban locals, as young as twenty and as old as sixty, feel about their own commitments to Europe being called into question, especially in light of rural attacks on urban values. In the popular imagination, as should be clear, rural newcomers are noted for their criminality and corruption, their nationalism and radical religiosity. They appear as the origin of all the trouble in Sarajevo, and serve as a counterpoint to both religiously devout supporters of Stand for Justice and many Bosniaks who regard themselves as secular, for example, supporters of the MFS-Emmaus.

3 New Nationalist Leaders and the Authoritative State

The Mladi Muslimani organization was founded in Sarajevo in 1939, in an embittered response to the arrangement between Dragiša Cvetković, the then-Prime Minister of the Kingdom of Yugoslavia, and Vlatko Maček, a Croatian political leader, that founded the Banovina Hrvatska (the Banate of Croatia), and divided most of contemporary Bosnia between Serbia and the newly-independent Croatian province. This, according to Mladi Muslimani, "worsened the predicament of [...] Muslims in the Kingdom of Yugoslavia" (Kostić 2007, 65; see also F. Friedman 1996; Magnusson 1999). What was needed, therefore, was an Islamic revival or awakening, considered to be essential to the very existence of Muslims. In the aftermath of the Second World War, and forbidden by the Communist Party, Mladi Muslimani continued their activities clandestinely. They imagined an "Islamic state that would count [...] 400 million inhabitants belonging to the most diverse races and nations" (Muftić 1942, 92, cited in Bougarel 2008, 22). In this light, it is not surprising that their political program included references to pan-Islamist movements like the Muslim Brotherhood (Mladi Muslimani 2002). That said, in Bosnia as elsewhere, political pan-Islamism was "nothing but a form of proto-nationalism," as illustrated by Mladi Muslimani's resistance to the "Yugoslav" idea after the Second World War, their interest in the Islamic Republic of Pakistan, which was born out of a larger multiethnic entity, and, above all, "their role in the founding of the SDA" (Bougarel 1997, 2–3).[7]

Mirnes is the General Secretary of Mladi Muslimani. In 2013, he welcomed me to his office in Morića Han, a former inn, the courtyard of which is now filled with Oriental carpets for sale and a café that is favored by poor and lower-income supporters of Mladi Muslimani and the Salafi movement. Over Turkish coffee, Mirnes talked about his past, his commitment to Mladi Muslimani, and what he considered to be the organization's role in the struggle for Palestine. He was born in 1972 in Nova Varoš, a city in Sandžak. After he graduated from the Faculty of Philosophy, University of Montenegro, he worked for *Ljiljan*, a weekly newspaper founded by the SDA as a successor to *Muslimanski Glas*, the official communiqué of the party. Mirnes joined Mladi Muslimani after he moved to Sarajevo. This move was compelled by the immense pressure Mirnes was under as an Islamic activist in Nova Varoš. He recounted how, although he believed the signing of the Dayton Agreement to be a window to political and religious freedom in Nova Varoš—he even ran for the local

---

7 In 1949, a wave of arrests shattered Mladi Muslimani. The organization was reestablished three decades later amid political liberalization and national affirmation of Muslims. This breathed new life into the organization, allowing it to mobilize students at the city's madrasas, a phenomenon I addressed at some length in chapter 3. One of the leading figures of the loose Islamic revival movement was the late Alija Izetbegović. In 1983, he was accused of fundamentalism and sentenced to a prison term. The persecution of Izetbegović, and twelve other members of Mladi Muslimani, established them as martyrs in the public eye, allowing them to overcome their marginality in relation to secular authority, and, seven years after their arrests, play a key role in the founding of the SDA. Although founded by pan-Islamists, the party's base included urban intellectuals, former Communist Party networks, and more secular-minded Bosniaks (see Bougarel 1997). During the war, it began to convey conservative meanings of Bosniak national identity, advocating a major political and cultural role for Islam, therefore, driving the wedge between religious and secular nationalists.

council as an SDA representative—in 1996, police harassment, profiling, and threatening phone calls started, and soon became staples of his everyday life.

It all came to head in the aftermath of the NATO bombing of the former Yugoslavia. During an interview, Mirnes explained his comments in these terms, "Serb nationalism experienced a boost that manifested in the persecution of members of the political opposition, like myself. My goal was to make a difference in the life of Muslims in Nova Varoš. But I was at it alone, so it was an impossible task. There was no *hajra* [benefit] in what I was doing. At the same time, it cost my family a lot." Mirnes went on to recount how his father died young from a heart attack. "He never asked me to stop, but he was worried. He experienced difficulty at work because of me. We lived in a small community, so everyone knew what I was up to, and their disapproval manifested in prejudice toward my family." The final straw, so to say, was an encounter with a former thesis supervisor. "I was late for class," Mirnes began. "On my way up the stairs I met this professor. He is an intelligent man, a professor of Philosophy and Theology." Mirnes continued, "He is also a Serb nationalist, and when we met, he would not speak to me. He had a look in his eyes that said, 'You are not welcomed.' That was it for me. I moved to Sarajevo five days later."

According to urban locals, those I described earlier, in the first half of this chapter, Sandžaklije like Mirnes enjoyed the protection of, and had taken over, the SDA that endorsed their migration in order to "increase the Bosniak population in Sarajevo" (Stefansson 2007, 72). For Mirnes, however, his engagement with the SDA in general, and Mladi Muslimani in particular, was an outcome of the bitterness and resentment that he carried over from Nova Varoš. His desires and aspirations, in this regard, were similar to Azim's. "The founders of Mladi Muslimani had experiences that I related to," Mirnes said. "They spent years in prison because they defied the state, declared themselves as 'Muslims,' and refused to back down in the face of extreme social and political hardship. They worked in the interest of Muslims who were marginalized and discriminated against. They suffered because of it. Same as me." In many ways, Mirnes's story rehearses a popular narrative within which one's discovery of Islam chafes against the secular rationalities of the state, a friction that results in new vocabularies of "ethics, religion, and politics" (Hirschkind 2006, 41). In these vocabularies, one's discovery of Islam is understood to provide a particular intelligibility to one's actions, making them morally meaningful. Let me elaborate.

Mirnes noted that he "returned" to Islam in 1994. "I say 'returned' to describe how I discovered Islam—willingly and contentedly. My friend gave me Mustafa Mahmud's *Understanding the Qur'an: A Contemporary Approach*." This book, according to Mirnes, led him to think critically about the virtue of submission to God, and the lack of this disposition in his life.[8] "It took time to 'mature' in the sense of knowing what the existence of God meant for me. At first, I was satisfied with just knowing that God existed, without following rituals. This was part of my 'maturing,' little by little." In 1998, Mirnes started praying and fasting. He explained to me that these outward practices "awakened a new kind of religiosity." In this Mirnes echoes a widely shared view that religiosity is the product of outward practices, rituals, and acts of worship, rather than just an expression of them. Notably, the moral rectitude that follows these transformations has social and political connotations that are significant to the community as a whole. Again, in Mirnes's words, "I realized what the prescribed path was. I had to do more for Muslims, and mimic the Islamic activism of Alija Izetbegović and others who founded Mladi Muslimani."

When Mirnes joined Mladi Muslimani in 1999, he volunteered, distributed leaflets, and organized conferences. "I tried to get involved as much as possible." Mirnes continued, "It was hard. I still needed to make money on the side. I had several jobs, and was struggling to make ends meet." Ten years later, however, the head of Mladi Muslimani offered Mirnes a secretary position. He recounted how one of his first duties was related to Palestine. "I worked on the International Quds Day, an event held on the last Friday of Ramadan. In London, for example, this event generates media coverage, and takes the form of protest. In Sarajevo, we show a documentary on Palestine, we invite an expert to speak about the Israeli–Palestinian conflict, or we promote a book about it. What we do is symbolic. But we do it regardless because history has to record that we were on the 'right' side." Mirnes continued, "In 1941, Mladi Muslimani signed a petition demanding that the Independent State of Croatia stops slaughtering Serbs, Jews, and Roma. At a time when Europe was overtaken by fascism, the organization acted in the interest of the needy." This tradition, according to Mirnes, must continue. "We want our descendants to be proud of how we acted in regard to the Israeli–Palestinian conflict like we are proud of what our ancestors did back in 1941." That said, Mirnes's nostalgic desire to emulate a bygone past is problematized by the fact that current supporters of Mladi Muslimani have rather low profiles that differ from the organization's image in the past as the hub of Bosniak political elite.

A number of scholars have argued that the past image of Mladi Muslimani lives on through organized forms of social engagement, such as giving meat to

---

8 For a detailed analysis of Mahmud's popularity as an Islamic moral authority, see Salvatore 2000.

the poor during Eid al-Adha (see Foschetti 2010). The lack of political power, the argument goes, is caused by Mladi Muslimani's inability to attract younger generations. I argue instead that younger generations are not the immediate targets of Mladi Muslimani. During an interview, Mirnes explained that they can attend conferences, like he did when he was younger. "But when it comes to BDS, for example, it makes more sense to focus on older generations. They can convert their moral values into money terms, and punish companies tied up in ethnic cleansing, land seizure, and military occupation. But they are passive. They claim to support Palestinians, but will not follow through." Mirnes paused for a moment to make sure I understood and then continued, "Mladi Muslimani have been printing BDS pamphlets since 2006. We hand them out on the streets outside of mosques and bus stations to brothers and sisters who seem enthusiastic to get involved. Not many do." After he heard about my work in Tower Hamlets, Mirnes compared this example to Bangladeshis who "spend an extra hour in a supermarket going though objects on offer in order to make an ethical choice."

3.1 State Politics and the Islamization of Society

The idea of passive, submissive, and uncritical older generations, especially those from the middle- and upper-middle income strata, frequently emerged in conversations I had with Mirnes, and many others like him, as we shall see later. I found it to be problematic for a variety of reasons, not the least of which is the fact that older generations participate in BDS, as in the case of well-to-do supporters of the MFS-Emmaus. Rather, I believe that the failure of Mladi Muslimani to mobilize among this specific group stems from their opposition to the idea of a secular Muslim identity and, more importantly, their links to the SDA, whose cadres are derided as corrupt schemers, "only out for personal gain, and engaged in [...] morally compromising activities" (Helms 2007, 238).[9]

Nedžad, who joined Mladi Muslimani right after the war, presented a very different account. For Nedžad, the problem was that Bosniaks have been *uskraćeni* (deprived) of Islam. "Whatever little Islam we had, the communists suppressed it. Bosniaks know nothing about Islam but have become its biggest critics. They criticize the SDA, for affirming Islam as key to our national identity, for being too conservative, but fail to recognize that without it, Bosnia and Bosniaks would not have survived." Before I proceed with the rest of his

---

9 Politics are seen as an "ethnically devalued universe" consisting of "immoral actions and immoral persons" (Kolind 2007, 126). This discourse is not limited to the SDA but extends to all nationalist and, to a lesser extent, non-nationalist parties.

discussion, which merits our serious attention, let me focus for a moment on Nedžad. He was born in Kiseljak, a small city in central Bosnia. He moved to Sarajevo in 1980, and grew up on the same street as Irfan. "I come from a merchant family. We had shops in Baščaršija before the communists nationalized them. I had to take care of myself, so I started selling souvenirs in 1984, during the Olympics. I have my own shop now." Seated in his shop on a rainy Wednesday morning, Nedžad vented his frustration with Bosniaks, most of whom he described as "secularized and Eurocentric."

Nedžad remarked to me that to relegate Islam to the supposedly "normal" domain of private worship was an "attempt to 'make good' with Europe." When I asked him to elaborate in more detail, Nedžad responded, "I do not understand Bosniaks who cling to Europe. Europe turned a blind eye to the slaughter of Bosniaks." Such anger with Europe often emerged where the nation had emptied religion of its content. In this sense, "Islamization" of Bosniaks during the war was de facto "nationalization" of Islam under a specific Bosnian cap. Those who developed a well-defined national identity began to cultivate, at the same time, anti-European sentiments. In contrast to supporters of the MFS-Emmaus, who consider Europe to be a symbol of the ultimate good that exceeds historical experience, and supporters of Stand for Justice, who consider it to be flawed from the current, historically relative perspective, supporters of Mladi Muslimani, like Nedžad above, "turn Islam into a political and religious ideology, a complete *Weltanschauung*," and perceive its relationship to Europe in terms of structural opposition (Bougarel 2007b, 115).

For example, Adnan Jahić, the SDA's official spokesperson and board member of Mladi Muslimani, who Mirnes calls "brother," argues that the war was a final confrontation between the autochthonous national and cultural values of the Bosniaks and the alien ones, "imported from the west, which have been imposed on us and presented as our own" (Jahić 1995a, 52–53, cited in Bougarel 2007b, 112). He continues, "We belong in terms of geography and [...] civilization, but in no way do we belong culturally and spiritually." This leads Jahić to argue, "We want Islam to be our moral, cultural, and intellectual impetus, as we do not consider that it could be the western culture and civilization. For this reason, it is important to understand that Islam is a collective issue and not an individual one, an issue that requires the largest possible consensus, and not any subjective free will" (Jahić 1995b, 390–391, cited in Bougarel 2007b, 114–115). Clearly, Jahić rejects the understanding of Islam as individual faith, and proposes an ethic of collective responsibility rather than an inner ethic. Similarly, he contrasts the western concept of democracy with the Islamic one. In the western concept, "human rights and liberties constitute the greatest value of the community." According to Jahić, here lies the weakness of the western culture and civilization—"there is no progress at the spiritual and ethical level." In contrast, Islamic democracy is understood to be grounded in "positive ethical values" that contribute to the fulfilment of the Islamic idea within the community (Jahić 1996, 247–254, cited in Bougarel 2007b, 112).

This account appears to be Foucauldian in that it conceives of ethics as a set of practical activities that are germane to a certain way of life. "Those who believe that it is possible to be linked with Islam in an irregular and superficial way," Jahić argues, "should be aware of their inconsistency." That said, if Islam becomes a criterion of differentiation within the community, "Jahić has no [...] choice but to entrust its implementation to the political power, and the 'positive ethical values' to which he refers become [...] an implicit state ideology" (Bougarel 2007b, 115). Indeed, Jahić struggles to define these values, and recognizes that it is important to "move from the ideal of political theory toward the reality of what is workable and possible." The maintenance, reproduction, and dissemination of Islam, in this view, is conditioned by the restoration of a party-state within a democratic political arena, and its ability to "encourage [...] forms of subtle Islamization of the society." As we saw earlier in this chapter, supporters of Stand for Justice claim responsibility for the moral and political direction of the society, especially in light of the state's failure to perform this role. In contrast, supporters of Mladi Muslimani view the state as the form of agency through which the society is to be transformed. Debates over the proper Muslim response to the Israeli–Palestinian conflict are a productive site to which one can turn to bring out multiple forms of agency, the diversity of "Bosnian Islam" these forms assume and require, "and the cleavages along which this diversity is structured" (Bougarel 2007b, 98).

In order to develop this point further, I turn to a conversation with Hamdija, a fifty-one-year-old representative in the SDA-led cantonal government, who was displaced from Biljača, a village in eastern Bosnia, and now lives in Kovači. Sitting at the Divan Café in Morića Han, he remarked to me, "Europeans promote human rights, but fail to prevent ethnic cleansing in Bosnia. It is the same with Palestine. This is a time of crisis, a fight for Palestinian survival, much like the war was a fight for the survival of Bosnia and Bosniaks." Note that Hamdija's evocation of "survival," strikingly evident in Nedžad's discussion reported earlier, allows him to infuse a sense of duty into his political activity, and reject the possibility that he had any desire for personal gain, status, and power when he joined the SDA, "the only party able to defend the 'Bosniak interests,' including the prominence of Islam." As our conversation wound down, Hamdija reiterated that he was not interested in politics, "but had to answer the call of duty to his nation amid Serb atrocities and European indifference echoed around them." Both were said to be "just because we are Muslims."

The fact that discourses of nation and religion are ineluctably intertwined, as in the quote above, must be understood in light of the broad impact the SDA has had in "Islamizing" the meaning of the war. At times, the late Alija Izetbegović, one of the eight members of Mladi Muslimani who later went on to found the SDA, even stated that the war had happened "only because we are 'bad' Muslims." For example, in October 1994, the then-President of the newly independent Bosnia, told the soldiers of the Seventh Muslim Brigade that "We had to endure this inferno to return to the right path, to remember who we are and what we are, to remember that we carry the legacy of Islam, and that we have the duty to protect it" (Izetbegović 1994, cited in Bougarel 2007a, 170). Such attempts by Bosniak nationalists in and around the SDA to recast their national sentiments in religious idioms continue today.

3.2 Critical Commentary and the Act of Remembrance

In an interview with me, Nedžad complained that decades after the slaughter of more than 8,000 men in Srebrenica, "suffering is not over." He said, "In the aftermath of the September 11 attacks, and the rise of anti-Islamic sentiments that have followed since, the international community, and especially the European Union, has tightened its leash on us. I believe that Europe has created a 'ghetto' in Bosnia that is similar to the one in Palestine. We see this in the territorial partition of Bosnia and various travel restrictions that are meant to keep us away from Europe." The issue seems to be even more pronounced given the often-cited docility of Bosniaks. Latif, a fifty-three-year-old columnist from Tuzla, most famous for his opinion pieces in *Saff*, a magazine with ties to the Salafi movement, used the terms *razbošnjačenje* ("de-Bosniakization") and *razmuslimovanje* ("de-Muslimization," but "de-Islamization" is more apt) when I met him. He said, "Bosniaks reject Islam and flee from their 'true' identity. Personally, I would love for the struggle for Palestine to awaken us politically, to give us a sense of unity. But we are not united, and never will be. Bosniaks are pushed into a corner by Europe, and believe that there is no way out other than to accept the imposed project of 'self-hatred.' Bosniaks celebrate their *podanački mentalitet* [submissive mentality]. They blame Islam for their stagnation and marginalization. They are the biggest Islamophobes." Such "rejection" of Islam, or even its "downplaying," as Nedžad described it earlier in this chapter, are seen as threats to the core of Bosniak nationalists in and around the SDA.

Comments such as these are also striking in another respect. During an interview, Mirnes explained that Bosniaks are compelled to "deny the suffering of their nation." He explained his comments in these terms, "I wrote about the Srebrenica genocide, and spoke with mothers who witnessed their fourteen-year-old sons get slaughtered by Serb forces. There is no greater loss than that. But they stay silent about the perpetrators—this is how sure they are that nothing will be done if they speak up. The courts fail to bring the perpetrators to justice. No justice, no truth. If you speak up, you are considered to be against a multiethnic Bosnia." At the same time, Mirnes voiced his frustration with "Bosniaks who associate with Europe," and care more about the suicide bombings in London than they do about Srebrenica. "They share posts on the Internet in solidarity with London, but have no interest to do the same for Srebrenica. In this 'post-Dayton prison,' we are compelled to forget genocide. This is especially egregious when it comes from our own people." Then, barely hiding his anger, Mirnes asked, "Within this context of avoidance and denial, how can we expect Bosniaks to speak up against the suffering of Palestinians?"

In December 2010, Latif invited me to the "Let us Remember Gaza" conference. The conference organized by Mladi Muslimani, and moderated by Mirnes, commemorated the second-year anniversary of Israeli attacks on the Gaza Strip, known as the Gaza Massacre, that left more than 1,400 Palestinians dead. It took place in a packed Bosnian Cultural Centre. In the audience, I noticed older men and a few older women dressed in contemporary styles of *hijab* (veil). Latif provoked tears and sadness among the audience as he drew parallels between the Gaza Massacre and the Srebrenica genocide, and discussed the ways in which Bosniaks were discouraged to commemorate and remember important episodes from recent history. These episodes, in turn, were understood to be opportunities for reflection and critical commentary on docility of Bosniaks, the term that has come to be associated with the abandonment of agency.

Speaking slowly and steadily, Latif began, "Tomorrow will mark two years since five of our sisters, aged four to fifteen, were killed in the Gaza Strip. But this will not be discussed anywhere, except for here, tonight. What I want to emphasize here is that no one cares about children killed in the Gaza Strip. No one treats them as a lesson of history. Our children will be taught human rights by reading the *Diary of Anne Frank*. I am not against this, but I am against living in the society of double standards and hypocrisy, where we cannot read about five of our sisters killed in the Gaza Strip, because they are Palestinians, they are Muslims. You see, they cannot be a lesson of history." Latif continued, "The question is what will the society do in regard to the decades-long killing of Palestinians. The society that does not care is sick, and needs to be cured. But we cannot cure it, because we are a part of it." At this point, Muhammad Velić, the imam of the Ferhadija Mosque and columnist for *Preporod*, a monthly newspaper published by the Islamska Zajednica, briefly interjected, "Look around, brothers and sisters, and ask yourselves: who do we emulate? We emulate westerners. We are Muslims, but our acts are not those of Muslims."

As the sound of applause filled the Bosnian Cultural Center, Latif called upon the audience to remember the victims of the Gaza Massacre. "But to do so, we must first remember our own victims. Those Muslims killed in Srebrenica, those Muslims displaced, and those we are losing today, who are 'de-Muslimized,' who reject Islam in favor of Europe and secularism." In this instance, episodes from recent history are invoked in order to urge Bosniaks to affirm their religious faith, and therefore their national unity. "Bosniaks and Palestinians," Latif concluded, "are too divided to raise their victimhood to the status of a 'memory imperative,' as is done by Jews. Time and again, enemies have used this to their advantage. You see, Israel and the Republic of Srpska have the same genesis. Both created on the back of genocide, and no one is willing to speak up. The perpetrators of atrocities enjoy impunity. Europe knows about this. But Bosniaks cling to Europe. Because they are passive, submissive, and uncritical. They have descended into a state of listlessness, and have no regard for their families, their friends, and the community as a whole." It is worth remembering that supporters of Stand for Justice take on themselves the responsibility to urge others to action, the correctness of which is argued and justified in the face of moral apathy and indifference. In contrast, supporters of Mladi Muslimani entrust this responsibility to the traditional centers of religious learning and authority under direct state control, notably madrasas and mosques.

Following the conference, I spoke with Mirhuniza, a forty-four-year-old receptionist at state-owned transport company GRAS, who fled to Sarajevo from Vranjevići, a village in eastern Bosnia. In tears, she told me, "I hear a lot of Bosniaks say, 'We want to join Europe.' I do not want that. Europe failed to stop the war." As we chatted outside the Bosnian Cultural Center, we were joined by Mirhuniza's husband, Durmo, a man in his mid-fifties who survived the war as a Bosnian Army soldier. "Europe has made it clear, time and again, that it does not care about us. During the war, Europe instigated a weapons embargo. I had to use a self-made gun against Serb forces that had inherited all the hardware and munition of the Yugoslav People's Army." Mirnes expressed a similar view when he argued, "The Bosnian Army had to organize from scratch. Europe refused to help." He went on to extend his idea, "Is this not similar to what is happening in the Gaza Strip? I see men throwing rocks at tanks."

The image of brave men defending their nation was often complemented with that of self-sacrificing mothers. In short, during the war, the men were said to be "heroic defenders," while women's roles were restricted to the reproduction and nurturing of "new (loyal) members of the nation"—future soldiers and mothers (Helms 2013, 52). Both were deemed necessary for the survival of Bosnia and Bosniaks. These descriptions bear considerable similarity to the gendered logic inhered in the First Intifada, as I discussed in chapter 2.

What is important to note is that the metaphor of "self-sacrificing mothers," concerned for their loved ones and children, was not just popular in war-circumstances. It remained one of the central aspects of post-war claims to victimhood. Women like Mirhuniza, who were members of the SDA, and saw their work with Mladi Musliman as an extension of this, emphasized women's sacrifice through the loss of sons and husbands, "and having to support families under conditions of danger, hunger, and insecurity" (Helms 2007, 252). In this logic, victimhood implies a negation of responsibility, which in turn establishes a sense of morality and incites solidarity with other victims. For example, I was told over and over that women in Bosnia, and specifically Bosniak women, developed strong emotional bonds with women in Palestine, who, as Mirhuniza once remarked, "buried their sons and husbands." I should also point out, however, that women do not hold monopoly over claims to victimhood. Indeed, war-related social categories, which inform the thinking of many of the men and women I knew in Stari Grad, are based on claims to victimhood at the hands of other ethno-national groups, European (non) interventions, and foreign influences. At the same time, although not always coded as such, these claims also reinforce categories that had existed before the war—urban versus rural, educated versus uneducated, modern versus backward, and so on.

4 Salafis and the Return to the "True" Islam

In the context of tensions that constitute one of the central aspects of everyday life in Stari Grad, both religious nationalists and more secular-minded Bosniaks, for whom religious practice had limited relevance outside of personal devotion, sought to position themselves against a small but visible community of religious believers who took on a version of Islam linked to mujahideen and humanitarian workers from the Middle East and South Asia who came during the war. They are often labeled "Wahhabis," although they themselves reject this label and are more correctly referred to as "Salafis." It is beyond the aim and scope of this book to provide an account of mujahideen efforts to "re-Islamize" their co-fighters in the Bosnian Army and return them to the tradition of the *salaf* (the virtuous predecessors who lived at the time of the Prophet), but what I do want to point to is that their critique of the secularizing trend among Bosniaks, especially those from the middle- and upper-middle-class, resonated with conservatives who sought refuge from the war in Islam. They could not receive guidance from the Islamska Zajednica, whose employees were "preoccupied with individual survival" (Karčić 2010, 155). That said, the Islamska Zajednica lobbied for assistance, and while diplomatic assistance was often lacking, countries in the Middle East and South Asia, notably Iran, Saudi Arabia, and Pakistan, sent food, medicine, and money. Like mujahideen, humanitarian workers in charge of allocating donations assessed that Bosniaks were not "Muslim enough," having drifted away from the "true" Islam—first because of the communists and then because of the secularized champions of Bosnia's European prospects. For this reason, food, medicine, and money that were allocated were accompanied by complimentary Salafi literature.

In the years that followed the war, the Salafi movement continued to mobilize among more conservative Bosniaks, notably the veterans of the El-Mujahid unit of the Bosnian Army. While primarily concerned with the correctness of the Islamic practice, they were also fiercely patriotic. The role model for many was the former military commander, Nezim Halilović, the imam of the King Fahd Mosque in Alipašino Polje, a socialist-era housing estate in the western outskirts of Sarajevo. Halilović is not a Salafi himself, but a renowned member of the Islamska Zajednica and director of its pilgrimage to Mecca.[10] His sermons, reposted on the Islamska Zajednica website, are an affective synthesis of the struggle for "faith, honor, and the state" (Halilović 2012a). On many occasions, such as anniversaries of the founding of military units and celebrations of major battles, Halilović tapped into collective grief and anger with the "aggressors and domestic traitors," as well as Europe that "supported them by denying Bosnia arms for self-defense" (Halilović 2012b). Consider, for example, his popular sermon delivered on the twentieth anniversary of the start of the Bosnian war. In a packed King Fahd Mosque, built with Saudi donations, Halilović condemned *gluha* (deaf) and *ćorava* (blind) Europe that ignored the "biological termination of Bosniaks," and sent food aid packages as an amnesty for its "inaction and immorality." He used an example of Žepa, where he was born and raised, to suggest that, instead of arms, Europeans sent Bibles and

---

10   A number of scholars have observed that "diehards" of the Salafi movement, those outside of the auspices of the Islamska Zajednica, tend to mobilize and operate in diaspora (see Clark 2010; Merdjanova 2013).

food aid packages with pork "although they knew that the city was 100 percent Muslim."

Notably, his fiery sermons have found uses beyond the context of the Friday prayer as a rhetorical form oriented toward politics as it is traditionally understood—their purpose is to mobilize voters. "Brothers and sisters," Halilović chanted, "we must fight for Srebrenica and our beautiful eastern Bosnia politically, by registering and voting there. But our struggle is also through prayers [...]. We pray that all traces of aggressors and domestic traitors be lost. That God punishes them as they deserve, and they deserve to be destroyed, just as they destroyed the male descendants of my people" (Halilović 2012c). Note that the whole question of ethical attitudes and sensibilities that underlie the actions of Stand for Justice, which are political in that they give vitality to the Muslim collective and shape the conditions of its existence, was dropped, as Halilović, instructed by the state (the governing party; see note four), focused on voting. This former student of al-Azhar University directed his warnings of divine punishment at younger generations as well, calling them "lifeless," unable to defend themselves, "let alone their nation." By emphasizing national goals and priorities, Halilović articulated a vision of what it means to act politically notably different to the one articulated by Stand for Justice.

The union of Islam and patriotism was the hallmark of the Aktivna Islamska Omladina (AIO), an organization founded by the veterans of the El-Mujahid unit of the Bosnian Army. As should be clear from what I stated above, those associated with the AIO generally supported the SDA. They used inflammatory rhetoric against other ethno-national groups, and Bosniaks who did not share their political views. Mirsad, whom I cited earlier in this chapter, voiced his concerns about the AIO, "and its ties to the Arab missionaries, who came to Bosnia with the intent to teach Islam to Bosniaks." To illustrate his point, Mirsad gave the example of male students who refused to sit with female students in class. "This is what they were told about Islamic practice by the Arab missionaries they met during the war." Mirsad explained to the students that such behavior was not practiced in their school because, "We belong to Europe." Durmo, who was less charmed with Europe, similarly complained how these "extreme" Islamic attitudes "have no place in Bosnia," and how he, as a veteran of the Bosnian Army, "is nothing like the neophyte and aggressive mujahideen." In contrast, Alen, a thirty-two-year-old taxi driver, who fled to Sarajevo from Kolići, a village in central Bosnia, proudly asserted that his older brother fought alongside mujahideen. Sitting at the Divan Café, a place in Morića Han I came to know well, he praised the dignity and heroism of mujahideen who helped when no one else did. "To now distance ourselves from them would be hypocritical."[11]

Alen worked at a taxi stand close to Morića Han. It was common for us to continue our conversations as we drove to my parents' home. In one such instance, Mirnes indicated how the AIO was supported by money that was left over after the El-Mujahid unit disassembled. When money ran out, the AIO turned to the Saudi High Commission for support. In the aftermath of the September 11 attacks, however, the AIO came under strict state surveillance. The influx of money from abroad was interrupted, forcing the AIO to close down in 2006. Its magazine *Saff* stopped publishing its printed version and made its online version free. At the same time, other Salafi-oriented organizations that struggled to stay active turned to the Internet as a new public space in which their message was easily spread. This led to an audience shift from those who were recruited in and right after the war through the AIO, and were now in their forties and fifties, to those in their twenties and thirties who were originally attracted by scholarships and free courses offered by the King Fahd Mosque. There was a clear shift of importance as well. Gone was the obsession with national survival. The emphasis was now on global political issues like the Israeli–Palestinian conflict. As I describe below, the demands of the nation were stymied and overshadowed by the demands of the umma, a universal collective body that provides dignity and comfort. During one of our conversations, Alen explained to me that he was drawn to the idea of "brotherhood" before he was familiar with the theological doctrine of Salafism.

4.1 *Mujahideen in Cyberspace*

IslamBosna.ba was established in 1997 as an Islamic charitable organization. It morphed into an Islamic website two years later when it became clear that there were numerous Islamic organizations "but not enough 'good' Islamic media in Bosnia." According to Alban, IslamBosna.ba's administrator, the website receives around 200,000 hits per month. When I first visited the website in 2010, there was a hyperlink to Ikhwanweb.org—the English website of the Muslim Brotherhood—and a collection of boycott fatwas copied from InMinds.com (see chapter 2). Alban noted that "in the eyes of the audience, 'external authorities' are attractive. They speak about the collective religious deviance that must be corrected, but has been ignored by imams of the Islamska Zajednica who tolerate 'occasional' Muslims who lead secular lives." To emphasize his point,

---

11 The ambiguities related to mujahideen were summed up by the late Alija Izetbegović when he noted that "on the whole, they did more harm than good" (Izetbegović 2002, cited in Merdjanova 2013, 63).

Alban mentioned an online poll that posed the following question, "Which of the Islamic movements/organizations do you trust the most?" The Salafi movement was most trusted by the audience, with 35 percent of votes. Muhammad Abduh and his mentee Rashid Rida, both of whom participated in founding the Salafi movement at the end of the nineteenth century and the start of the twentieth century, were lauded for their interpretation of the founding texts, the Qur'an and the Sunna, in accord with European modernity, rationality, and science. Their ideas were crystalized by the Muslim Brotherhood under the leadership of Hassan al-Banna (Skovgaard-Petersen 1997, 155–156). Importantly, this is a legacy that Yusuf al-Qaradawi lays claim to.[12]

In chapter 2, I argued that modern religious reformers like al-Qaradawi urge younger generations to read for themselves, exercising good judgment and trusting their own opinions "as to what the texts mean for Islam today" (Mandaville 2003, 136). Almost without exception, younger generations cited al-Qaradawi's "Boycotting Israeli and American Goods" as having an impact on their decision to participate in BDS and thus in the umma's productive life. Alban recited al-Qaradawi's fatwa when explaining to me an ethic of mutual assistance and collective responsibility, revealed in the Qur'an and demonstrated in the Sunna. Ajla and Aida drew on it when expressing a concern for the maintenance of public morality. Although al-Qaradawi's fatwa provides a primary source of reference for younger generations, and thus helps me flesh out the pedagogy of BDS, this does not imply a uniformity of thought and action.

Looking at a boycott list on IslamBosna.ba, I count tens of products not available in Sarajevo. This list was copied from InMinds.com, and while IslamBosna.ba published a new call for boycott in 2014, thereby referencing al-Qaradawi's fatwa, it did not revise this list (see chapter 2). This points to a rather wide circulation of popular Islamic materials that leads to inconsistencies of action and a lack of coherence with local situations and conditions. This, coupled with low purchasing power of its audience, suggests that, in the

---

12 The term "Salafi" is attributed both to earlier reformist trends associated with Abduh and Rida and the ultra-conservative teachings of Muhammad Ibn Abd al-Wahhab that are popular among the veterans of the El-Mujahid unit, and Saudi-financed groups and networks in diaspora and remote villages throughout Bosnia, such as Bočinje, Briješče, and Gornja Maoča. While supporters of IslamBosna.ba benefited from scholarships and free courses offered by the King Fahd Mosque, and were exposed to the teachings of al-Wahhab in this way, they tend toward Abduh and Rida, and modern religious reformers like al-Qaradawi "who reread, reassess, and reassert the validity of Qur'anic teachings in new contexts" (Mandaville 2003, 136). For an excellent discussion of the blurring of these trends in Europe, see Nielsen 2003.

case of IslamBosna.ba, participation in BDS is symbolic. For Alban, however, posting, liking, and sharing popular Islamic materials on Facebook, Twitter, and so on, accommodates the demands of pious living, that is, living in accord with what is believed to be God's will. We might remind ourselves that Ajla participates with the same assumption that BDS is germane to her life as a Muslim. She cites and uses the same materials. She is, however, critical of all those who "hide like mice in public," whether behind computer screens, as in the case of IslamBosna.ba, or in supermarket aisles, as in the case of the MFS-Emmaus.[13] What is striking here is that popular Islamic materials are imparted different meanings and usages as they cross the hierarchical divisions of class, gender, education, and social status.

4.2 Activism in the Valorized Space of Self-Reflection

Dževad was a young man in his early twenties whom I had come to know through Alen. He lived with his aunt in Kovači. His father was killed during the war, and his mother died of cancer two years before I met him. Dževad had a makeshift stand in front of the King Fahd Mosque. Together with tape-recorded sermons, some of which I discussed in chapter 2, Dževad and his friend Kadir sold photos and videos of battles in Afghanistan and Iraq. During one of my visits with Dževad, he handed me a DVD titled "Why is Israel Attacking the al-Aqsa Mosque," and said, "Witchcraft is forbidden, so Solomon wanted to bury books of black magic. They are under the al-Aqsa Mosque where the Solomon's Temple was located. That is why Jews are digging tunnels there." In chapter 4, I briefly indicated the place and significance of the al-Aqsa Mosque in the BDS activities of younger generations. It is worth remembering that these activities do not target Jews, and are instead directed at Israel due to its violations of Palestinian rights and international law. Dževad was an exception to this. This is what he had to say, "In Judaism, 'chosenness' is a belief that Jews are the 'chosen people.' This has led to arrogance. Jews believe that they can desecrate sacred sites like the al-Aqsa Mosque. The Qur'an warns in the seventy-fifth *ayat* [verse] of the third *surah* [chapter] that Jews will take what is not theirs, lie upon God, and demoralize Muslims." At this point, Dževad redirected his attention to the theme of Muslim solidarity, "Muslims who buy Israeli goods

---

13 Consuming one thing rather than another is a decision generally relegated to the private sphere of individual lifestyles, as in the case of well-to-do supporters of the MFS-Emmaus (see Bennett 2004; Norris 2009). This does not make them less political than those who protest, especially as consuming has become increasingly political (see Gudeman 2008; Micheletti 2003; Johnston 2008). That said, if consuming is an isolated form of participation driven by self-directed choices and goals, as in the case of well-to-do supporters of the MFS-Emmaus, it lacks the collective or public dimension (see Carrier 2012).

add salt to the wound. The Prophet said, 'The umma is like one body. When one of the limbs is in pain, the whole body responds with fever and weakness.' When brothers and sisters are starving, caged behind apartheid walls, Muslims everywhere feel it." He concluded, "We cannot be passive, because we let our body suffer." As we have seen, supporters of Stand for Justice consider BDS to be a form of public engagement in the name of Islam that is concordant with the secular state framework. The fact that BDS mobilizes across divisions of political and religious affiliations, moreover, speaks to their desire to discover connections between the majority society and their search for proper Islamic conduct therein. In contrast, supporters of IslamBosna.ba consider such an engagement to be especially dangerous after years of state surveillance and socioeconomic exclusion. They reject active participation and engagement with the majority society in favor of the valorization of private life. Despite their focus on inward disposition or orientation, it would be wrong to describe supporters of IslamBosna.ba as "apolitical." Rather, their political agency is a contingent and unanticipated consequence of the effects their ethical practices "have produced in the social field" (Mahmood 2012, 35).

Kadir was brought up in a pious family. He attended *maktab* (primary religious school), where he memorized portions of the Qur'an and learned the rudimentary skills of recitation. He accepted his first invitation to a Salafi lecture out of curiosity, which led to several more. When Dževad, his best friend, signed up for free courses at the King Fahd Mosque, he did too. "Did you hear about the 'Palestine: Trial for Humanity' conference," Kadir asked me shortly after we met. "Halilović was the first imam in Bosnia to call for BDS. He emphasized the importance of ending Israel's impunity, especially in regard to the desecration of the al-Aqsa Mosque." The conference was organized in February 2008 by Mladi Muslimani. What struck me when watching the conference on YouTube was the extent to which Halilović's call for BDS was influenced by al-Qaradawi's fatwa. This was clear in Halilović's position that women should play a central role in BDS, with the important caveat that this role be restricted to what he described as women's "natural status" as mistresses of the house and guardians of the children and moral purity. In espousing this position, Halilović echoed the views of Bosniak nationalists in and around the SDA. Specifically, he condemned "secularized and Eurocentric" Bosniaks who strive to free women from their "natural status" and thus reject religion, morality, and tradition, in short, "the essence of Bosniak [national] identity" (Helms 2008, 99). While Halilović elaborated al-Qaradawi's fatwa in national terms, Kadir's interpretation clearly drew sustenance from the broader moral project of the umma. "Arabs buy Marlboro cigarettes to the tune of 100 million USD each day. Philipp Morris, the owner of Marlboro cigarettes, gives 15 million USD to Israel. You see, al-Qaradawi warns that Arabs are bankrolling the suffering of brothers and sisters in Palestine." Kadir paused reflectively for a moment and then continued, "Oh, my umma, you take pride in 1.5 billion members, *a nizašta se ne pitaš i ne učestvuješ u globalnim pitanjima* [but you are not consulted over, nor take part in, global political issues]. Oh, my umma, you are weak. Israel does not fear you, nor gives you any importance."

I asked him what constituted the best solution to the problem at hand. Kadir responded, "Each individual has to go back to the Qur'an and the Sunna, discover the value of the divine word, and transform it into a practical reality." Unlike Ajla, Kadir was not interested in creating a social space where Muslims come to learn how to act and speak for the sake of the umma. I noticed instead a strong individualizing impetus that requires each individual to engage with the founding texts, a process that inserts knowledge into the heart and expresses it through the performance of ethical practices. These practices have profound, if unintended, consequences for how politics is imagined and lived. Indeed, my arguments in this chapter suggest that political projects like BDS presuppose not only critical deliberation. They also depend on the ethical sensibilities or virtues that ground and contextualize various discourses on the demands of Islamic piety within post-war Bosnian realities.

CHAPTER 6

Conclusion

This concluding chapter marks the completion of a thematic exploration of BDS activism among Europe's Muslims, one that has entailed not only an intellectual journey into what are often viewed as distinct domains of ethics and politics, each supposedly sequestered in the private and public domains, but also a physical journey into the field. During this journey, I encountered many people who became informants, from lower-income Bangladeshi settlers to well-to-do Bosniak urbanites. Following the arc of their experience revealed diverse modes of engaging with BDS activism, some grounded in a secular discourse of human rights, others imbued with a language of Islam. Their engagement, moreover, spoke directly to the conditions and transformations of "being Muslim," but it was embedded in other activities, whether in the context of employment, education, or domestic life. It was also marked by the ongoing conflicts over social and religious authority, by the fervent attempts to invigorate some notion of a global Muslim community, and by the myriad interventions from the state, the ulama, and so forth. These ethnographic tracings are instructive for at least two reasons. One, they help us think in new ways about the articulations of "being Muslim" through the negotiation of global political discourses. Two, they remind us that solidarity, and the possibility for engagement it opens up, is an extensive category that takes different and even conflicting forms. But rather than a story of opposition, the story of BDS activism among Europe's Muslims is one of imbrication—individual and collective, private and public, ethical and political. It therefore needs to be told in terms of exchanges and attachments that this imbrication generates. This story is best traced, I want to suggest further, through close attention to the historical rhythms and sociopolitical processes that inject distant political commitments into the lives of Europe's Muslims and make solidarity happen, as a lived everyday practice.

In many ways, *Lives in Solidarity* is an exploration of competing claims to solidarity in Tower Hamlets and Stari Grad, and specific modes of being and acting these claims presuppose and enable. Indeed, one of my central arguments is that BDS is not simply an expression of solidarity but also a site of struggle over the nature of that solidarity. Working toward such an argument requires a certain amount of reflection on competing claims to solidarity in Tower Hamlets and Stari Grad, as well as an understanding of how they work in practice. To this end, this concluding chapter presents some final thoughts on the significance of practical context to the labor and practice of solidarity. The emphasis on the thick texture of my informants' lives provides an intimate, on-the-ground interpretation that incites the inversion and subversion of "concepts the ethnographer brings to and encounters in the field" (Strathern 1990, 205). This concluding chapter compares, connects, and counterposes the two contexts through which the terms and concepts that inform the actions of my informants gain their specific meaning. In short, it revisits some of the ways in which BDS is modulated by, and refracted through, recent historical and sociopolitical circumstances in order to elucidate different contextual factors that shape the actions, as well as the concerns, public duties, and character of my informants, and draw out the implications for existing and future research.

1 Social Authority and the Ethics of Freedom

By focusing on how BDS is "localized" through reference to "being Muslim," and living in accordance with what are considered to be Islamic values and ethics, this book offers a unique perspective on the manner in which global political discourses connect to lived experiences and self-expressions in Tower Hamlets and Stari Grad. As such, it provides an unexpected but useful lens for approaching Muslim lives across divisions of class, gender, and generation. In addition, by exploring how BDS is deliberated locally as it becomes part of what is entailed in "being Muslim," this book proposes an alternative reading of BDS that is not only about activism. It is also—if not predominantly—about the connection between BDS and Muslim practices and ethics. Indeed, if we examine the material presented in this book about the "localization" of BDS in Tower Hamlets and Stari Grad, it is clear that this particular strand of a larger struggle for Palestinian rights is oriented not only toward the recognition and elaboration of frames that connect the suffering of Palestinians to the plight of Muslims, but also toward the "retraining" of ethical sensibilities so as to move Muslims toward correct forms of conduct and moral responsibility.

A central aspect of the program of ethical self-cultivation pursued by my informants is that it entails a profound alteration in, and reorganization of, social and political life. In order to elaborate this point, let me focus for a moment on the relationship between social authority and individual freedom that is part of this complex disciplinary program. Specifically, I argue that debates about character formation and moral correctness in Tower Hamlets and Stari Grad enfold contrasting understandings of individual freedom—understandings that have radically different implications for the organization of political life within private and public spheres. These debates, furthermore, presuppose different relations to forms of social authority that are multiplied by generational differences in each context. Here, we might consider the example of middle-aged and middle-class Bosniaks who regard BDS to be an expression of self-guided choice and action. Notably, the capacity to realize one's personal choice, and by extension autonomous will, is conditioned upon both the acquisition and the consummation of self-esteem and self-confidence, which Bosniaks in this age and income bracket derive from their work and professional achievement. Self-guided choice and action, and the concomitant realization of autonomous will as a social ideal, are not only regarded as distinctly European attributes, but also as impervious to, and unencumbered by, social influences from rural and supposedly "non-cultured" newcomers. In this sense, the desire for self-government reflects the exacerbation of social divides and conflicts in a post-war context. Let me elaborate.

When middle-aged and middle-class Bosniaks call for solidarity with Palestinians, they articulate not only patterns of sensibility, affect, and memory that I explore in chapter 5, but also fears of losing control over their lives and destinies. Let me remind the reader that those I spoke to had stayed in Star Grad during the siege but, given its present-day cultural and moral deterioration, felt like their patriotism was in vain. Their disillusionment is channeled through BDS in a way that foregrounds the importance of personal choice, one generally formulated in accord with the dictates of "self-interest," and that seeks to assert not only the autonomy of middle-aged and middle-class Bosniaks in a post-war context, but also their cultural capital and social prestige, as expressed in the styles of consumption and the forms of political and associational life characteristic of Europe. What is notable here is that, although the notion of autonomy is central to the exercise of freedom, my analysis lays bare the social and historical conditions that are necessary for its inculcation and realization.

The remarks on freedom, and the ability to autonomously "choose" one's desires, that I discuss above can be usefully compared to the views of first-generation Bangladeshis from working-class families. Here, the exercise of freedom requires a certain understanding of the self that is sustained in conversation with others or "through the common understanding which underlines the practices of our society" (Taylor 1985, 209, cited in Mahmood 2012, 150). In other words, the exercise of freedom "turns not only on the ability to distance oneself from the social," as in the case of middle-aged and middle-class Bosniaks, but also, more importantly, "on the capacity to turn one's gaze critically to reflect upon oneself in order to determine the horizon of possibilities and strategies through which one acts upon the world" (Taylor 1985, 229, cited in Mahmood 2012, 150). What this formulation draws attention to is how particular relations to social authority constitute both the subjectivities and the actions of first-generation Bangladeshis. Delicately poised in relation to the state and society, and in fear of antagonism and future insecurity, they confine actions to the invisibility and silence of private life. Such quietist tendencies find expression in BDS, especially in its description as an individual matter, guided by personal choice, rather than a collective one.

Although the use of the notion of personal choice reflects how the secular ethos has permeated the lives of my informants, I want to echo Mahmood and argue that neither the field of choices nor the agents who exercise it simply "reproduce [its] assumptions" (Mahmood 2012, 85). Younger generations of Bosniaks across class and social positions, for example, cite al-Qaradawi when trying to explain their decision to participate in BDS—some refer to an ethic of mutual assistance and collective responsibility, other cite a concern for the maintenance of public morality. The range of choices they outline, in this sense, are dictated by the scholarly opinions grounded in Islamic ethical and pedagogical materials that provide the bases for any decision. As such, personal choice is understood not to be an expression of one's will but "something one exercises in following the prescribed path to becoming a better Muslim" (Mahmood 2012, 85).

The differences between these two positions are significant and, as I indicated earlier, have consequences for how the horizon of politics is imagined and debated in Tower Hamlets and Stari Grad. Note that BDS is understood to be one among a collection of acts that serve as a means to the realization of a pious self, and that are regarded as the critical instruments in a program of self-cultivation. Rather than an atomistic or individual act devoid of intentionality, BDS is understood as an act through which pious dispositions are formed. This understanding is well captured in generational differences that I explore in chapter 4. Younger generations of Bangladeshis, who oppose the way their parents handle Islam as a series of rituals to perform without regard for how they contribute to the realization of piety, describe piety as the quality of "being close to God," a way of being and acting that saturates all of one's acts. At a basic level, it requires every Muslim to engage in acts like BDS that are considered mandatory. In addition, the manner and attitude with which these acts are performed is important—sincerity and fear of God are emotions by which excellence in piety is evaluated. Since the point is not simply that one acts virtuously but also how one enacts a virtue—with intent, commitment, and so forth—constant vigilance and monitoring is a critical element in ethical self-cultivation.

1.1 Public Islam and the Politics of Authenticity

Scholars have often argued that an increased interest in the correctness and virtuosity of one's performance is best understood as an expression of recent "emancipation" or "coming out" among Europe's Muslims (see Boubekeur 2007; Dassetto and Nonneman 1996; Leman 2000; Waardenburg 1996). While this interpretation is not entirely wrong, and captures an important aspect of living in a non-Muslim society, it nonetheless fails to take into account a longer and more complex process of reform that raises interesting questions about religious authority and knowledge, which in turn help elaborate the emergence of a social and public Islam in Tower Hamlets and Stari Grad.

My ethnographic analysis of the discussions that enfold within the context of activism in Tower Hamlets and Stari Grad paint a picture of the kind of authority commanded by a new generation of idealistic activists whose profile is not fixed in a social, class, or gender location but traverses a wide terrain of the social landscape. As I hope I have made clear, they invoke greater knowledge and moral authority than their parents, who are accused of dogmatism and traditional scripturalism that hold little hope of providing resources for the issues and problems faced in daily life. As a result, the Islam of the parents is confronted with intellectualized and localized views, in the sense of a recourse to the founding texts and a reflection on what it means to be Muslim in a non-Muslim society, put forward by the children, "under the label of an 'authentic' Islam" (Amir-Moazami and Salvatore 2003, 70–71). This generational conflict also contributes to changes in religious authority toward more flexible and pluralized forms. The ensuing politics of authenticity, to quote Amir-Moazami and Salvatore, serves to further fragment traditional sources of authority, "to the extent that the locus of the 'real' Islam and the identity of those who are allowed to speak on its behalf are becoming elusive" (Amir-Moazami and Salvatore 2003, 71).

As is evident from the preceding chapters, this tendency is reinforced by the relatively high degree of social power and competence among Europe's younger generations of Muslims, as manifest in their social networking, familiarity with political tools, and media knowledge. Traditional sources of authority are thereby not always directly attacked, but challenged from "within," as younger generations step up to reinterpret and reformulate the central precepts of Islam such that they speak directly to the contingencies of today, a task they believe has been abandoned by traditional sources of authority. As I described in chapter 1, this points to an incessancy in the manner in which a discursive Muslim tradition is shaped and redefined via internal interventions.

In a wider perspective, these processes initiate more general shifts from ritual to social forms of Islam in Tower Hamlets and Stari Grad—as Islam is becoming an all-encompassing source that finds expression not only within different moments of daily life but also within different forms of public engagement. It is precisely this different comprehension of Islam that inspires younger generations to render public issues that their parents confine to the private sphere of personal choice, notably the obviously political issues like the Israeli–Palestinian conflict. I want to push this argument further and suggest that the discussion about the proper locus of Islam, that is, the proper coordination between a privatized interiority of belief and a public exteriority that is regarded as an expression of this belief, is based on different arrangements of power and authority, which in turn enfold contrasting visions of what it means to act politically. Younger generations emphasize community participation, social responsibility, and greater activism in the name of Islam that differs considerably from the so-called "quiet Islam" of their parents (Cesari 1995, 34, cited in Amir-Moazami and Salvatore 2003, 69). What is meaningful here is that newly emergent forms of Islamic public engagement are not only expressions of inner beliefs and values, but also means of acquiring them. In other words, it is through public engagement, of which BDS is only a small part, that the pious subjects of this book come to be formed.

As should be clear from what I stated above, younger generations treat Islam as a set of values and ethics that are to be cherished, but that are also relevant to all aspects of one's life—political and religious. They posit a different relationship between outward, and public, practices and inward, and private, belief. Not only are the two regarded as inseparable, but, more importantly, inward belief is the product of outward practices rather than a manifestation of them. Why is this difference consequential? Because, to quote Mahmood, "it affects the way people live and order their lives, their sense of self [...], their understanding of authority and its [...] relationship to individual desires and capacities" (Mahmood 2012, xv). As I suggested earlier, it has profound consequences for how politics is imagined and debated. Such reversal of direction, in short, draws attention to practices that make particular kinds of subjects and sociopolitical imaginaries possible. This insight should be of interest to scholars working on Europe's Muslims in general, and their struggle to negotiate the demands of piety in secularized and pluralized societies in particular. Through ethnographic detail, I show that newly emergent forms of Islamic public engagement, with BDS as a case in point, meet the demands of secular existence, but are nonetheless rooted in the larger project of realizing piety. The picture that emerges from this analysis is one of a symbiosis between Islamic and European culture, "and one that flies in the face of popular accounts of a 'clash of civilizations' or of some inherently adversarial contest" (Mandaville 2003, 128).

2 Solidarity and the Everyday Spatialities of Activism

This book shares many of the questions and concerns that scholars and commentators writing on Europe's Muslims have pursued. For example, how do Europe's Muslims practically work upon themselves in order to become the desirous subjects of specific traditions of teaching and Islamic practice? Clearly, my informants wish to render all aspects of their lives into a means of realizing God's will. But the task of living in accordance with this understanding is not a simple matter—it is mediated not only by debates internal to the Islamic tradition but also by recent historical and sociopolitical circumstances. Part of my objective in this book has been to explore the assumptions and suppositions of this tradition, as well as the day-by-day contexts through which this tradition is enacted and lived. To this end, I have looked at the manner in which hierarchies of class, gender, and generation intersect with BDS, and how they differ in their conceptualization and their role in stimulating activism. Younger generations, as I hope I have made clear, believe that BDS externalizes a different kind of Islam, one marked by, among other things, greater activism. They take on themselves the task of urging fellow Muslims to participate in BDS as a way of reflecting over the meaning and implication of their commitment to piety. It is worth recalling that these acts of guidance are considered crucial to the restoration and strengthening of the umma, as a community riven with moral corruption. Here, I build my analysis up from smaller scales, investigating how my informants deploy BDS within a larger moral project of the umma. In doing so, I move away from an analytical framework that treats the umma as fictional or imagined, and provide instead a set of practical images through which its sense of globality is articulated. That said, a grounded and reflexive approach to political discourses that invoke a collective Muslim subject, particularly those undergirded by the ideas of moral improvement, has largely been eclipsed by the overwhelming attention devoted to the state and, more concretely, its place as a constituent unit of political analyses. It is true that many states, notably Turkey, claim to speak on behalf of a collective Muslim subject, which they at times instrumentalize for their own sovereign interests (Başkan and Taşpınar 2021, 5). I am not concerned, however, with competing visions of the umma or championing the veracity of one claim over another. Rather, I am interested in one particular dynamic integral to its realization, that centered around BDS.

I should make clear that my point is not to dismiss the importance of the state, but to inquire into an entire dimension of politics that remains poorly understood and undertheorized within the literature on solidarity activism, BDS or otherwise. Importantly, as I have suggested, going beyond the state does not mean escaping the state altogether. This is best illustrated in chapter 5, particularly the manner in which the state, or the governing party, utilizes BDS to promote, co-opt, impede, or isolate forms of Islam and "good" or "bad" Muslims. But this rich landscape of conflicting and overlapping historical developments is left illegible if our choice of conceptual categories is limited to the state. Indeed, one of the basic premises of this book is that in order to understand how a secular movement for Palestinian rights becomes enmeshed in the complex ways of "being Muslim," one must turn not to the traditional spaces of political struggle, such as the state and formal politics, but to arguments about what constitutes a proper way of living ethically. In Tower Hamlets and Stari Grad today, this normative ethical project is centered upon questions of affectivity, social responsibility, and pious conduct.

2.1 Translocal Mobilization and the Imaginaries of Struggle

As should now be clear, much of the analytical labor of this book is directed at exploring how a transnational discourse on Palestinian rights has been woven into local efforts to live and act in accord with standards of Islamic piety. Consequently, this book contributes to debates about how to research translocal phenomena through the fine grain of ethnographic fieldwork. As I have discussed elsewhere, the concept of translocality, which describes today's struggle for freedom, justice, and equality, refers to relationships designed to "create new spaces of agency and overcome the constraints posed by a nation-state bounded view. [...] They both transgress and transcend locality, and have the ability to change the local spaces from which they emerge" (Banerjee 2011, 325). Translocality, viewed in this way, encourages new social and political relationships and bases of authority, and helps shift attention from global to local scales, "where these relationships are more visible and valued." Importantly, as sociologist Jackie Smith has astutely observed, translocality is a practice developed through struggle, as people have learned to "work across [...] divisions to build unity and advance shared goals" (J. Smith 2021). This is a point that resonates with my insight that BDS is at once an iconic struggle for Palestinian rights and a catalyst for thinking about struggle in a larger context. Unlike most of what has been written on this topic, this book sidelines questions of antisemitism, and asks instead how the localization of BDS in Tower Hamlets and Stari Grad can help us understand the difficulties and challenges of "being Muslim" differently than we might have otherwise.

Worth mentioning here is that my informants live under conditions of economic stress and political uncertainty. In spite of their direct involvement in local politics, Bangladeshis suffer from unemployment, lack of public services, and poor housing conditions. Bosniaks, at the same time, harbor memories of mass killing and forced migration. Against this backdrop, BDS becomes emblematic of "dissent by the dispossessed and impoverished" (Nash 2004, 3). That said, the manner in which BDS is brought into complex settings and implicated in aspects of life exceed the question of dissent and, for that matter, resistance. To be clear, resistance is an important conceptual category, one I pay considerable attention to in chapters 1 and 2. It is the operative term in a century of popular struggle for Palestinian rights. Furthermore, how my informants practice BDS counts as resistance. But BDS is a movement that gets entangled with lifetimes of migration, memories of war, and other experiences. As such, the analysis of that resistance is connected to the question of local histories, biographies, and "being Muslim," and can only be conceived in relation to "ethical and political conditions" within which that resistance acquires its specific meaning (Mahmood 2012, 9). I pursue the direction opened up by this approach—not only because I find it analytically rich but also because it draws attention to conditions that sustain an entire way of being and acting that, while not always enunciable, is nonetheless efficacious in regard to the organization of BDS in Tower Hamlets and Stari Grad.

There are two interrelated issues that are important to emphasize here. One, the effort to illustrate how BDS, a secular translocal movement connected both in discourse and practice to historical precedents, such as the anti-apartheid movement in South Africa, is brought into conversations about "being Muslim" in two distinct cultural settings casts light on how issues of struggle are negotiated in ways that both inform and are informed by local dynamics. Two, these local dynamics are the scaffolding, if you will, through which the labor and practice of solidarity is realized. They are not simply instances of social cleavages and antagonisms around class, gender, and generation—they also point to distinct forms of experience, memory, and affect that inform how solidarity is imagined, articulated, and practiced. Consequently, this approach commands particular weight in the theorization of solidarity, especially in response to revitalized Black and Indigenous-led radical movements. Let me elaborate.

As I note in the introduction to this book, through its use of justice and rights frames, BDS has come to represent a "progressive action program" that is both locally relevant and transnationally framed (Barghouti 2011, 58). In particular, there are intersections through the languages of liberation and human rights, tactics of boycott and divestment, "and decentralized, horizontal, and networked organizational forms, along with similar targets" (Morrison 2022, 17). Consider, for example, the following statement by the BNC in Ramallah in support of BLM:

> The Palestinian BDS National Committee (BNC) stands resolutely in solidarity with our Black brothers and sisters across the United States who are calling for justice in the wake of the latest wave of insufferable police murders of Black Americans. [...] As indigenous people of Palestine, we have firsthand experience with settler-colonialism and racist violence wielded by Israel's regime of oppression—with the military funding and unconditional support of the United States government—to dispossess us, ethnically cleanse us, and reduce us to lesser humans. [...] The indiscriminate, extrajudicial murder of Black Americans, the unconscionable United States prison system, and the inhumane and racist treatment of migrants and asylum seekers are all symptoms of an increasingly militarized security state that is wreaking havoc and destruction against communities of color in the United States and around the world. As long as this system of oppression continues, it is up to our [...] movements to work collectively and intersectionally to dismantle it, from the United States to Palestine. [...] We call on our community to recognize the connections between the United States domestic racial oppression and its racialized imperial oppression against people of color around the world.
> BOYCOTT, DIVESTMENT, AND SANCTIONS NATIONAL COMMITTEE 2020

In shifting the focus from occupation alone to struggle for freedom, justice, and equality, BDS has created a framework for solidarity that has restored relations between Palestinian and Black activists on a scale not seen since the 1967 Arab–Israeli War when the PLO and the Black Panther Party drew comparisons between "racial capitalism in Israel and in the United States," as well as between the United States imperialism around the world, "in which Israeli politics [...] were implicated" (Lubin 2014, 17). At the same time, it should be noted that the police killing of Michael Brown, and subsequent uprising in Ferguson, sparked demonstrations across the United States just as the uproar against a fifty-day war in Gaza reached its fever pitch. "Protestors from Oakland to New York chanted 'from Ferguson to Palestine, occupation is a crime,' and began to highlight connections between the two struggles" (Davis Bailey 2015, 1017). As I indicated earlier, Palestinian and Black activists have been in solidarity long before Ferguson. Consider, for example, the following statement by Rabab Abdulhadi, a prominent scholar of race and resistance, in which she explains, "These expressions are not new, and they are not because of the excitement of the moment. They [...] have historical precedents in the connections that organically brought together the anti-colonial, anti-racist, anti-capitalist—very clearly revolutionary politics" (Abdulhadi 2014, 10, cited in

Davis Bailey 2015, 1018). That said, the most recent chapter in Palestinian–Black solidarity—the Ferguson–Gaza moment—indicated an increase in mainstream political awareness in the United States and momentum shift for both Palestinian and Black liberation struggles. This moment created a new opportunity for "multidirectional solidarity both on the ground and online," one that was represented in statements of support between communities bearing the brunt of state repression (Davis Bailey 2015, 1019). I should make clear that my brief overview of Palestinian–Black solidarity illustrates both the kind of exchanges and public interactions for which BDS plays a constitutive role, and explicates what I earlier referred to as distinct forms of experience, memory, and affect that inform how solidarity is imagined, articulated, and practiced.

As many examples in this book show, the grounded nature of solidarity is part of its messiness. What solidarity looks like is different depending on the ground where one stands, "and who one's closest adversaries are" (Li 2020). It may be explicitly politically motivated, and it may be deeply imbued with political potential. My informants, however, describe and practice solidarity in ways that often do not cohere easily with grand narratives of politics. This presents an analytical dilemma outlined by anthropologist Heath Cabot—to what extent should I apply an "external interpretive frame to solidarity," such as an approach that claims solidarity for politics? And to what extent should I highlight "internal meanings of solidarity" by trusting my informants to interpret solidarity for me (Cabot 2015, 3)? *Lives in Solidarity* invites us to think through this conundrum. In particular, it invites us to seriously explore what it means to recognize local interpretations of solidarity that engage not only the rational-critical faculties but also address the heart—the site of ethical sensibilities, affective orientations, and passionate attachments. Let us remember that ethical sensibilities have been treated as inconsequential in most analyses of solidarity activism, BDS or otherwise. Even in those cases where they are considered within political analyses, "they are understood as symbols deployed by social movements toward political ends" (Mahmood 2012, 119). The specific conception of ethical sensibilities, and the shape they take, are not in themselves seen to have political implications. And yet, as the preceding chapters have made clear, their cultivation and expression are critical to the organization of BDS in Tower Hamlets and Stari Grad. This project, moreover, does not take an intellectualist form but is carried out within the fabric of everyday life where questions about the proper Muslim response to the Israeli–Palestinian conflict are clothed in local history and culture. Local interpretations of solidarity, viewed in this way, are not easily translated into the realm of politics, but they are nonetheless crucial for the realization of solidarity in practice.

They help elaborate why my informants engage in solidarity, what it means to them, and how they enact it in their day-to-day lives. To ignore the ethical and emotional texture of these interpretations bears the risk of eliding crucial perspectives on what makes solidarity possible in the first place.

Bibliography

Abdel-Shafi, Heydar, Hanan Ashrawi, Mustafa Barghouti, Azmi Bishara, Rana Nashashibi, Eyad Sarraj, Khader Shkirat, and Raji Sourani. 2002. "Urgent Call to World Civil Society: Break the Conspiracy of Silence, Act Before it is Too Late." *MIFTAH*, March 30. Accessed May 10, 2023. http://miftah.org/Display.cfm?DocId=686&CategoryId=32.

Abdulla, Rasha A. 2007. "Islam, Jihad, and Terrorism in Post-9/11 Arabic Discussion Boards." *Journal of Computer-Mediated Communication* 12 (3): 1063–1081. https://doi.org/10.1111/j.1083-6101.2007.00363.x.

Abrahamian, Ervand. 1979. "The Causes of the Constitutional Revolution in Iran." *International Journal of Middle East Studies* 10 (3): 381–414. https://doi.org/10.1017/S0020743800000179.

Abu-Lughod, Lila. 1990. "The Romance of Resistance: Tracing Transformations of Power Through Bedouin Women." *American Ethnologist* 17 (1): 41–55. https://doi.org/10.1525/ae.1990.17.1.02a00030.

Abu-Sunaynah, Yusuf. 2008. "Islaam, Between the Enemies' Plans and the Muslims' Betrayal." *Al Minbar*, July 1. Accessed December 22, 2022. https://alminbar.com/khutbaheng/2284.htm.

Aburish, Said K. 1993. *Cry Palestine: Inside the West Bank*. Boulder: Westview Press.

Adams, Caroline. 1987. *Across Seven Seas and Thirteen Rivers: Life Stories of Pioneer Sylheti Settlers in Britain*. London: THAP.

Afary, Janet. 1996. *The Iranian Constitutional Revolution, 1906–1911: Grassroots Democracy, Social Democracy, and the Origins of Feminism*. New York: Columbia University Press.

Afary, Janet, and Kevin B. Anderson. 2005. *Foucault and the Iranian Revolution: Gender and the Seductions of Islam*. Chicago: University of Chicago Press.

Ahmed, Nilufar. 2005. "Tower Hamlets: Insulation in Isolation." In *Muslim Britain: Communities Under Pressure*, edited by Tahir Abbas, 194–208. London: Zed Books.

al-Fawzan, Saleh. 2006. "The System of Commandments Regarding Denmark by Sheikh Saleh al-Fawzan." *Sahab Salafi Network*, February 10. Accessed December 20, 2022. http://www.sahab.net/forums/showthread.php?p=513663.

al-Qaradawi, Yusuf. 2001. "Sheikh Yusuf al-Qaradawi Condemns Attacks Against Civilians: Forbidden in Islam." *Islam Online,* September 13. Accessed December 10, 2022. https://archive.islamonline.net/?p=17698.

al-Qaradawi, Yusuf. 2002. "Boycotting Israeli and American Goods." *Islam Online*, April 4. Accessed December 10, 2022. https://archive.islamonline.net/?p=993.

al-Qaradawi, Yusuf. 2006. "Duties of Muslims Living in the West." *Islam Online*, March 7. Accessed December 20, 2022. https://archive.islamonline.net/?p=1008.

Ali, Shaheen S. 2016. *Modern Challenges to Islamic Law*. Cambridge: Cambridge University Press.

Alvarez, Sonia E. 1998. "Latin American Feminisms 'Go Global': Trends of the 1990s and Challenges for the New Millennium." In *Cultures of Politics/Politics of Cultures: Re-Visioning Latin American Social Movements*, edited by Sonia E. Alvarez, Evelina Dagnino, and Arturo Escobar, 293–324. Boulder: Westview Press.

Amir-Moazami, Schirin, and Armando Salvatore. 2003. "Gender, Generation, and the Reform of Tradition: From Muslim Majority Societies to Western Europe." In *Muslim Networks and Transnational Communities in and across Europe*, edited by Stefano Allievi and Jørgen S. Nielsen, 52–77. Leiden and Boston: Brill.

Amnesty International. 2001. *Broken Lives: A Year of Intifada*. London: Amnesty International.

Anderson, Jon W. 2003. "The Internet and Islam's New Interpreters." In *New Media in the Muslim World: The Emerging Public Sphere*, 2nd edition, edited by Dale F. Eickleman and Jon W. Anderson, 41–55. Bloomington: Indiana University Press.

Anwar, Muhammad. 1998. *Between Cultures: Continuity and Change in the Lives of Young Asians*. London and New York: Routledge.

Aran, Amnon, and Roni Ginat. 2014. "Revisiting Egyptian Foreign Policy Towards Israel Under Mubarak: From Cold Peace to Strategic Peace." *Journal of Strategic Studies* 37 (4): 556–583. https://doi.org/10.1080/01402390.2014.923766.

Arsejinević, Damir. 2014. "After 22 Years of Being Bullied Bosnians are Desperate, and Must Protest." *The Guardian*, February 28. Accessed May 10, 2023. https://www.theguardian.com/commentisfree/2014/feb/28/bosnia-protest-citizens-change-corruption.

Asad, Talal. 1986. *The Idea of an Anthropology of Islam*. Washington: Center for Contemporary Arab Studies at Georgetown University.

Asad, Talal. 2003. *Formations of the Secular: Christianity, Islam, Modernity*. Stanford: Stanford University Press.

Awwad, Hind. 2012. "Six Years of BDS: Success." In *The Case for Sanctions Against Israel*, edited by Audrea Lim, 77–84. London and New York: Verso.

Back, Les, Michel Keith, Azra Khan, Kalbir Shukra, and John Solomos. 2009. "Islam and the New Political Landscape: Faith Communities, Political Participation, and Social Change." *Theory, Culture, and Society* 26 (4): 1–23. https://doi.org/10.1177/0263276409104965.

Bakan, Abigail B., and Yasmeen Abu-Laban. 2009. "Palestinian Resistance and International Solidarity: The BDS Campaign." *Race and Class* 51 (1): 29–54. https://doi.org/10.1177/0306396809106162.

Bakić-Hayden, Milica. 1995. "Nesting Orientalisms: The Case of Former Yugoslavia." *Slavic Review* 54 (4): 917–931. https://doi.org/10.2307/2501399.

Banerjee, Bobby. 2011. "Voices of the Governed: Towards a Theory of the Translocal." *Organization* 18 (3): 323–344. https://doi.org/10.1177/1350508411398729.

Barghouti, Omar. 2006. "Putting Palestine Back on the Map: Boycott as Civil Resistance." *Journal of Palestine Studies* 35 (3): 51–57. https://doi.org/10.1525/jps.2006.35.3.51.

Barghouti, Omar. 2011. *Boycott, Divestment, Sanctions: The Global Struggle for Palestinian Rights*. Chicago: Haymarket Books.

Barkun Michael. 1994. *Religion and the Racist Right: The Origins of the Christian Identity Movement*. Chapel Hill: University of North Carolina Press.

Barnett, Michael N. 1998. *Dialogues in Arab Politics: Negotiations in Regional Order*. New York: Columbia University Press.

Baron, Beth. 2005. *Egypt as a Woman: Nationalism, Gender, and Politics*. Berkeley: University of California Press.

Baroud, Ramzy. 2013a. "Palestine's Global Battle That Must be Won." In *Generation Palestine: Voices from the Boycott, Divestment and Sanctions Movement*, edited by Rich Wiles, 3–17. London: Pluto.

Baroud, Ramzy. 2013b. "Beit Sahour: Boycott is Historically Palestinian." *The Palestine Chronicle*, December 17. Accessed May 15, 2023. http://www.palestinechronicle.com/beit-sahour-boycott-is-historically-palestinian/.

Baroud, Ramzy. 2018. "What Palestinians Can Teach Us About Popular Resistance." *Al Jazeera*, April 11. Accessed May 15, 2023. https://www.aljazeera.com/opinions/2018/4/11/what-palestinians-can-teach-us-about-popular-resistance/.

Bartulović, Alenka. 2015. "Islam and Gender in Post-War Bosnia and Herzegovina: Competing Discourses and Everyday Practices of Muslim Women." In *(In)equality and Gender Politics in Southeastern Europe: A Question of Justice*, edited by Christine M. Hassenstab and Sabrina P. Ramet, 275–296. London and New York: Palgrave Macmillan.

Başkan, Birol, and Ömer Taşpınar. 2021. *The Nation or the Ummah: Islamism and Turkish Foreign Policy*. Albany: SUNY Press.

Baumgart-Ochse, Claudia. 2017. "Claiming Justice for Israel/Palestine: The Boycott, Divestment, Sanctions (BDS) Campaign and Christian Organizations." *Globalizations* 14 (7): 1172–1187. https://doi.org/10.1080/14747731.2017.1310463.

Baumgarten, Helga. 2005. "The Three Faces/Phases of Palestinian Nationalism, 1948–2005." *Journal of Palestine Studies* 34 (4): 25–48. https://doi.org/10.1525/jps.2005.34.4.25.

Bayat, Asef. 2005. "Islamism and Social Movement Theory." *Third World Quarterly* 26 (6): 891–908. https://doi.org/10.1080/01436590500089240.

Beaulieu, Alain. 2010. "Towards a Liberal Utopia: The Connection Between Foucault's Reporting on the Iranian Revolution and the Ethical Turn." *Philosophy and Social Criticism* 36 (7): 810–818. https://doi.org/10.1177/0191453710372065.

Beckford, James A. 1990. "The Sociology of Religion and Social Problems." *Sociological Analysis* 51 (1): 1–14. https://doi.org/10.2307/3711337.

Begum, Halima, and John Eade. 2005. "All Quiet on the Eastern Front? Bangladeshi Reactions in Tower Hamlets." In *Muslim Britain: Communities Under Pressure*, edited by Tahir Abbas, 179–194. London: Zed Books.

Beinin, Joel. 2012. "North American Colleges and Universities and BDS." In *The Case for Sanctions Against Israel*, edited by Audrea Lim, 61–75. London and New York: Verso.

Bekin, Caroline, Marylyn Carrigan, and Isabelle Szmigin. 2007. "Communities and Consumption." *International Journal of Sociology and Social Policy* 27 (3): 101–105. https://doi.org/10.1108/ijssp.2007.03127caa.001.

Bellah, Robert N., Richard Madsen, William M. Sullivan, Ann Swidler, and Steven M. Tipton. 1996. *Habits of the Heart: Individualism and Commitment in American Life*. 2nd edition. Berkeley: University of California Press.

Bennett, Lance W. 2004. "Branded Political Communication: Lifestyle Politics, Logo Campaigns, and the Rise of Global Citizenship." In *Politics, Products, and Markets: Exploring Political Consumerism Past and Present*, edited by Michele Micheletti, Andreas Follesdal, and Dietlind Stolle, 101–125. London: Transaction Publishers.

Berlan, Amanda. 2012. "Good Chocolate? An Examination of Ethical Consumption in Cocoa." In *Ethical Consumption: Social Value and Economic Practice*, edited by James G. Carrier and Peter G. Luetchford, 43–60. Oxford and New York: Berghahn.

Bird, Jon. 1993. "Dystopia on the Thames." In *Mapping the Futures: Local Cultures, Global Change*, edited by Jon Bird, Berry Curtis, Tim Putnam, George Robertson, and Lisa Tickner, 120–135. London and New York: Routledge.

Bot, Michiel. 2019. "The Right to Boycott: BDS, Law, and Politics in a Global Context." *Transnational Legal Theory* 10 (3): 421–445. https://doi.org/10.1080/20414005.2019.1672134.

Boubekeur Amel. 2007. "Political Islam in Europe." In *European Islam: Challenges for Public Policy and Society*, edited by Samir Amghar, Amel Boubekeur, and Michael Emerson, 14–37. Brussels: Center for European Political Studies.

Bougarel, Xavier. 1997. "From Young Muslims to Party of Democratic Action: The Emergence of a Pan-Islamist Trend in Bosnia-Herzegovina." *Islamic Studies* 36 (2): 533–549.

Bougarel, Xavier. 1999. "Yugoslav Wars: The 'Revenge of the Countryside' Between Sociological Reality and Nationalist Myth." *East European Quarterly* 33 (2): 157–175.

Bougarel, Xavier. 2007a. "Death and the Nationalist: Martyrdom, War Memory, and Veteran Identity Among Bosnian Muslims." In *The New Bosnian Mosaic: Identities, Memories, and Moral Claims in a Post-War Society*, edited by Xavier Bougarel, Elissa Helms, and Ger Duijzings, 167–191. Aldershot: Ashgate.

Bougarel. Xavier. 2007b. "Bosnian Islam as European Islam: Limits and Shifts of a Concept." In *Islam in Europe: Diversity, Identity and Influence*, edited by Aziz al-Azmeh and Effie Fokas, 96–124. Cambridge: Cambridge University Press.

Bougarel, Xavier. 2008. "Farewell to the Ottoman Legacy? Islamic Reformism and Revivalism in Inter-War Bosnia-Herzegovina." In *Islam in Inter-War Europe*, edited by Nathalie Clayer and Eric Germain, 313–343. London: Hurst.

Boycott, Divestment, and Sanctions National Committee. 2020. "We Cannot Breathe Until We Are Free! Palestinians Stand in Solidarity with Black Americans." *Boycott, Divestment, and Sanctions*, May 30. Accessed May 15, 2023. https://www.bdsmovement.net/news/we-cant-breathe-until-we-are-free-palestinians-stand-solidarity-with-black-americans.

Bringa, Tone. 1995. *Being Muslim the Bosnian Way: Identity and Community in a Central Bosnian Village*. Princeton: Princeton University Press.

British Muslim Initiative. 2006. "About Us." Accessed May 10, 2023. https://www.facebook.com/pg/BritishMuslimInitiative/about/.

Brown, Michael F. 1996. "On Resisting Resistance." *American Anthropologist* 98 (4): 729–735. https://doi.org/10.1525/aa.1996.98.4.02a00030.

Brownhill, Sue. 1990. *Developing London's Docklands: Another Great Planning Disaster?* London: Paul Chapman Publishing.

Brysk, Alison. 2000. *From Tribal Village to Global Village: Indian Rights and International Relations in Latin America*. Stanford: Stanford University Press.

Bunt, Gary R. 2003. *Islam in the Digital Age: E-Jihad, Online Fatwas and Cyber Islamic Environments*. London: Pluto.

Butler, Judith. 1990. *Gender Trouble: Feminism and the Subversion of Identity*. London and New York: Routledge.

Butler, Judith. 2006. "Academic Freedom and the ASA's Boycott of Israel: A Response to Michelle Goldberg." *The Nation*, December 8. Accessed May 15, 2023. https://www.thenation.com/article/archive/academic-freedom-and-asas-boycott-israel-response-michelle-goldberg/.

Burawoy, Michael. 1998. "The Extended Case Method." *Sociological Theory* 16 (1): 4–33. https://doi.org/10.1111/0735-2751.00040.

Burawoy, Michael. 2000. "Introduction: Reaching for the Global." In *Global Ethnography: Forces, Connections, and Imaginations in a Postmodern World*, edited by Michael Burawoy et al., 1–40. Berkeley: University of California Press.

Bunzl, Matti. 2005. "Between Anti-Semitism and Islamophobia: Some Thoughts on the New Europe." *American Ethnologist* 32 (4): 499–508. https://doi.org/10.1525/ae.2005.32.4.499.

Byrnes, Timothy A. 1991. *Catholic Bishops in American Politics*. Princeton: Princeton University Press.

Cabot, Heath. 2015. "The Banality of Solidarity." *Journal of Modern Greek Studies* 7 (1): 1–7.

Caeiro, Alexandre. 2011. "The Making of the Fatwa: The Production of Islamic Expertise in Europe." *Archives de Sciences Sociales des Religions* 155 (3): 81–100. https://doi.org/10.4000/assr.23312.

Cannon, Ellen. 2019. "The BDS and Anti-BDS Campaigns: Propaganda War vs. Legislative Interest-Group Articulation." *Jewish Political Studies Review* 30 (1): 5–64.

Caplan, Neil. 2009. *The Israel-Palestine Conflict: Contested Histories*. Hoboken: Wiley-Blackwell.

Carr, Helen. 2011. "The Right to Buy, the Leaseholder, and the Impoverishment of Ownership." *Journal of Law and Society* 38 (4): 519–541. https://doi.org/10.1111/j.1467-6478.2011.00557.x.

Carrier, James G. 2012. "Introduction." In *Consumption: Social Value and Economic Practice*, edited by James G. Carrier and Peter G. Leutchford, 1–37. Oxford and New York: Berghahn.

Carroll, William K., and Robert S. Ratner. 1996. "Master Framing and Cross-Movement Networking in Contemporary Social Movements." *The Sociological Quarterly* 37 (4): 601–625. https://doi.org/10.1111/j.1533-8525.1996.tb01755.x.

Carter Hallward, Maia. 2013. *Transnational Activism and the Israeli – Palestinian Conflict*. London and New York: Palgrave Macmillan.

Carter Hallward, Maia, and Patrick Shaver. 2012. "War by Other Means or Nonviolent Resistance? Examining the Discourses Surrounding Berkeley's Divestment Bill." *Peace and Change* 37 (3): 389–412. https://doi.org/10.1111/j.1468-0130.2012.00756.x.

Cauffman, Timothy. 2018. "The State Power to Boycott a Boycott: The Thorny Constitutionality of State Anti-BDS Laws." *Columbia Journal of Transnational Law* 57 (1): 115–173. http://dx.doi.org/10.2139/ssrn.3186369.

Chouhan, Karen, Stuart Speeden, and Undaleeb Qazi. 2011. "Experience of Poverty and Ethnicity in London." *Joseph Rowntree Foundation*, May 18. Accessed May 15, 2023. https://www.jrf.org.uk/report/experience-poverty-and-ethnicity-london.

Clark, Janine N. 2010. "Religion and Reconciliation in Bosnia-Herzegovina: Are Religious Actors Doing Enough?" *Europe-Asia Studies* 62 (4): 671–694. https://doi.org/10.1080/09668131003737019.

Clarke, John. 2007. "Unsettled Connections: Citizens, Consumers and the Reform of Public Services." *Journal of Consumer Culture* 7 (2): 159–178. https://doi.org/10.1177/1469540507077671.

Colenutt, Bob. 1991. "The London Docklands Development Corporation: Has the Community Benefited?" In *Hollow Promises: Rhetoric and Reality in the Inner City*, edited by Michael Keith and Alisdair Rogers, 31–41. London: Mansell.

Coles, Kimberley. 2007. "Ambivalent Builders: Europeanization, the Production of Difference, and Internationals in Bosnia-Herzegovina." In *The New Bosnian Mosaic:*

Identities, Memories, and Moral Claims in a Post-War Society, edited by Xavier Bougarel, Elissa Helms, and Ger Duijzings, 255–272. Aldershot: Ashgate.

Colla, Elliott. 2006. "Solidarity in the Time of Anti-Normalization: Egypt Responds to the Intifada." In *The Struggle for Sovereignty: Palestine and Israel, 1993–2005*, edited by Joel Beinin and Rebecca L. Stein, 249–259. Stanford: Stanford University Press.

Collins, Peter. 2012. "Ethical Consumption as Religious Testimony: The Quaker Case." In *Ethical Consumption: Social Value and Economic Practice*, edited by James G. Carrier and Peter G. Luetchford, 181–198. Oxford and New York: Berghahn.

Comaroff, Jean. 1985. *Body of Power, Spirit of Resistance: The Culture and History of a South African People*. Chicago: University of Chicago Press.

Connors Jackman, Michael, and Nishant Upadhyay. 2014. "Pinkwatching Israel, Whitewashing Canada: Queer (Settler) Politics and Indigenous Colonization in Canada." *Women's Studies Quarterly* 42 (3): 195–210. https://doi.org/10.1353/wsq.2014.0044.

Cook, Steven A. 2022. "The BDS Movement Has Already Lost." *Foreign Policy*, May 19. Accessed May 20, 2023. https://foreignpolicy.com/2022/05/19/bds-movement-boycott-israel-palestine-harvard-crimson/

Cooper, Davina, and Didi Herman. 2020. "Doing Activism Like a State: Progressive Municipal Government, Israel/Palestine, and BDS." *Politics and Space* 38 (1): 40–59. https://doi.org/ 10.1177/2399654419851187.

Coutin, Susan B. 1993. *The Culture of Protest: Religious Activism and the U.S. Sanctuary Movement*. Boulder: Westview Press.

Cunningham, Hilary. 1999. "Ethnography of Transnational Social Activism: Understanding the Global as Local Practice." *American Ethnologist* 26 (3): 583–604. https://doi.org/10.1525/ae.1999.26.3.583.

Darweish, Marwan, and Andrew Rigby. 2018. "The Internationalization of Nonviolent Resistance: The Case of the BDS Campaign." *Journal of Resistance Studies* 1 (4): 45–71.

Dassetto, Felice, and Gerd Nonneman. 1996. "Islam in Belgium and the Netherlands: Towards a Typology of 'Transplanted' Islam." In *Muslim Communities in the New Europe*, edited by Gerd Nonneman, Tim Niblock, and Bogdan Szajkowski, 187–218. Reading: Ithaca Press.

Davis Bailey, Kristian. 2015. "Black – Palestinian Solidarity in the Ferguson – Gaza Era." *American Quarterly* 67 (4): 1017–1026. doi:10.1353/aq.2015.0060.

de Hanas, Daniel N. 2014. "Immigration and Diversity in Tower Hamlets: A Brief Guide." *Public Spirit*, May 10. Accessed December 20, 2022. http://www.publicspirit.org.uk/assets/DN-DeHanas-Diversity-in-Tower-Hamlets-1st-May.pdf.

Diab, Khaled. 2012. "The Arab World's Missed Opportunities." *Haaretz*, November 4. Accessed May 15, 2023. http://www.haaretz.com/opinion/the-arab-world-s-missed-opportunities-1.474306.

Dilts, Andrew. 2011. "From 'Entrepreneur of the Self' to 'Care of the Self': Neoliberal Governmentality and Foucault's Ethics." *Foucault Studies* 12 (1): 130–146. https://doi.org/10.22439/fs.v0i12.3338.

Dinerstein, Ana C. 2015. *The Politics of Autonomy in Latin America: The Art of Organizing Hope*. London and New York: Palgrave Macmillan.

Donia, Robert J., and John V. A. Fine Jr. 1994. *Bosnia and Herzegovina: A Tradition Betrayed*. New York: Columbia University Press.

Downs, Donald D. 2006. "Political Mobilization and Resistance to Censorship." In *Academic Freedom at the Dawn of a New Century: How Terrorism, Governments, and Culture Wars Impact Free Speech*, edited by Evan Gerstmann and Matthew J. Streb, 61–78. Stanford: Stanford University Press.

Eade, John. 1991. "The Political Construction of Class and Community: Bangladeshi Political Leadership in Tower Hamlets, East London." In *Black and Ethnic Leadership in Britain: The Cultural Dimensions of Political Action*, edited by Pnina Werbner and Muhammad Anwar, 58–75. London and New York: Routledge.

Eade, John. 1997. "Reconstructing Places: Changing Images of Locality in Docklands and Spitalfields." In *Living the Global City: Globalization as the Local Process*, edited by John Eade, 127–146. London and New York: Routledge.

Eade, John. 2000. *Placing London: From Imperial Capital to Global City*. Oxford and New York: Berghahn.

Eade, John. 2007. "Economic Migrant or Hyphenated British? Writing About Difference in London's East End." In *The Cultures of Economic Migration: International Perspectives*, edited by Suman Gupta and Tope Omoniyi, 27–36. Aldershot: Ashgate.

Eade, John, and David Garbin. 2002. "Changing Narratives of Violence, Struggle, and Resistance: Bangladeshis and the Competition for Resources in the Global City." *Oxford Development Studies* 30 (2): 137–149. https://doi.org/10.1080/13600810220138258.

Eade, John, and David Garbin. 2006. "Competing Visions of Identity and Space: Bangladeshi Muslims in Britain." *Contemporary South Asia* 15 (2): 181–193. https://doi.org/10.1080/09584930600955291.

Ehn, Billy, and Orvar Löfgren. 2009. "Routines: Made and Unmade." In *Time, Consumption, and Everyday Life: Practice, Materiality, and Culture*, edited by Elizabeth Shove, Frank Trentmann, and Richard Wilk, 99–113. Oxford: Berg.

Eisenlohr, Patrick. 2012. "Media and Religious Diversity." *Annual Review of Anthropology* 41 (1): 37–55. https://doi.org/10.1146/annurev-anthro-092611-145823.

Emmaus International. n.d. "Who We Are." Accessed March 10, 2023. https://www.emmaus-international.org/en/who-we-are/.

Epstein, Arnold L. 1958. *Politics in an Urban African Community*. Manchester: Manchester University Press.

Evans, Peter. 2005. "Counter-Hegemonic Globalization: Transnational Social Movements in the Contemporary Global Political Economy." In *Handbook of Political Sociology*, edited by Thomas Janoski, Robert R. Alford, Alexander Hicks, and Mildred Schwartz, 655–672. Cambridge: Cambridge University Press.

Extortion for London. 2012. "Islamic Tower Hamlets." Accessed December 25, 2022. http://www.exfl.com/islamic-london/islamic-tower-hamlets-london.htm.

Favell, Adrian. 2003. "Games Without Frontiers? Questioning the Transnational Social Power of Migrants in Europe." *European Journal of Sociology* 44 (3): 397–427. https://doi.org/10.1017/S0003975603001334.

Feld, Marjorie N. 2014. *Nations Divided: American Jews and the Struggle Over Apartheid*. London and New York: Palgrave Macmillan.

Fishman, Joel S. 2012. "The BDS Message of Anti-Zionism, Anti-Semitism, and Incitement to Discrimination." *Israel Affairs* 18 (3): 412–425. https://doi.org/10.1080/13537121.2012.689521.

Fishman, Willian J. 1975. *East End Jewish Radicals, 1875–1914*. London: Duckworth.

Fleischmann, Ellen L. 2003. *The Nation and Its "New" Women: The Palestinian Women's Movement, 1920–1948*. Berkeley: University of California Press.

Fleming, Katherine E. 2000. "Orientalism, the Balkans, and Balkan Historiography." *The American Historical Review* 105 (4): 1218–1233. https://doi.org/10.1086/ahr/105.4.1218.

Fletcher, Robert. 2001. "What are we Fighting for? Rethinking Resistance in a Pewenche Community in Chile." *Journal of Peasant Studies* 28 (3): 37–66. https://doi.org/10.1080/03066150108438774.

Forman, Charlie. 1989. *Spitalfields: A Battle for Land*. London: Hilary Shipman.

Foschetti, Beatrice. 2010. "A Comparative Study of Four Different Groups of Young Practicing Muslims in the Post-War Sarajevo: From Nationalization to Islamization." Paper presented at the London School of Economics' First Joint Ph.D. Symposium on Modern and Contemporary South East Europe, London, June 7.

Foucault, Michel. 1978. *The History of Sexuality, Vol. 1: An Introduction*. Translated by Robert Hurley. New York: Pantheon.

Foucault, Michel. 1980. "Two Lectures." In *Power/Knowledge: Selected Interviews and Other Writings, 1972–1977, by Michel Foucault*, edited by Colin Gordon, 78–108. Translated by Colin Gordon, Leo Marshall, John Mepham, and Kate Soper. New York: Pantheon.

Foucault, Michel. 1982. "The Subject and Power." *Critical Inquiry* 8 (4): 777–795. https://doi.org/10.1086/448181.

Foucault, Michel. 1986. *The History of Sexuality, Vol. 2: The Use of Pleasure*. Translated by Robert Hurley. New York: Vintage.

Friedman, Francine. 1996. *The Bosnian Muslims: Denial of a Nation*. Boulder: Westview Press.

Friedman, Monroe. 1985. "Consumer Boycotts in the United States, 1970–1980: Contemporary Events in Historical Perspective." *Journal of Consumer Affairs* 19 (1): 96–117. https://doi.org/10.1111/j.1745-6606.1985.tb00346.x.

Friedman, Monroe. 1991. "Consumer Boycotts: A Conceptual Framework and Research Agenda." *Journal of Social Issues* 47 (1): 149–168. https://doi.org/10.1111/j.1540-4560.1991.tb01817.x.

Friends of al-Aqsa. n.d. "Who We Are." Accessed May 15, 2023. https://www.foa.org.uk/whoweare.

Friends of al-Aqsa. 2009. "Check the Label." Accessed May 15, 2023. https://www.foa.org.uk/campaign/checkthelabel-produce.

Gaffney, Patrick D. 1994. *The Prophet's Pulpit: Islamic Preaching in Contemporary Egypt.* Berkeley: University of California Press.

Gallagher, Tom. 2001. *Outcast Europe: The Balkans, 1789–1989, from the Ottomans to Milošević.* London and New York: Routledge.

Gamson, William A., and David S. Meyer. 1996. "Framing Political Opportunity." In *Comparative Perspectives on Social Movements: Political Opportunities, Mobilizing Structures, and Cultural Framings,* edited by Doug McAdam, John D. McCarthy, and Mayer N. Zald, 274–290. Cambridge: Cambridge University Press.

Garbaye, Romain. 2005. *Getting into Local Power: The Politics of Ethnic Minorities in British and French Cities.* Malden: Blackwell.

Gardner, Katy. 1995. *Global Migrants, Local Lives: Migration and Transformation in Rural Bangladesh.* Oxford: Oxford University Press.

Gardner, Katy, and Abdus Shakur. 1994. "I'm Bengali, I'm Asian, and I'm Living Here." In *Desh Pardesh: The South Asian Presence in Britain,* edited by Roger Ballard, 142–164. London: Hurst.

Garrett, Dennis E. 1987. "The Effectiveness of Marketing Policy Boycotts: Environmental Opposition to Marketing." *Journal of Marketing* 51 (2): 46–57. https://doi.org/10.1177/002224298705100204.

Gasper, Michael. 2001. "Abdallah Nadim, Islamic Reform, and 'Ignorant' Peasants: State-Building in Egypt?" In *Muslim Traditions and Modern Techniques of Power,* edited by Armando Salvatore, 75–92. New Brunswick: Transaction Publishers.

Gertheiss, Svenja. 2015. *Diasporic Activism in the Israeli – Palestinian Conflict.* London and New York: Routledge.

Gest, Justin. 2010. *Apart: Alienated and Engaged Muslims in the West.* London: Hurst.

Gidley, Ben. 2009. "The Ghosts of Kishinev in the East End: Responses to a Pogrom in the Jewish London of 1903." In *The Jew in Late-Victorian and Edwardian Culture: Between the East End and East Africa,* edited by Eitan Bar-Yosef and Nadia Valman, 98–112. London and New York: Palgrave Macmillan.

Glick Schiller, Nina, Linda Basch, and Cristina Blanc-Szanton. 1992. "Transnationalism: A New Analytic Framework for Understanding Migration." In *Toward a Transnational*

Perspective on Migration: Race, Class, Ethnicity, and Nationalism Reconsidered, edited by Nina Glick Schiller, Linda Basch, and Cristina Blanc-Szanton, 1–24. New York: New York Academic Sciences.

Gluckman, Max. 1958. *Analysis of a Social Situation in Modern Zululand*. Manchester: Manchester University Press.

Glynn, Sarah. 2002. "Bengali Muslims: The New East End Radicals?" *Ethnic and Racial Studies* 25 (6): 969–988. https://doi.org/10.1080/0141987022000009395.

Glynn, Sarah. 2008. "East End Bengalis and the Labour Party: The End of a Long Relationship?" In *New Geographies of Race and Racism*, edited by Clair Dwyer and Caroline Bressey, 67–82. Aldershot: Ashgate.

Goodman, Michael K. 2010. "The Mirror of Consumption: Celebritization, Developmental Consumption, and the Shifting Cultural Politics of Fair Trade." *Geoforum* 41 (1): 104–116. https://doi.org/10.1016/j.geoforum.2009.08.003.

Gonzalez-Quijano, Yves. 2003. "The Birth of a Media Ecosystem: Lebanon in the Internet Age." In *New Media in the Muslim World: The Emerging Public Sphere*, 2nd edition, edited by Dale F. Eickleman and Jon W. Anderson, 61–79. Bloomington: Indiana University Press.

Gorin, Julia. 2009. "Bosnian-Serb PM Milorad Dodik Sends Letter of Support to Israel." *Republican Riot*, January 22. Accessed December 20, 2022. http://www.juliagorin.com/wordpress/?p=2014.

Grace, Anne. 1990. "The Tax Resistance at Bayt Sahur." *Journal of Palestine Studies* 19 (2): 99–107. https://doi.org/10.2307/2537416.

Grassroots Palestinian Anti-Apartheid Wall Campaign. 2007. "Towards a Global Movement: A Framework for Today's Anti-Apartheid Activism." *Boycott, Divestment, and Sanctions*, June 10. Accessed May 15, 2023. https://bdsmovement.net/files/bds%20report%20small.pdf.

Green, Sarah F. 2005. *Notes from the Balkans: Locating Marginality and Ambiguity on the Greek-Albanian Border*. Princeton: Princeton University Press.

Grillo, Ralph, and Bruno Riccio. 2004. "Translocal Development: Italy – Senegal." *Population, Space, and Place* 10 (2): 99–111. https://doi.org/10.1002/psp.321.

Grimes, Kimberley M. 2004. "Changing the Rules of Trade with Global Partnerships: The Fair Trade Movement." In *Social Movements: An Anthropological Reader*, edited by June Nash, 237–249. Hoboken: Wiley-Blackwell.

Guarnizo, Luis E., Alejandro Portes, and Willian Haller. 2003. "Assimilation and Transnationalism: Determinants of Transnational Political Action Among Contemporary Migrants." *American Journal of Sociology* 108 (6): 1211–1248. https://doi.org/10.1086/375195.

Guarnizo, Luis E., and Michael P. Smith. 1998. "The Locations of Transnationalism." In *Transnationalism from Below*, edited by Michael P. Smith and Luis E. Guarnizo, 3–34. New Brunswick: Transaction Publishers.

Gudeman, Stephan. 2008. *Economy's Tension: The Dialectics of Community and Market*. Oxford and New York: Berghahn.

Guha, Ranajit. 1983. *Elementary Aspects of Peasant Insurgency in India*. Oxford: Oxford University Press.

Gutmann, Matthew. 2012. "Beyond Resistance: Raising Utopias from the Dead in Mexico City and Oaxaca." In *New Approaches to Resistance in Brazil and Mexico*, edited by John Gledhill and Patience A. Schell, 305–324. Durham: Duke University Press.

Halbfinger, David, Michael Wines, and Steven Erlanger. 2019. "Is BDS Anti-Semitic? A Closer Look at the Boycott Israel Campaign." *The New York Times*, July 27. Accessed May 10, 2023. https://www.nytimes.com/2019/07/27/world/middleeast/bds-israel-boycott-antisemitic.html.

Halevi, Leor. 2012. "The Consumer Jihad: Boycott Fatwas and Nonviolent Resistance on the World Wide Web." *International Journal of Middle East Studies* 44 (1): 45–70. https://doi.org/10.1017/S0020743811001243.

Halevi. Leor. 2019. *Modern Things on Trial: Islam's Global and Material Reformation in the Age of Rida, 1865–1935*. New York: Columbia University Press.

Halilović, Nezim. 2012a. "Dvadesetogodišnjica Armije RBiH [The Twentieth Anniversary of the Army of the Republic of Bosnia and Herzegovina]." *Islamska Zajednica*, April 13. Accessed December 20, 2022. http://www.rijaset.ba/index.php?option=com_content&view=article&id=14104:dvadesetogodisnjica-armije-rbih&catid=21&Itemid=602.

Halilović, Nezim. 2012b. "Dvadeset Godina od Početka Oružane Agresije i Genocida u Republici Bosni i Hercegovini [Twenty Years Since the Start of the Armed Aggression and Genocide in the Republic of Bosnia and Herzegovina]." *Islam Bosna*, April 6. Accessed December 20, 2022. http://www.islambosna.ba/dvadeset-godina-od-poetka-oruane-agresije-i-genocida-ubih-a.

Halilović, Nezim. 2012c. "Neka su Prokleti Dželati Naroda Moga [Let the Murderers of My People be Cursed"]." *Saff*, July 13. Accessed December 20, 2022. http://saff.ba/neka-su-prokleti-dzelati-naroda-mog/.

Hammami, Rema. 1997. "From Immodesty to Collaboration: Hamas, the Women's Movement, and National Identity in the Intifada." In *Political Islam: Essays from Middle East Report*, edited by Joel Beinin and Joe Stock, 194–210. Berkeley: University of California Press.

Hann, Chris. 1988. "Christianity's Internal Frontier: The Case of the Uniates of South-East Poland." *Anthropology Today* 4 (3): 9–13. https://doi.org/10.2307/3032640.

Hannigan, John A. 1991. "Social Movement Theory and the Sociology of Religion: Toward a New Synthesis." *Sociological Analysis* 52 (4): 311–331. https://doi.org/10.2307/3710849.

Hayden, Robert M. 1996. "Imagined Communities and Real Victims: Self-Determination and Ethnic Cleansing in Yugoslavia." *American Ethnologist* 23 (4): 783–801. https://doi.org/10.1525/ae.1996.23.4.02a00060.

Helms, Elissa. 2007."Politics is a Whore: Women, Morality, and Victimhood in Post-War Bosnia-Herzegovina." In *The New Bosnian Mosaic: Identities, Memories, and Moral Claims in a Post-War Society*, edited by Xavier Bougarel, Elissa Helms, and Ger Duijzings, 235–254. Aldershot: Ashgate.

Helms, Elissa. 2008. "East and West Kiss: Gender, Orientalism, and Balkanism in Muslim-Majority Bosnia-Herzegovina." *Slavic Review* 67 (1): 88–119. https://doi.org/10.2307/27652770.

Helms, Elissa. 2013. *Innocence and Victimhood: Gender, Nation, and Women's Activism in Post-War Bosnia-Herzegovina*. Madison: University of Wisconsin Press.

Herrera, Linda, and Mark Lotfy. 2012. "E-Militias of the Muslim Brotherhood: How to Upload Ideology on Facebook." *Jadaliyya*, September 5. Accessed May 15, 2023. https://www.jadaliyya.com/Details/27013/E-Militias-of-the-Muslim-Brotherhood-How-to-Upload-Ideology-on-Facebook.

Hervieu-Léger, Danièle, 1997. "Faces of Catholic Transnationalism: In and Beyond France." In *Transnational Religion and Fading States*, edited by Susanne H. Rudolph and James P. Piscatori, 104–118. Boulder: Westview Press.

Hever, Shir. 2019. "BDS Suppression Attempts in Germany Backfire." *Journal of Palestine Studies* 48 (3): 86–96. https://doi.org/10.1525/jps.2019.48.3.86.

Hilal, Jamil. 2010. "The Polarization of the Palestinian Political Field." *Journal of Palestine Studies* 39 (3): 24–39. https://doi.org/10.1525/jps.2010.xxxix.3.24.

Hiltermann, Joost R. 1991. *Behind the Intifada: Labor and Women's Movements in the Occupied Territories*. Princeton: Princeton University Press.

Hilton, Matthew. 2008. "The Banality of Consumption." In *Citizenship and Consumption*, edited by Kate Soper and Frank Trentmann, 87–103. London and New York: Palgrave Macmillan.

Hirschkind, Charles. 2006. *The Ethical Soundscape: Cassette Sermons and Islamic Counterpublics*. New York: Columbia University Press.

Hofheinz, Albrecht. 2005. "The Internet in the Arab World: Playground for Political Liberalization." *Internationale Politik und Gesellschaft* 3 (1): 78–96.

Holloway, John. 2002. *Change the World Without Taking Power*. London: Pluto.

Holz, Klaus, and Michael Kiefer. 2010. "Islamistischer Antisemitismus Phänomen und Forschungsstand [The Phenomenon of Islamist Antisemitism and the Current State of Research]." In *Konstellationen des Antisemitismus: Antisemitismusforschung und Sozialpädagogische Praxis* [*The Patterns of Antisemitism: The Research on Antisemitism and the Socio-Educational Practice*], edited by Wolfram Stender, Guido Follert, and Mihri Özdoğan, 109–138. Wiesbaden: Vs. Verlag für Sozialwissenschaft.

Hondagneu-Sotelo, Pierrette, Genelle Gaudinez, Hector Lara, and Billie C. Ortiz. 2004. "There's a Spirit That Transcends the Border: Faith, Ritual, and Postnational Protest at the US – Mexico Border." *Sociological Perspectives* 47 (2): 133–159. https://doi.org/10.1525/sop.2004.47.2.133.

Hooker, Berry M. 2003. *Indonesian Islam: Social Change Through Contemporary Fatawa*. Honolulu: University of Hawaii Press.

Horstmann, Alexander. 2007. "The Tablighi Jama'at, Transnational Islam, and the Transformation of the Self Between Southern Thailand and South Asia." *Comparative Studies of South Asia, Africa and the Middle East* 27 (1): 26–40. https://doi.org/10.1215/1089201x-2006-041.

Hudson, Alan. 2006. "Whitechapel Road Revisited." *Rising East*, April 22. Accessed December 20, 2022. https://www.uel.ac.uk/risingeast/archive04/debate/hudson_marriott_owens_dench.htm.

Hudson, Leila. 1994. "Coming of Age in Occupied Palestine: Engendering the Intifada." In *Reconstructing Gender in the Middle East: Tradition, Identity, and Power*, edited by Fatima Müge Göçek and Shiva Balaghi, 123–136. New York: Columbia University Press.

Humphrey, Caroline. 1983. *Karl Marx Collective: Economy, Society, and Religion in a Siberian Collective Farm*. Cambridge: Cambridge University Press.

Huq, Maimuna. 2009. "Talking Jihad and Piety: Reformist Exertions Among Islamist Women in Bangladesh." *The Journal of the Royal Anthropological Institute*. 15 (1): 163–182. https://doi.org/10.1111/j.1467-9655.2009.01548.x.

Hussain, Delwar. 2006. "Bangladeshis in East London: From Secular Politics to Islam." *Open Democracy*, July 6. Accessed May 10, 2023. https://www.opendemocracy.net/faith-protest/bangladeshi_3715.jsp.

Innovative Minds. n.d. "Boycott Israel Campaign." Accessed May 15, 2023. http://www.inminds.com/boycott-israel.html.

Innovative Minds. 2006. "Fatwas Given by Islamic Scholars on the Boycott of Israel." Accessed May 15, 2023. http://www.inminds.com/boycott-fatwas.html.

International Court of Justice. 2004. "International Court of Justice Advisory Opinion Finds Israel's Construction of Wall Contrary to International Law." Accessed May 15, 2023. https://www.un.org/press/en/2004/icj616.doc.htm.

Islam Bosna. 2014. "Islamsko Stanovništvo: Da li Nam je Dozvoljeno Bojkotovati Izraelske Proizvode [Islamic Citizens: Are We Allowed to Boycott Israeli Products]?" Accessed December 20, 2022. http://islambosna.ba/islamsko-stanoviste-da-li-nam-je-dozvoljeno-bojkotovati-izraelske-proizvode.

Jacob, Christian. 2009. "Fatah Sixth General Conference Resolutions: Pursuing Peace Option Without Relinquishing Resistance or Right to Armed Struggle." *The Middle East Media Research Institute*, August 31. Accessed May 15, 2023. https://www

.memri.org/reports/fatah-sixth-general-conference-resolutions-pursuing-peace-option-without-relinquishing.

Jad, Islah. 2005. "Between Religion and Secularism: Islamist Women of Hamas." In *Shifting Ground: Muslim Women in the Global Era*, edited by Fereshteh Nouraie-Simone, 172–198. New York: Feminist Press at the City University of New York.

Jamal, Amaney. 2005. *The Palestinian National Movement: Politics of Contention, 1967–2005*. Bloomington: Indiana University Press.

Jansen, Stef. 2009. "After the Red Passport: Towards an Anthropology of the Everyday Geopolitics of Entrapment in the EU's 'Immediate Outside'." *Journal of the Royal Anthropological Institute* 15 (4): 815–832. https://doi.org/10.1111/j.1467-9655.2009.01586.x.

Janson, Marloes. 2005. "Roaming About for God's Sake: The Upsurge of the Tablīgh Jamā'at in the Gambia." *Journal of Religion in Africa* 35 (4): 450–481. http://dx.doi.org/10.1163/157006605774832199.

Jelen, Ted G., and Clyde Wilcox. 2002. "The Political Roles of Religion." In *Religion and Politics in Comparative Perspective: The One, The Few, and The Many*, edited by Ted G. Jelen and Clyde Wilcox, 314–124. Cambridge: Cambridge University Press.

Jevtić, Jana. 2015. "Politics of Consumption: Boycott, Divestment, and Sanctions Campaign and 'Being' Muslim in Tower Hamlets." In *Everyday Life Practices of Muslims in Europe*, edited by Erkan Toğuşlu, 75–97. Leuven: Leuven University Press.

Jevtić, Jana. 2017. "Bosnian Muslims and the Idea of 'European Islam' in Post-War Sarajevo: Generation, Class, and Contests Over Religious Authority." *Journal of Muslims in Europe* 6 (1): 52–75. https://doi.org/10.1163/22117954-12341335.

Johnson, Mark. 1998. "Global Desirings and Translocal Loves: Transgendering and Same-Sex Sexualities in the Southern Philippines." *American Ethnologist*, 25 (4): 695–711. https://doi.org/10.1525/ae.1998.25.4.695.

Johnston, Josée. 2008. "The Citizen-Consumer Hybrid: Ideological Tensions and the Case of Whole Foods Market." *Theory and Society* 37 (1): 229–70. https://doi.org/10.1007/s11186-007-9058-5.

Joyner, Christopher C. 1984. "The Transnational Boycott as Economic Coercion in International Law: Policy, Place, and Practice". *Vanderbilt Journal of International Law* 17 (2): 206–286.

Kabeer, Naila. 2000. *The Power to Choose: Bangladeshi Women and Labor Market Decisions in London and Dhaka*. London and New York: Verso.

Kadish, Sharman. 1992. *Bolsheviks and British Jews*. London: Frank Cass.

Kaplan, Edward H., and Charles A. Small. 2006. "Anti-Israel Sentiment Predicts Anti-Semitism in Europe." *Journal of Conflict Resolution* 50 (4): 548–561. https://doi.org/10.1177/0022002706289184.

Karahasan, Dževad. 1994. *Sarajevo, Exodus of a City*. Translated by Slobodan Drakulić. New York: Kodansha International.

Karčić, Harun. 2010. "Globalization and Islam in Bosnia: Foreign Influences and the Effects." *Totalitarian Movements and Political Religions* 11 (2): 151–166. https://doi.org/10.1080/14690764.2010.511467.

Karić, Enes. 1997. "Islam u Suvremenoj Bosni [Islam in Contemporary Bosnia]." In *Bosna Sjete i Zaborava: Eseji o Zemlji Neiscrpnih inspiracija* [Bosnia of Remembering and Forgetting: Essays on the Country of Endless Inspiration], edited by Enes Karić, 88–95. Zagreb: Durieux.

Karim, Karim H. 2002. "Muslim Encounters with New Media," In *Islam Encountering Globalization*, edited by Ali Mohammadi, 1–14. London and New York: Routledge.

Kaye, Dalia D. 2001. *Beyond the Handshake: Multilateral Cooperation in the Arab – Israeli Peace Process*. New York: Columbia University Press.

Keddie, Nikki R. 1966. *Religion and Rebellion in Iran: The Tobacco Protest of 1891–1892*. London: Frank Cass.

Kershen, Anne J. 2012. *Strangers, Aliens and Asians: Huguenots, Jews and Bangladeshis in Spitalfields 1666–2000*. London and New York: Routledge.

Khalidi, Rashid. 2006. *Iron Cage: The Story of the Palestinian Struggle for Statehood*. Oxford: Oneworld Publications.

Khalidi, Rashid. 2014. *Under Siege: PLO Decisionmaking During the 1982 War*. 2nd edition. New York: Columbia University Press.

Khalidi, Rashid. 2020. *The Hundred Years' War on Palestine: A History of Settler Colonialism and Resistance, 1917–2017*. London: Profile Books.

King, Esther. 2020. "Europe Seeks Own Response to Black Lives Matter." *Politico*, June 10. Accessed May 15, 2023. https://www.politico.eu/article/us-style-civil-rights-protests-come-to-europe-george-floyd-black-lives-matter/.

King, Mary E. 2007. *A Quiet Revolution: The First Palestinian Intifada and Nonviolent Resistance*. New York: Nation Books.

Kivisto, Peter. 2001. "Theorizing Transnational Immigration: A Critical Review of Current Efforts." *Ethnic and Racial Studies* 24 (4): 549–577. https://doi.org/10.1080/01419870120049789.

Kligman, Gail. 1988. *The Wedding of the Dead: Ritual, Poetics, and Popular Culture in Transylvania*. Berkeley: University of California Press.

Klug, Brian. 2004. "The Myth of the New Anti-Semitism." *The Nation*, January 15. Accessed May 15, 2023. https://www.thenation.com/article/archive/myth-new-anti-semitism/.

Kober, Avi. 2002. *Coalition Defection: The Dissolution of Arab Anti-Israeli Coalitions in War and Peace*. New York: Praeger.

Kolind, Torsten. 2007. "In Search of 'Decent People': Resistance to the Ethnicization of Everyday Life Among the Muslims of Stolac." In *The New Bosnian Mosaic: Identities, Memories, and Moral Claims in a Post-War Society*, edited by Xavier Bougarel, Elissa Helms, and Ger Duijzings, 123–138. Aldershot: Ashgate.

Kolind, Torsten. 2008. *Post-War Identification: Everyday Muslim Counterdiscourse in Bosnia Herzegovina*. Aarhus: Aarhus University Press.

Kostić, Roland. 2007. "Ambivalent Peace: External Nation-Building, Threatened Identity, and Reconciliation in Bosnia and Herzegovina." Doctoral Dissertation. Uppsala: Uppsala University.

Kulick, Don. 1996. "Causing a Commotion: Public Scandal as Resistance Among Brazilian Transgendered Prostitutes." *Anthropology Today* 12 (6): 3–7. https://doi.org/10.2307/2783401.

Kupferschmidt, Uri M. 1987. *The Supreme Muslim Council: Islam Under the British Mandate for Palestine*. Leiden and Boston: Brill.

Kuttab, Eileen S. 1993. "Palestinian Women in the Intifada: Fighting on Two Fronts." *Arab Studies Quarterly* 15 (2): 69–85.

Lambek, Michael. 2000. "The Anthropology of Religion and the Quarrel Between Poetry and Philosophy." *Current Anthropology* 41 (3): 309–302. https://doi.org/10.1086/300143.

Lambton, Ann K. S. 1987. *Qajar Persia: Eleven Studies*. London and New York: I. B. Tauris.

Latour, Vincent. 2017. "Between Consensus, Consolidation, and Crisis: Immigration and Integration in 1970s Britain." *Revue Française de Civilisation Britannique* 22 (1): 1–15. https://doi.org/10.4000/rfcb.1719.

Leibowitz, Rebecca. 2005. "Defeating Anti-Israeli and Anti-Semitic Activity on Campus. A Case Study: Rutgers University." *Jewish Political Studies Review* 17 (1): 199–213.

Leman, Johan. 2000. "Minority Leadership, Science, Symbols, and the Media: The Belgian Islam Debate and its Relevance for Other Countries in Europe." *Journal of International Migration and Integration* 1 (3): 351–372. https://doi.org/10.1007/s12134-000-1018-0.

LeVine, Mark. 2003. "Human Nationalisms Versus Inhuman Globalisms: Cultural Economies of Globalization and the Re-Imagining of Muslim Identities in Europe and the Middle East." In *Muslim Networks and Transnational Communities in and across Europe*, edited by Stefano Allievi and Jørgen S. Nielsen, 78–126. Leiden and Boston: Brill.

Levitt, Peggy, and Nina Glick Schiller. 2004. "Conceptualizing Simultaneity: A Transnational Social Field Perspective on Society." *International Migration Review* 38 (3): 1002–1039. https://doi.org/10.1111/j.1747-7379.2004.tb00227.x.

Li, Darryl. 2019. *The Universal Enemy: Jihad, Empire, and the Challenge of Solidarity*. Stanford: Stanford University Press.

Li, Darryl. 2020. "The Universal Enemy: A Reply." *The Immanent Frame*, July 8. Accessed May 10, 2023. https://tif.ssrc.org/2020/07/08/the-universal-enemy-a-reply/.

Lichterman, Paul. 1996. *The Search for Political Community: American Activists Reinventing Commitment.* Cambridge: Cambridge University Press.

Lillie, Nathan, and Ian Greer. 2007. "Industrial Relations, Migration, and Neoliberal Politics: The Case of the European Construction Sector." *Politics and Society* 35 (4): 551–581. https://doi.org/10.1177/0032329207308179.

Lipman, Vivian D. 1990. *A History of the Jews in Britain Since 1858*. Leicester: Leicester University Press.

Lipton, Eric, and Eric Lichtblau. 2004. "Even Near Home, a New Front is Opening in the Global Terror Battle." *The New York Times*, September 23. Accessed May 10, 2023. https://www.nytimes.com/2004/09/23/world/worldspecial2/even-near-home-a-new-front-is-opening-in-the-terror.html.

Littler, Jo. 2005. "Beyond the Boycott: Anti-Consumerism, Cultural Change and the Limits of Reflexivity." *Cultural Studies* 19 (2): 227–252. https://doi.org/10.1080/0950 2380500077771.

Lofranco, Zaira. 2017. "Negotiating 'Neighborliness' in Sarajevo Apartment Blocks." In *Migrating Borders and Moving Times: Temporality and the Crossing of Borders in Europe*, edited by Hastings Donnan, Madeleine Hurd, and Carolin Leutloff-Grandits, 42–57. Manchester: Manchester University Press.

Lorde, Audre. 1984. *Sister Outsider: Essays and Speeches by Audre Lorde.* Berkeley: Ten Speed Press.

Losman, Donald L. 1972. "The Arab Boycott of Israel." *International Journal of Middle East Studies* 3 (2): 99–122. https://doi.org/10.1017/S0020743800024831.

Louis, William R., and Avi Shlaim. 2012. "Introduction." In *The 1967 Arab – Israeli War: Origins and Consequences*, edited by Willian R. Louis and Avi Shlaim, 1–22. Cambridge: Cambridge University Press.

Lubin, Alex. 2014. *Geographies of Liberation: The Making of an Afro-Arab Political Imaginary.* Chapel Hill: The University of North Carolina Press.

Luetchford, Peter G. 2012. "Fair Trade and Small Farmers." In *Ethical Consumption: Social Value and Economic Practice*, edited by James G. Carrier and Peter G. Luetchford, 60–81. Oxford and New York: Berghahn.

Lybarger, Loren D. 2007. *Identity and Religion in Palestine: The Struggle Between Islamism and Secularism in the Occupied Territories.* Princeton: Princeton University Press.

Lyon, Sarah. 2009. "What Good Will Two More Trees Do? The Political Economy of Sustainable Coffee Certification, Local Livelihoods and Identities." *Landscape Research* 34 (2): 223–240. https://doi.org/10.1080/01426390802390673.

MacIntyre, Alasdair 1981. *After Virtue: A Study in Moral Theory.* Notre Dame: University of Notre Dame Press.

Maček, Ivana. 2001. "Predicament of War: Sarajevo Experiences and Ethics of War." In *Anthropology of Violence and Conflict*, edited by Bettina E. Schmidt and Ingo W. Schröder, 127–224. London and New York: Routledge.

Maček, Ivana. 2007. "Imitation of Life: Negotiating Normality in Sarajevo Under Siege." In *The New Bosnian Mosaic: Identities, Memories, and Moral Claims in a Post-War Society*, edited by Xavier Bougarel, Elissa Helms, and Ger Duijzings, 39–57. Aldershot: Ashgate.

Magnusson, Kjell. 1999. "Bosnia and Herzegovina." In *Islam Outside the Arab World*, edited by David Westerlund and Ingvar Svanberg, 295–314. Richmond: Curzon.

Mahmood, Saba. 2012. *Politics of Piety: The Islamic Revival and the Feminist Subject*. 2nd edition. Princeton: Princeton University Press.

Maira, Sunaina. 2018. *Boycott: The Academy and Justice for Palestine*. Berkeley: University of California Press.

Maisel, Peggy. 2003. "Lessons from the World Conference Against Racism: South Africa as a Case Study." *Oregon Law Review* 81 (3): 739–770.

Malcom, Noel. 1994. *Bosnia: A Short History*. New York: New York University Press.

Mandaville, Peter. 2001. *Transnational Muslim Politics: Reimagining the Umma*. London and New York: Routledge.

Mandaville, Peter. 2003. "Towards a Critical Islam: European Muslims and the Changing Boundaries of Transnational Religious Discourse." In *Muslim Networks and Transnational Communities in and across Europe*, edited by Stefano Allievi and Jørgen S. Nielsen, 127–145. Leiden and Boston: Brill.

Mansoor, Sanya. 2020. "The Trump Administration is Cracking Down Against a Global Movement to Boycott Israel. Here's What You Need to Know About BDS." *Time*, December 4. Accessed May 15, 2023. https://time.com/5914975/what-to-know-about-bds/.

Marcus, Kenneth. 2015. "Is BDS Anti-Semitic." In *The Case Against Academic Boycotts of Israel*, edited by Cary Nelson and Gabriel N. Brahm, 243–258. Detroit: Wayne State University Press.

Markowitz, Fran. 2010. *Sarajevo: A Bosnian Kaleidoscope*. Urbana: University of Illinois Press.

Marriott, John. 2006. "Family and Kinship in the New East End." *Rising East*, April 22. Accessed December 20, 2022. https://www.uel.ac.uk/risingeast/archive04/debate/hudson_marriott_owens_dench.htm.

McCarthy, Justin. 1993. "Ottoman Bosnia, 1800–1878." In *The Muslims of Bosnia-Herzegovina: Their Historic Development from the Middle Ages to the Dissolution of Yugoslavia*, edited by Mark Pinson, 54–83. Cambridge: Harvard University Press.

McFarland, Horace N. 1967. *The Rush Hour of the Gods: A Study of New Religious Movements in Japan*. London and New York: Macmillan Press.

McLoughlin, Sean. 2005. "The State, New Muslim Leaderships and Islam as a Resource for Public Engagement in Britain." In *European Muslims and the Secular State*, edited by Jocelyne Cesari and Sean McLoughlin, 55–69. Aldershot: Ashgate.

McMahon, Sean. 2014. "The Boycott, Divestment, Sanctions Campaign: Contradictions and Challenges." *Race and Class* 55 (4): 65–81. https://doi.org/10.1177/0306 396813519939.

Measuring Anti-Muslim Attacks. 2014. "Anti-Muslim Hate Crimes, 2012–2014 in London: An Analysis of the Situation." Accessed May 15, 2023. https://tellmamauk .org/anti-muslim-hate-crimes-2012-2014-in-london-an-analysis-of-the-situation.

Medjunarodni Forum Solidarnosti-Emmaus. n.d. "O Nama [About Us]." Accessed May 15, 2023. https://mfs-emmaus.ba/o-nama/.

Meghji, Ali. 2020. "Britain's Postcolonial Crisis: The Denial of Racism in Little England." *Europe Now*, December 7. Accessed May 15, 2023. https://www.europenowjournal .org/2020/12/07/britains-postcolonial-crisis-the-denial-of-racism-in-little-england/.

Merdjanova, Ina. 2013. *Rediscovering the Umma: Muslims in the Balkans Between Nationalism and Transnationalism*. Oxford: Oxford University Press.

Mesarić, Andreja. 2013. "Wearing Hijab in Sarajevo: Dress Practices and the Islamic Revival in Post-War Bosnia-Herzegovina." *Anthropological Journal of European Cultures* 22 (2): 13–34. https://doi.org/10.3167/ajec.2013.220202.

Messick, Brinkley. 1996. "Media Muftis: Radio Fatwas in Yemen." In *Islamic Legal Interpretation: Muftis and their Fatwas*, edited by Muhammad K. Masud, Brinkley Messick, and David S. Powers, *Islamic Legal Interpretation: Muftis and their Fatwas*, 310–320. Cambridge: Harvard University Press.

Mi'Ari, Mahmoud. 1999. "Attitudes of Palestinians Toward Normalization with Israel." *Journal of Peace Research* 36 (3): 339–348. https://doi.org/10.1177/00223 43399036003006.

Micheletti, Michele. 2003. *Political Virtue and Shopping: Individuals, Consumerism, and Collective Action*. London and New York: Palgrave Macmillan.

Micheletti, Michele, and Didem Oral. 2019. "Problematic Political Consumerism: Confusions and Moral Dilemmas in Boycott Activism." In *The Oxford Handbook of Political Consumerism*, edited by Magnus Boström, Michele Micheletti, and Peter Oosterveer, 699–720. Oxford: Oxford University Press.

Mishal, Shaul, and Reuven Aharoni. 1994. *Speaking Stones: Communiqués from the Intifada Underground*. Syracuse: Syracuse University Press.

Mishal, Shaul, and Avraham Sela. 2000. *The Palestinian Hamas: Vision, Violence, and Coexistence*. New York: Columbia University Press.

Mitchell, Richard P. 1969. *The Society of the Muslim Brothers*. Oxford: Oxford University Press.

Mladi Muslimani. 2002. "Prvi Nastup [The First Appearance]." Accessed May 15, 2023. http://www.mm.co.ba/index.php/bs/udruzenje-danas/historijat/241-prvi-nastup.

Moaddel, Mansoor. 1994. "Shi'i Political Discourse and Class Mobilization in the Tobacco Movement of 1890–1892." In *A Century of Revolution: Social Movements in Iran*, edited by John Foran, 1–20. Minneapolis: University of Minnesota Press.

Moore, Donald S. 1998. "Subaltern Struggles and the Politics of Place: Remapping Resistance in Zimbabwe's Eastern Highlands." *Cultural Anthropology* 13 (3): 344–381. https://doi.org/10.1525/can.1998.13.3.344.

Morawska, Ewa. 2004. "Exploring Diversity in Immigrant Assimilation and Transnationalism: Poles and Russian Jews in Philadelphia." *International Migration Review* 38 (4): 1372–1412. https://doi.org/10.1111/j.1747.7379.2004.tb00241.x.

Morrison, Suzanne. 2022. "Border-Crossing Repertoires of Contention: Palestinian Activism in a Global Justice Movement." *Globalizations* 19 (1): 17–33. https://doi.org/10.1080/14747731.2020.1844973.

Mujkić, Asim. 2016. "Bosnian Days of Reckoning: Review of the Sequence of Protests in Bosnia and Herzegovina 2013–14, and Future Prospects of Resistance." *Southeastern Europe* 40 (2): 217–242. https://doi.org/10.1163/18763332-04002004.

Mukhaymar, Fuad. 2000. "Ulama's Fatwa on Boycotting Israeli and American Products." *Islam Online*, October 21. Accessed December 20, 2022. https://archive.islamonline.net/?p=861.

Nagengast, Carole, and Michael Kearney. 1990. "Mixtec Ethnicity: Social Identity, Political Consciousness, and Political Activism." *Latin American Research Review* 25 (2): 61–91.

Nash, June. 2004. "Introduction: Social Movements and Global Processes." In *Social Movements: An Anthropological Reader*, edited by June Nash, 1–26. Hoboken: Wiley-Blackwell.

Nehamas, Alexander. 1998. *The Art of Living: Socratic Reflections from Plato to Foucault*. Berkeley: University of California Press.

Nielsen, Jørgen S. 2003. "Transnational Islam and the Integration of Islam in Europe." In *Muslim Networks and Transnational Communities in and across Europe*, edited by Stefano Allievi and Jørgen S. Nielsen, 28–51. Leiden and Boston: Brill.

Norman, Julie M. 2011. "Introduction: Nonviolent Resistance in the Second Intifada." In *Nonviolent Resistance in the Second Intifada: Activism and Advocacy*, edited by Maia Carter Hallward and Julie M. Norman, 1–11. London and New York: Palgrave Macmillan.

Norris, Pippa. 2009. "Political Activism: New Challenges, New Opportunities." In *The Oxford Handbook of Comparative Politics*, edited by Carles Boix and Susan C. Stokes, 628–649. Oxford: Oxford University Press.

O'Hanlon, Rosalind. 1988. "Recovering the Subject: Subaltern Studies and Histories of Resistance in Colonial South Asia." *Modern Asian Studies* 22: 189–224. https://doi.org/10.1017/S0026749X00009471.

Ochs, Juliana. 2011. *Security and Suspicion: An Ethnography of Everyday Life in Israel*. Philadelphia: University of Pennsylvania Press.

Ong, Aihwa. 1987. *Spirits of Resistance and Capitalist Discipline: Factory Women in Malaysia*. Albany: State University of New York Press.

Office of the United Nations High Commissioner for Human Rights. 2018. "UN Rights Office Issues Report on Business and Human Rights in Settlements in the Occupied Palestinian Territory." Accessed May 15, 2022. https://www.ohchr.org/en/press-releases/2018/01/un-rights-office-issues-report-business-and-human-rights-settlements.

Office of the United Nations High Commissioner for Human Rights. 2022. "Special Rapporteur on the Situation of Human Rights in the Occupied Palestinian Territories: Israel has Imposed Upon Palestine an Apartheid Reality in a Post-Apartheid World." Accessed August 18, 2022. https://www.ohchr.org/en/press-releases/2022/03/special-rapporteur-situation-human-rights-occupied-palestinian-territories.

Omid, Homa. 1994. *Islam and the Post-Revolutionary State in Iran*. London and New York: Palgrave Macmillan.

Organization for Security and Cooperation in Europe. 2003. "Anti-Semitism Conference, 2003." Accessed May 15, 2023. https://www.osce.org/node/65986.

Ortner, Sherry B. 1995. "Resistance and the Problem of Ethnographic Refusal." *Comparative Studies in Society and History* 37 (1): 173–193. https://doi.org/10.1017/S0010417500019587.

Palestinian Campaign for the Academic and Cultural Boycott of Israel. 2006. "The PACBI Call for Academic Boycott Revised: Adjusting the Parameters of the Debate." *Boycott, Divestment, and Sanctions*, July 6. Accessed May 15, 2023. https://bdsmovement.net/pacbi/pacbi-call.

Palestinian Campaign for the Academic and Cultural Boycott of Israel. 2011. "Israel's Exceptionalism: Normalizing the Abnormal." *Boycott, Divestment, and Sanctions*, October 31. Accessed May 15, 2023. https://bdsmovement.net/news/israel's-exceptionalism-normalizing-abnormal.

Palestinian Civil Society Organizations. 2002. "A Call to Boycott Israel Issued by Palestinian Civil Society Organizations." *BADIL Resource Center for Palestinian Residency and Refugee Rights*, August 28. Accessed May 15, 2023. https://badil.org/press-releases/2362.html.

Palestinian Information Center. 2015. "Their Humanity Forced Them to Sing and Make Promises. Let's Say it Louder. Let's All Boycott Israel and Stop Apartheid." Accessed May 15, 2023. https://www.facebook.com/PalinfoEN/videos/971632742856194.

Palestine Solidarity Campaign. 2021. "Veolia." Accessed May 15, 2023. https://www.palestinecampaign.org/wp-content/uploads/2012/12/Veolia-bigcampaign-website-revised-draft-update-16-5-13-3.pdf.

Pappé, Ilan. 2004. *A History of Modern Palestine: One Land, Two Peoples*. 2nd edition. Cambridge: Cambridge University Press.

Pargeter, Alison. 2008. *The New Frontiers of Jihad: Radical Islam in Europe*. Philadelphia: University of Pennsylvania Press.

Patterson, Patrick H. 2003. "On the Edge of Reason: The Boundaries of Balkanism in Slovenian, Austrian, and Italian Discourse." *Slavic Review* 62 (1): 110–41. https://doi.org/10.2307/3090469.

Peace, Timothy. 2013. "Muslims and Electoral Politics in Britain: The Case of the Respect Party." In *Muslim Political Participation in Europe*, edited by Jørgen S. Nielsen, 299–321. Edinburgh: Edinburgh University Press.

Penaloza, Lisa, and Linda L. Price. 1993. "Consumer Resistance: A Conceptual Overview." In *Advances in Consumer Research, Vol. 20*, edited by Leigh McAlister and Michael L. Rothschild, 123–128. Provo: Association for Consumer Research.

Peteet, Julie. 1997. "Icons and Militants: Mothering in the Danger Zone." *Signs: Journal of Women in Culture and Society* 23 (1): 103–129. https://doi.org/10.1086/495237.

Pickering, Paula M. 2006. "Generating Social Capital for Bridging Ethnic Divisions in the Balkans: Case Studies of Two Bosniak Cities." *Ethnic and Racial Studies* 29 (1): 79–103. https://doi.org/10.1080/01419870500352397.

Pieterse, Jan N. 1995. "Globalization as Hybridization." In *Global Modernities*, edited by Mike Featherstone, Scott Lash, and Roland Robertson, 45–69. London: Sage.

Pinson, Mark. 1993. "The Muslims of Bosnia-Herzegovina under Austro-Hungarian Rule, 1878–1918." In *The Muslims of Bosnia-Herzegovina: Their Historical Development from the Middle Ages to the Dissolution of Yugoslavia*, edited by Mark Pinson, 84–128. Cambridge: Harvard University Press.

Portes, Alejandro, and Rubén Rumbaut. 1996. *Immigrant America: A Portrait*. 2nd edition. Berkeley: University of California Press.

Prakash, Gyan. 1990. *Bonded Histories: Genealogies of Labor Servitude in Colonial India*. Cambridge: Cambridge University Press.

Purdam, Kingsley. 1996. "Settler Political Participation: Muslim Local Councilors." In *Political Participation and Identities of Muslims in Non-Muslim States*, edited by Wasif A. R. Shadid and Sjoerd P. van Koningsveld, 129–143. Kampen: Kok Pharos.

Putnam, Todd, and Timothy Muck. 1991. "Wielding the Boycott Weapon for Social Change." *Business and Society Review* 78 (2): 5–8.

Qumsiyeh, Mazin. 2011. *Popular Resistance in Palestine: A History of Hope and Empowerment*. London: Pluto.

Rabasa, José. 2010. *Without History: Subaltern Studies, the Zapatista Insurgency, and the Specter of History*. Pittsburgh: University of Pittsburgh Press.

Rabbani, Mouin. 2006. "Palestinian Authority, Israeli Rule." In *The Struggle for Sovereignty: Palestine and Israel, 1993–2005*, edited by Joel L. Beinin and Rebecca L. Stein, 75–83. Stanford: Stanford University Press.

Ramet, Sabrina P. 1996. "Nationalism and the 'Idiocy' of the Countryside: The Case of Serbia." *Ethnic and Racial Studies* 19 (1): 70–87. https://doi.org/10.1080/01419870.1996.9993899.

Raynolds, Laura T. 2002. "Consumer/Producer Links in Fair Trade Coffee Networks." *Sociologia Ruralis* 42 (4): 404–424. https://doi.org/10.1111/1467-9523.00224.

Respect Party. 2005. "Peace, Justice, Equality: The Respect Manifesto for the May 2005 Election." *The British Broadcasting Corporation*, May 10. Accessed May 10, 2023. http://news.bbc.co.uk/1/shared/bsp/hi/pdfs/RESPECT_uk_manifesto.pdf.

Robbins, Thomas, Dick Anthony, and James Richardson. 1978. "Theory and Research on Today's 'New Religions'." *Sociological Analysis* 39 (2): 95–122. https://doi.org/10.2307/3710211.

Robinson, Glenn E. 1997. *Building a Palestinian State: The Incomplete Revolution*. Bloomington: Indiana University Press.

Roseberry, William. 1996. "The Rise of Yuppie Coffees and the Reimagination of Class in the United States." *American Anthropologist* 98 (4): 762–775. https://doi.org/10.1525/aa.1996.98.4.02a00070.

Rouse, Roger. 1992. "Making Sense of Settlement: Class Transformations, Cultural Struggle, and Transnationalism Among Mexican Immigrants in the United States." *Annals of the New York Academy of Sciences* 645 (1): 25–52. https://doi.org/10.1111/j.1749-6632.1992.tb33485.x.

Roy, Sara. 2011. *Hamas and Civil Society in Gaza: Engaging the Islamist Social Sector*. Princeton: Princeton University Press.

Rucker-Chang, Sunnie. 2014. "The Turkish Connection: Neo-Ottoman Influence in Post-Dayton Bosnia." *Journal of Muslim Minority Affairs* 34 (2): 152–164. https://doi.org/10.1080/13602004.2014.911586.

Sabeel-Kairos. n.d. "About Us." Accessed May 10, 2023. https://www.sabeel-kairos.org.uk/category/about-us/about-sabeel-kairos/.

Sahlins, Michael. 2002. *Waiting for Foucault, Still*. Chicago: Prickly Paradigm Press.

Said, Edward W. 1978. *Orientalism: Western Conceptions of the Orient*. New York: Pantheon.

Salem, Walid. 2005. "The Anti-Normalization Discourse in the Context of Israeli – Palestinian Peace- Building." *Palestine-Israel Journal of Politics, Economics, and Culture* 12 (1): 100–109.

Salvatore, Armando. 2000. "Social Differentiation, Moral Authority, and Public Islam in Egypt: The Path of Mustafa Mahmud." *Anthropology Today* 16 (2): 12–15. https://doi.org/10.1111/1467.8322.00014.

Salvatore, Armando. 2004. "Making Public Space: Opportunities and Limits of Collective Action Among Muslims in Europe." *Journal of Ethnic and Migration Studies* 30 (5): 1013–1031. https://doi.org/10.1080/1369183042000245679.

Sarajlić, Eldar. 2009. "Europe as a Media Myth: The Case of Bosnian Muslims." In *Mutual Misunderstandings? Muslims and Islam in the European Media*, edited by Karem Öktem and Reem Abou-El-Fadl, 53–78. Oxford: European Studies Center.

Sarajlić, Eldar. 2011. "Return of the Consuls: Islamic Networks and Foreign Policy Perspectives in Bosnia and Herzegovina." *Southeast European and Black Sea Studies* 11 (2): 173–190. https://doi.org/10.1080/14683857.2011.587251.

Sarna, Aaron J. 1986. *Boycott and Blacklist: A History of Arab Economic Warfare Against Israel*. Lanham: Rowman and Littlefield.

Sayigh, Rosemary. 2007. *Palestinians: From Peasants to Revolutionaries*. London: Zed Books.

Schanzer, Johnathan. 2008. *Hamas vs. Fatah: The Struggle for Palestine*. London and New York: Palgrave Macmillan.

Schielke, Samuli. 2009. "Being Good in Ramadan: Ambivalence, Fragmentation, and the Moral Self in the Lives of Young Egyptians." *The Journal of the Royal Anthropological Institute* 15 (1): 24–40. https://doi.org/10.1111/j.1467-9655.2009.01540.x.

Sandoval, Chela. 2000. *Methodology of the Oppressed*. Minneapolis: University of Minnesota Press.

Schiffauer, Werner. 2007. "From Exile to Diaspora: The Development of Transnational Islam in Europe." In *Islam in Europe: Diversity, Identity, and Influence*, edited by Aziz al-Azmeh and Effie Fokas, 68–95. Cambridge: Cambridge University Press.

Schulze, Kirsten A. 2017. *The Arab – Israeli Conflict*. 3rd edition. London and New York: Routledge.

Scott, James C. 1990. *Domination and the Arts of Resistance: Hidden Transcripts*. New Heaven: Yale University Press.

Segev, Tom. 2011. "The Makings of History: The Blind Misleading the Blind." *Haaretz*, October 21. Accessed May 10, 2023. https://www.haaretz.com/2011-10-21/ty-article/the-makings-of-history-the-blind-misleading-the-blind/0000017f–db5e–d3a5-af7f-fbfe049b0000.

Seitz, Charmaine. 2006. "Coming of Age: Hamas's Rise to Prominence in the Post-Oslo Era." In *The Struggle for Sovereignty: Palestine and Israel, 1993–2005*, edited by Joel Beinin and Rebecca L. Stein, 112–129. Stanford: Stanford University Press.

Sen, Sankar, Zaynep Gürhan-Canli, Vicki Morwitz. 2001. "Withholding Consumption: A Social Dilemma Perspective on Consumer Boycotts." *Journal of Consumer Research* 28 (3): 399–417. https://doi.org/10.1086/323729.

Seymour, Susan 2006. "Resistance." *Anthropological Theory* 6 (3): 303–321. https://doi.org/10.1177/1463499606066890.

Sherbiny, Naiem A. 1976. "Arab Oil Production Policies in the Context of International Conflicts." In *Arab Oil: Impact on the Arab Countries and Global Implications*, edited by Mark A. Tessler and Naiem A. Sherbiny, 35–57. New York: Praeger.

Shindler, Colin. 2008. *A History of Modern Israel*. Cambridge: Cambridge University Press.

Sinha, Shamser. 2008. "Seeking Sanctuary: Exploring the Changing Postcolonial and Racialized Politics of Belonging in East London." *Sociological Research Online* 13 (5): 102–116. https://doi.org/10.5153/sro.1799.

Sivaramakrishan, Kalyanakrishnan. 2005. "Some Intellectual Genealogies for the Concept of Everyday Resistance." *American Anthropologist* 107 (3): 346–355. https://doi.org/10.1525/aa.2005.107.3.346.

Siniora, Hanna. 1988. "An Analysis of the Current Revolt." *Journal of Palestine Studies* 17 (3): 3–13. https://doi.org/10.2307/2537455.

Silverstein, Paul A. 2008. "The Context of Antisemitism and Islamophobia in France." *Patterns of Prejudice* 42 (1): 1–26. https://doi.org/10.1080/00313220701805877.

Skovgaard-Petersen, Jakob. 1997. *Defining Islam for the Egyptian State: Muftis and Fatwas of the Dār al-Iftā*. Leiden and Boston: Brill.

Smith, Christian. 1996. "Correcting a Curious Neglect, or Bringing Religion Back In." In *Disruptive Religion: The Force of Faith in Social Movement Activism*, edited by Christian Smith, 1–25. London and New York: Routledge.

Smith, Jackie. 2021. "The Power of Translocal Organizing." *Great Transition Initiative*, August 23. Accessed May 15, 2023. https://greattransition.org/gti-forum/global-solidarity-smith.

Smith, Michael P. 1992. "Postmodernism, Urban Ethnography, and the New Social Space of Ethnic Identity." *Theory and Society* 21 (4): 493–531. https://doi.org/10.1007/BF00993487.

Smith, Michael P. 2000. *Transnational Urbanism: Locating Globalization*. Hoboken: Wiley-Blackwell.

Snow, David A., and Robert D. Benford. 1992. "Master Frames and Cycles of Protest." In *Frontiers in Social Movement Theory*, edited by Aldon D. Morris and Carol McClurg, 133–155. New Haven: Yale University Press.

Solberg, Anne R. 2007. "The Role of Turkish Islamic Networks in the Western Balkans." *Comparative Southeast European Studies* 55 (4): 429–461. https://doi.org/10.1515/soeu-2007-550406.

Sorabji, Cornelia. 1993. "Ethnic War in Bosnia?" *Radical Philosophy* 63 (1): 33–35.

Sorabji, Cornelia. 1994. "Mixed Motives: Islam, Nationalism and Mevluds in an Unstable Yugoslavia." In *Muslim Women's Choices: Religious Belief and Social Reality*, edited by Camilla F. El-Solh and Judy Mabro, 108–127. Oxford: Berg.

Sorabji, Cornelia. 2006. "Managing Memories in Post-War Sarajevo: Individuals, Bad Memories, and New Wars." *Journal of the Royal Anthropological Institute* 12 (1): 1–18. https://doi.org/10.1111/j.1467-9655.2006.00278.x.

Sorabji, Cornelia. 2008. "Bosnian Neighborhoods Revisited: Tolerance, Commitment and Komšiluk in Sarajevo." In *On the Margins of Religion*, edited by Frances Pine and João de Pina-Cabral, 97–112. Oxford and New York: Berghahn.

Sourani, Raji. 2013. "Why Palestinians Called for BDS." In *Generation Palestine: Voices from the Boycott, Divestment and Sanctions Movement*, edited by Rich Wiles, 61–71. London: Pluto.

Speed, Shannon. 2008. *Rights in Rebellion: Indigenous Struggle and Human Rights in Chiapas*. Stanford: Stanford University Press.

Spivak, Gayatri C. 1988. "Can the Subaltern Speak?" In *Marxism and the Interpretation of Culture*, edited by Cary Nelson and Larry Grossberg, 271–313. Urbana: University of Illinois Press.

Stand for Justice. 2012. "Hvala Svima [Thank You All]." Accessed May 10, 2023. https://www.facebook.com/media/set/?set=a.408723265865360.92948.208101009260921&type=3.

Starr, Deborah. 2009. *Remembering Cosmopolitan Egypt: Literature, Culture, and Empire*. London and New York: Routledge.

Starrett, Gregory. 2010. "Islam and the Politics of Enchantment." In *Islam, Politics, Anthropology*, edited by Filippo Osella and Benjamin Soares, 213–230. Hoboken: Wiley-Blackwell.

Stefansson, Andres H. 2007. "Locals, Newcomers and the Cultural Transformation of Sarajevo." In *The New Bosnian Mosaic: Identities, Memories, and Moral Claims in a Post-War Society*, edited by Xavier Bougarel, Elissa Helms, and Ger Duijzings, 59–78. Aldershot: Ashgate.

Stefansson, Andres H. 2010. "Coffee After Cleansing? Coexistence, Cooperation, and Communication in Post-Conflict Bosnia and Herzegovina." *Focaal* 1 (57): 62–76. https://doi.org/10.3167/fcl.2010.570105.

Stephan, Maria J. 2003. "People Power in the Holy Land: How Popular Nonviolent Struggle Can Transform the Israeli – Palestinian Conflict." *Journal of Public and International Affairs* 14 (1): 1–26.

Stephan, Maria J. 2009. "Introduction." In *Civilian Jihad: Nonviolent Struggle, Democratization, and Governance in the Middle East*, edited by Maria J. Stephan, 1–14. London and New York: Palgrave Macmillan.

Stephen, Lynn. 1996. "The Creation and Re-Creation of Ethnicity: Lessons from the Zapotec and Mixtec of Oaxaca." *Latin American Perspectives* 23 (2): 17–37. https://doi.org/10.1177/0094582X9602300202.

Stockton, Ronald R. 2015. "Presbyterians Divest." *Middle East Policy* 22 (1): 41–65. https://doi.org/10.1111/mepo.12111.

Stoner, Kathryn L. 1991. *From the House to the Streets: The Cuban Women's Movement for Legal Reform, 1898–1940*. Durham: Duke University Press.

Strathern, Marilyn. 1990. "Negative Strategies in Melanesia." In *Localizing Strategies: Regional Traditions of Ethnographic Writing*, edited by Richard Fardon, 204–216. Edinburgh: Scottish Academic Press.

Taguieff, Pierre-André. 2004. *Rising from the Muck: The New-Antisemitism in Europe*. Translated by Patrick Camiller. Chicago: Ivan R. Dee.

Tarrow, Sidney. 1994. *Power in Movement: Social Movements, Collective Action and Politics*. Cambridge: Cambridge University Press.

Tatari, Eren. 2014. *Muslims in British Local Government: Representing Minority Interests in Hackney, Newham, and Tower Hamlets*. Leiden and Boston: Brill.

Tessler, Mark A. 2009. *A History of the Israeli – Palestinian Conflict*. 2nd edition. Bloomington: Indiana University Press.

Thayer, Millie. 2001. "Transnational Feminism: Reading Joan Scott in the Brazilian Sertão." *Ethnography* 2 (2): 243–271. https://doi.org/10.1177/14661380122230911.

Thompson, Craig J. 2004. "Marketplace Mythology and Discourses of Power." *Journal of Consumer Research* 31 (1): 162–180. https://doi.org/10.1086/383432.

Thrall, Nathan. 2018. "Boycott, Divestment, Sanctions: How a Controversial Nonviolent Movement Has Transformed the Israeli – Palestinian Debate." *The Guardian*, August 24. Accessed May 15, 2023. https://www.theguardian.com/news/2018/aug/14/bds-boycott-divestment-sanctions-movement-transformed-israeli-palestinian-debate.

Tilly, Charles. 1986. *The Contentious French*. Cambridge: Harvard University Press.

Todorova, Maria. 1997. *Imagining the Balkans*. Oxford: Oxford University Press.

Toth, James. 2004. "Local Islam Gone Global: The Roots of Religious Militancy in Egypt and its Transnational Transformation." In *Social Movements: An Anthropological Reader*, edited by June Nash, 117–145. Hoboken: Wiley-Blackwell.

Tower Hamlets Council's Corporate Research Unit. 2013. "Population by Age and Ethnicity Tool." *Tower Hamlets Council*, May 20. Accessed May 15, 2023. https://www.towerhamlets.gov.uk/Documents/Borough_statistics/Research-tools-and-guidance/Tool-2011-Census-TH-Ethnicity-by-Age.xlsx.

Tower Hamlets Council's Corporate Research Unit. 2015. "Religion in Tower Hamlets. 2011 Census Update." *Tower Hamlets Council*, February 26. Accessed May 15, 2023. https://www.towerhamlets.gov.uk/Documents/Borough_statistics/Ward_profiles/Census-2011/2015-04-21-Faith-key-facts-Revised-data.pdf.

Trust for London. 2017. "Tower Hamlets. Poverty and Inequality Data." Accessed May 15, 2023. https://www.trustforlondon.org.uk/data/boroughs/tower-hamlets-poverty-and-inequality-indicators.

Turner, Alwyn W. 2008. *Crisis? What Crisis? Britain in the 1970s*. London: Aurum.

Urban, Kristen. 1994. "Blueprint for a Democratic Palestinian State: UNLU Communiqués and the Codification of Political Values for the First Two Years of the Intifada." *Arab Studies Quarterly* 16 (3): 67–82.

van Bruinessen, Martin. 2010. "Producing Islamic Knowledge in Western Europe: Discipline, Authority, and Personal Quest'. In *Producing Islamic Knowledge: Transmission and Dissemination in Western Europe*, edited by Martin van Bruinessen and Stefano Allievi, 1–27. London and New York: Routledge.

van de Port, Mattijs. 1998. *Gypsies, Wars and Other Instances of the Wild: Civilization and its Discontents in a Serbian Town.* Amsterdam: Amsterdam University Press.

van der Geest, Sjaak, Trudie Gerrits, and Flore S. Åslid. 2012. "Introduction: Ethnography and Self-Exploration." *Medische Antropologie*, 24 (1): 5–22.

van Velsen, Jaap. 1960. "Labor Migration as a Positive Factor in the Continuity of Tonga Tribal Society." *Economic Development and Cultural Change* 8 (3): 265–278. https://doi.org/10.1086/449846.

Visram, Rozina. 2002. *Asians in Britain: 400 Years of History.* London: Pluto.

Waardenburg, Jacques. 1996. "Muslims as Dhimmis: The Emancipation of Muslim Immigrants in Europe. The Case of Switzerland." In *Muslims in the Margin: Political Responses to the Presence of Islam in Western Europe*, edited by Wasif A. R. Shadid and Sjoerd P. van Koningsveld, 145–164. Kampen: Kok Pharos.

Wagner, Walter H. 2008. *Opening the Qur'an: Introducing Islam's Holy Book.* Notre Dame: University of Notre Dame Press.

Walden, Raphael. 2004. "The Drafting of the Articles on the Middle East and Anti-Semitism at the Durban Conference Against Racism." In *Racism and Human Rights*, edited by Raphael Walden, 165–170. Leiden: Martinus Nijhoff.

Ward, Ian. 2009. *Law, Text, Terror.* Cambridge: Cambridge University Press.

Warf, Barney, and Peter Vincent. 2007. "Multiple Geographies of the Arab Internet." *Area* 39 (1): 83–96. https://doi.org/10.1111/j.1475-4762.2007.00717.x.

Wemyss, Georgie. 2008. "White Memories, White Belonging: Competing Colonial Anniversaries in 'Postcolonial' East London." *Sociological Research Online* 13 (5): 50–67. https://doi.org/10.5153/sro.1801.

Werbner, Pnina. 1997. "Essentializing Essentialism, Essentializing Silence: Ambivalence and Multiplicity in the Constructions of Race and Ethnicity." In *Debating Cultural Hybridity: Multi-Cultural Identities and the Politics of Anti-Racism*, edited by Pnina Werbner and Tariq Modood, 226–254. London: Zed Books.

White, Ben. 2020. "Delegitimizing Solidarity: Israel Smears Palestine Advocacy as Anti-Semitic." *Journal of Palestine Studies* 49 (2): 65–79. https://doi.org/10.1525/jps.2020.49.2.65.

Williams, Rhys H. 2006. "Collective Action, Everyday Protest, and Lived Religion." *Social Movement Studies* 5 (1): 83–89. https://doi.org/10.1080/14742830600630465.

Wilson, Bryan R. 1970. *Religious Sects: A Sociological Study.* London: Weidenfeld and Nicholson.

Wilson, John K. 2008. *Patriotic Correctness: Academic Freedom and its Enemies.* Boulder: Paradigm.

Wistrich, Robert S. 2012. *From Ambivalence to Betrayal: The Left, the Jews, and Israel.* Lincoln: University of Nebraska Press.

Wood, Richard. 1994. "Faith in Action: Religious Resources for Political Success in Three Congregations." *Sociology of Religion* 55 (4): 397–417. https://doi.org/10.2307/3711979.

Wuthnow, Robert. 1976. "The New Religions in Social Context." In *The New Religious Consciousness*, edited by Charles Y. Glock and Robert N. Bellah, 267–293. Berkeley: University of California Press.

Wuthnow, Robert. 1991. *Acts of Compassion*. Princeton: Princeton University Press.

Young, Marion I. 1990. *Justice and the Politics of Difference*. Princeton: Princeton University Press.

Younge, Gary. 2020. "What Black America Means to Europe." *The New York Review of Books*, June 6. Accessed May 10, 2023. https://www.nybooks.com/daily/2020/06/06/what-black-america-means-to-europe/.

Zacher, Mark W. 1979. *International Conflicts and Collective Security, 1946–1977. The United Nations, Organization of American States, Organization of African Unity, and Arab League*. New York: Praeger.

Zibechi, Raúl. 2012. *Territories in Resistance: A Cartography of Latin American Social Movements*. Translated by Ryan Ramor. Oakland: AK Press.

Index

AAM (anti-apartheid movement)   27, 131
AAUP (American Association of University Professors)   25
Abduh, Muhammad   119
Abdulhadi, Rabab   132
Abu-Lughod, Lila   7
Abu-Sunaynah, Yusuf   39
academics, boycotts by   25, 70
ACLU (American Civil Liberties Union)   22
Across Seven Seas and Thirteen Rivers: Life Stories of Pioneer Sylheti Settlers in Britain (Adams)   46
activism
   everyday spatialities of   129–130
   see also boycott, divestment and sanctions; boycotts
Adams, Caroline   46
ADC (American – Arab Anti-Discrimination Committee)   24
agency   6–8, 111
AIO (Aktivna Islamska Omladina)   117–118
AIPU (Council of the Arab Inter-Parliamentary Union)   31
Aktivna Islamska Omladina (AIO)   117–118
Ali, Altab   74–75
AlMinbar.com   39–40
American Association of University Professors (AAUP)   25
American Civil Liberties Union (ACLU)   22
American – Arab Anti-Discrimination Committee (ADC)   24
Amir-Moazami, Schirin   15–16
Andoni, Raed   30
anti-apartheid movement (AAM)   27, 131
anti-colonial movements   6
anti-Muslim hate crimes   45
anti-normalization movements   29
anti-racist movements   6, 24, 71, 72
antisemitism   1, 43, 120
apartheid   10n6, 27
apartment blocks   51–52
apathy, moral   104, 114
   see also docility, of Bosniaks
al-Aqsa Mosque   77, 81, 120, 121
Arab Boycott Bureau   31
Arab League   26, 27–28, 30–31
Arab states   22, 27–28
Arabism   28
Association of University Teachers (AUT)   70
Awami League   69

Back, Les   66
Bangladesh Liberation War   61, 65
Bangladeshi community (Tower Hamlets)
   establishment of   45
   leadership of
      by British-born activists   61–62
      by East London Mosque's leaders   49–50
      by first generation immigrants   48, 61
      by second generation immigrants   48–49, 61
   marginalization of   47–48
   origins of   45–46
   redevelopment of Docklands and   47
   see also Bangladeshis; Tower Hamlets; United Kingdom
Bangladeshi Welfare Association   48
Bangladeshis (Tower Hamlets)
   British-born
      BDS activities of   76–86
      criticism on religious leadership   80–81
      criticism on Tower Hamlets Council   76
      Hizb ut-Tahrir and   83
      leadership by   61–62
      moral reform and   82–86
      Muslim identity of   49, 83–84
      political activism of   77–79
      relationship with British state   79
      religious knowledge of   81–82
   democracy and   61
   first-generation
      BDS activities of   62–66, 68
      ethno-national heritage of   60–61, 65, 66–68
      experiences of   46
      individualization of responsibility and   62–68
      leadership by   48, 61

Bangladeshis (Tower Hamlets) (*cont.*)
  second-generation
    BDS activities of   68–76
    ethnic absolutism and   68–69
    hybrid belonging of   72, 73
    Islam and   69
    leadership by   48–49, 61
    racism and   73–75
    secular nationalist view   75
    use of term   4n4
    see also Bangladeshi community (Tower Hamlets); Tower Hamlets; United Kingdom
al-Banna, Hassan   34, 119
Banovina Hrvatska (Banate of Croatia)   105
Barghouti, Omar   6, 9–10, 25, 27, 30, 31, 91
Baroud, Ramzy   6–7, 10, 30
Bayat, Asef   15
BDS National Committee (BNC)   2, 131–132
Beckford, James A.   14
"being Muslim"
  anti-racist movements and   131–132
  articulations of   123
  BDS and   6, 17, 124, 131
  European life and   40, 41
  social contexts and   131
Beit Sahour   30
Bengali, use of term   4n4
Bethnal Green (London)   60
Bethnal Green Mosque (London)   67
Birkbeck University (UK)   73
Black Americans   132
Black radical movements   131–132
BMI (British Muslim Initiative)   77
BNC (BDS National Committee)   2, 131–132
BNP (British National Party)   47
Bosnia
  displacements in   51, 55–56, 88
  Muslim organizations in   89
    see also under specific organizations
  Muslims in *see* Bosniaks
  nationalist leaders of   105
  nationalist parties in   93–94
  rural newcomers *see* rural newcomers
  Srebrenica genocide   3, 18, 104–105, 113–114
  urbanites in *see* urbanites
  see also Sarajevo

Bosniaks (Stari Grad)
  democracy and   54, 110–111
  docility of   101, 104, 109, 112, 113, 114
  Europe and *see under* Europe
  Islam and
    Islamization   110–112, 115–116
    patriotism and   117
    rejection of   112, 114
    Salafism *see* Salafism
    understanding of   52–54
  Mladi Muslimani *see* Mladi Muslimani
  Muslim identity of   58, 109
  older middle-class
    BDS activities of   92–98
    disappointments of   93–94
    European identity of   96
    local patriotism   92–93
    MFS-Emmaus *see* MFS-Emmaus
    on religious duties   95–96
    on rural newcomers   94–95
    vs. rural newcomers   96–97
    siege of Sarajevo, BDS and   92
    social prestige and   56n4, 96
    on state intervention into religious practices of   95
    women's freedoms and   97
  patriotism of   93, 117, 125
  socialism and   53–54
  solidarity among   3, 52
  use of term   4n4, 52n2
  victimhood of   18, 19, 87, 114, 115
  younger middle-class
    BDS activities of   19, 98–115
    criticism on older generation   109
    criticism on religious leadership   101
    disappointment with Europe of   104–105
    Islamic virtues and   99–100
    political activism of   102–104
    religious knowledge of   101
    siege of Sarajevo, BDS and   99
    sociability and   101–102
    Stand for Justice *see* Stand for Justice
  see also Bosnia; Mladi Muslimani; Stari Grad
Bow Central Mosque (London)   69
boycott, divestment and sanctions (BDS)
  in general   1–2, 43–44, 123–124

INDEX 167

by academics 70
anti-apartheid movement and 27, 131
antisemitism and 1, 43, 120
democracy and 72
as dissent by impoverished/
 dispossessed 131
effectiveness of 6
generational differences and *see under*
 generational differences
insider vs. outsider struggles and *see*
 insider vs. outsider struggles
Islamic piety and *see under* piety, Islamic
Islamic virtues and *see under* virtues,
 Islamic
literature on 4
localization of 2, 9–10, 130
master frames in 11, 131
organizations active in *see under specific*
 organizations
pedagogical materials on 37–42, 64, 79
personal experience of suffering
 and 65–66
private engagement with *see under*
 private engagement
public engagement with *see under* public
 engagement, Islamic
resistance as 131
 see also resistance, civil
results of 13, 22–23
secularism and 13–14, 130, 131
as self-managed change 9
sociability and 101–102
solidarity and *see* solidarity/solidarity
 movements
in Stari Grad *see* Stari Grad
tolerance and friendship and 84
in Tower Hamlets *see* Tower Hamlets
umma and *see under* umma
see also boycotts
Boycott, Divestment, Sanctions: The
 Global Struggle for Palestinian Rights
 (Barghouti) 6
"Boycotting Israeli and American Goods"
 (al-Qaradawi) 34, 41, 119
boycotts
 in general 13
 by academics 25
 fatwas and 33, 34–37, 38, 40–41, 42, 119

gender and 35–36
of Israel
 by Arab League 27–28, 30–31
 fatwas and 35–37
 online calls for 33–42
 religious scholars' calls for 32–33
 transnational solidarity and 23–27
 as religious obligations 26, 32–33, 34–35
of Russia 39
trade unions and 37
of UK 34, 39
websites dedicated to 37–42
women's roles in 35
see also boycott, divestment and
 sanctions
British Muslim Initiative (BMI) 77
British National Party (BNP) 47
Britishness 68, 72, 73
Brown, Michael 132
bumpkins/hillbillies (*papci*) 56
Burawoy, Michael 17

Cabot, Heath 133
Cairo (Egypt) 90
Carrier, James G. 13
cartoons controversy 33*n*3
Central Office for the Boycott of Israel (CBO
 of Arab League) 28, 30–31
'Check the Label' campaign 85
Christianity 24–25, 66*n*1
Church of England 25
civil resistance *see* resistance, civil
class
 middle-class *see under* Bosniaks
 working-class *see* white working-class
 see also insider vs. outsider struggles
Coca-Cola 91
Colborne, Sarah 77
collective responsibility 110–111, 119, 126
colonial exploitation 10, 47–48
Columbia Road Flower Market
 (London) 60
Columbia University (USA) 24
Communist Party (Yugoslavia) 55
community, Muslim *see* umma
compassion 64, 82, 94
Conference of Arab Regional Offices of
 Liaison Officers (2004) 31

Conference of the Scholars of Islam
  (2002) 32
consumption, ethical 12–13
Corbyn, Jeremy 77
Council of the Arab Inter-Parliamentary
  Union (AIPU) 31
Croatia 54, 105, 108
cultured vs. non-cultured 3, 57, 58, 88, 125
Cvetković, Dragiša 105

dates 84–85
"de-Bosniakization" (*razbošnjačenje*) 112
decency 94, 98
"defensive religiosity" 66–67
Deif, Muhammad 39
"de-Islamization" (*razmuslimovanje*) 112, 114
  see also Islamization
democracy
  Bangladeshis and 61
  BDS and 72
  Bosniaks and 54, 110–111
  Palestinian struggle and 65
Denmark 33n3
Devareaux, Derek T. 74
Diary of Anne Frank (Frank) 113
displacements, in Bosnia 51, 55–56, 88
dissemination, of religious knowledge 38, 41–42
divestment campaigns 24–25
dobra, stara porodica ("good, old family") 55
docility, of Bosniaks 101, 104, 109, 112, 113, 114
Docklands (London) 47
Dodik, Milorad 102
došljaci ("those who have arrived") 56
Duke University (USA) 24

East End (London) 44–45
East London Mosque 48–49, 67
Easy Talk 85
Egypt
  activist entering the Gaza Strip through 90
  anti-normalization movement in 28
  Arab League and 28
  boycott of UK by 34
  Israel and 28–29
  radical religious movement 15

Ehn, Billy 62
Emmaus International Network 89
England *see* United Kingdom
ethical consumption 12–13
ethics
  of collective responsibility 110–111, 119, 126
  political discourse and 4–5, 14
  "ethnic absolutism" 68
Europe
  Bosniaks and
    association with 54–55, 58–59, 96, 104–105, 110, 113–114
    rejection of 111–112, 114, 116–117
    Stand for Justice and 105
    Yugoslav longing for 58
"extended case method" 17
Extortion for London 74

Fadlallah, Muhammad Hussein 37
family prestige 56n4, 96
Faradhi, Muslehuddin 50
fatwas
  boycotts and 33, 34–37, 38, 40–41, 42, 119
  dissemination of 38
  on duties of European Muslims 40–41
al-Fawzan, Saleh 36–37, 42
fear of God 32, 53, 64, 82, 87, 94, 95, 103, 126
Ferguson (Missouri; USA) 131–132
fieldwork, methodology of 19–21
Fleming, Katherine E. 58
FOA (Friends of al-Aqsa) 18–19, 77, 81
Foucault, Michel 7–8, 97n4
Frank, Anne 113
free subjects 8
Friends of al-Aqsa (FOA) 18–19, 77, 81
Friends of Sabeel Ecumenical Liberation
  Theology Center (UK) 70
friendship 84
fundamentalism 54, 57, 58, 106n7

Galloway, George 49–50, 77
Gaza flotilla raid 77
Gaza Massacre 113–114
Gaza Strip 90
gender 35–36, 97
  see also women

General Federation of Trade Unions in
 Palestine (GFTUP) 23
generational differences
 BDS and
  in Stari Grad 125
  in Tower Hamlets 35–36, 61, 67–68,
   77–78, 82, 126
  Islam and 15, 49–51, 59, 127
  umma and 53–54
Georgetown University (USA) 24
"good, old family" (*dobra, stara
 porodica*) 55
Gorinjac, Zemira 91

Halevi, Leor 34
Halilović, Nezim 116–117, 121–122
Hamas 26, 32, 35, 39
Harvard University (USA) 24
Helms, Elissa 18
Hercegovci (people from Herzegovina) 56
Heseltine, Michael 47
Hezbollah 32
Hirschkind, Charles 63, 82
Hizb ut-Tahrir (Islamic Liberation Party) 83
honesty 94, 98
Hudson, Alan 48
Huguenot immigrants 2, 44
human rights violations, by Israel 1, 22–23
al-Husseini, Ibrahim Salih 40
al-Husseini, Mohammed Amin 34
hypocrisy 95–96, 113

ICJ (International Court of Justice) 26, 27
IDF (Israel Defense Forces) 23, 26
IFE (Islamic Forum of Europe) 49–50
Ikhwanweb.org 118
India 34
Indigenous radical movements 131–132
InMinds.com 41, 118
insider vs. outsider struggles
 BDS and
  in Stari Grad 55–57, 87–88
  in Tower Hamlets 73
International Court of Justice (ICJ) 26, 27
International Quds Day 108
International Women's Strike 84
Internet 33–34, 38n5, 118
interviews, methodology of 21

Iran 8n5, 34
Irish immigrants 44
Islam
 of Bosniaks *see under* Bosniaks
 critical discourse on 16–17
 democracy and 110–111
 Europe and 105
 gender and 97
 generational differences and 15, 49–51,
  59, 127
 new media and *see* new media
 piety in *see* piety, Islamic
 politics and 111
 private engagement with 14, 101, 110, 128
 public engagement with 41, 59, 70, 82,
  121, 128
 racism and 75
 reforms in Ottoman Empire 16
 religious obligations in *see* religious
  obligations
 rituals in 52, 80, 126
 secularism and *see* secularism
 as system of values 53, 111, 128
 virtues in *see* virtues, Islamic
 see also Muslims
IslamBosna.ba 19, 41–42, 118–120, 121
Islamic Community of Bosnia and
 Herzegovina (Islamska Zajednica Bosne i
 Hercegovine) 54, 114, 116
Islamic Forum of Europe (ife) 49–50
Islamic Liberation Party (Hizb ut-Tahrir) 83
Islamization 110–112, 115–116
 see also "de-Islamization"
  (*razmuslimovanje*)
IslamOnline.net 40
Islamophobia 38–39, 77
Islamska Zajednica Bosne i Hercegovine
 (Islamic Community of Bosnia and
 Herzegovina) 54, 114, 116
Israel
 boycotts of
  by Arab League 27–28, 30–31
  fatwas and 35–37
  online calls for 33–42
  religious scholars calls for 32–33
  transnational solidarity and 23–27
  see also boycott, divestment and
   sanctions

Israel (*cont.*)
  building of separation wall 26
  Declaration of Independence of 28
  Egypt and 28–29
  human rights violations by 1, 22–23
  Palestinians in *see* Palestinians
  Qatar and 31*n*2
  Saudi Arabia and 31*n*2
Israel Defense Forces (IDF) 23, 26
Izetbegović, Alija 106*n*7, 108, 112, 118*n*11
Izetbegović, Bakir 93*n*2, 102

Jamiat Ulama-i-Hind's fatwa 34
Jansen, Stef 92
Jewish immigrants 2, 44–45
Jewish Voice for Peace (JVP) 84
Jews for Israeli – Palestinian Peace (JIPF) 84
jihadi acts 26, 32–33, 34–35, 39
  see also religious obligations
Judaism/Jews 120
justice frames 11, 17, 131
JVP (Jewish Voice for Peace) 84
Jyllands-Posten (newspaper) 33*n*3

Kafa movement 78
Kahf, Monzer 40
Keffiyeh project 77
Kershen, Anne 45
al-Khalili, Ahmad bin Hamad 37
Khamenei, Sayyid Ali Hosseini 41
Khan Yunis massacre 98–99
Khazaa, Ahmad 31
killings, racist 74
King Fahd Mosque (Sarajevo) 116, 118, 119*n*12, 121
Kober, Avi 27–28
Krajišnici (people from Krajina) 56

Labour Party (UK) 46, 47, 48
"Let us Remember Gaza" conference (2010) 113
"living traditions" 16
Livingstone, Ken 77
Ljiljan (SDA newspaper) 106
localization, of BDS 2, 9–10, 130
Löfgren, Orvar 62

London (UK) 44–45, 47
  see also Tower Hamlets
London Docklands Development Corporation 47
London Muslim Centre 49, 50
longevity, in family history 56*n*4, 96

Maček, Vlatko 105
MacIntyre, Alasdair 16
madrasas 53
Mahmood, Saba 7, 97*n*4
Mahmud, Mustafa 107–108
Massachusetts Institute of Technology (MIT) 24
master frames 11, 131
Mavi Marmara (MV) 77, 90
Mawlawi, Faysal 37, 40
MCB (Muslim Council of Britain) 70–71
Medjunarodni Forum Solidarnosti (MFS-Emmaus) 19, 89–91, 109, 110, 120
methodology of fieldwork 19–21
MFS-Emmaus (Medjunarodni Forum Solidarnosti) 19, 89–91, 109, 110, 120
migration laws (UK) 48, 75
Mirza Shirazi 34
Mladi Muslimani
  in general 19
  BDS activities of 108–109
  conferences of 113, 121
  founding of 105
  illegality of 106
  Islam's role in 110–111
  past image of 108
  politics and 105–109
  target group of 109
  volunteers of 107, 108, 114, 115
modesty 53
moral actions/life 79–80
moral reform 82–86
moral values, Islamic 53, 111, 128
mothers, self-sacrificing 114–115
MPAC (Muslim Public Affairs Committee) 70–71
Mukhaymar, Fuad 40
multiethnicity 51–52
Muslim Brotherhood 34, 106, 119
Muslim community *see* umma

Muslim Council of Britain (MCB)   70–71
Muslim identity
  of Bosniaks   58, 109
  of British-born Bangladeshis   49, 83–84
  as European identity   58
  secular   109–110
Muslim Public Affairs Committee (MPAC)   70–71
Muslim solidarity *see* solidarity/solidarity movements
Muslimanski Glas (SDA newspaper)   106
Muslims
  in general   123
  antisemitism and   43, 120
  in Bosnia *see* Bosniaks
  fatwas on duties of   40–41
  hypocrisy towards/of   95–96, 113
  identity of *see* Muslim identity
  interpretations of Islam by   16–17
  new media and   15, 33–34, 38, 43–44, 118
    see also websites
  piety of *see* piety, Islamic
  racism against   47–48, 71–72, 73–75
  reforms in Ottoman Empire   16
  religiosity of *see under* religiosity
  religious obligations of *see* religious obligations
  solidarity of *see under* solidarity/solidarity movements
  in UK *see* Bangladeshi community
  use of term   4n4, 52n2
  see also Islam; umma
mutual assistance   52, 119, 126
Muzaffar, Chandra   41
MV (*Mavi Marmara*)   77, 90

Nakaš, Bakir   93
National Front (UK)   71
nationalism   37
  economic   37
  secularism and   28, 33, 49, 61, 69, 75
  in Serbia   107
  see also proto-nationalism
Nelson, Cary   25
Nestlé   91
new media   15, 33–34, 38, 43–44, 118
  see also websites

9/11 attacks   32, 38–39, 40
non-cultured vs. cultured   3, 57, 58, 88, 125
Nova Varoš   106–107
Nuh, Sayyid Muhammad   40

Occupied Territories (OT) *see* Palestine
Ohio State University (USA)   24
OnIslam.net   40
online resistance   33–42
Operation Defensive Shield (2002)   23
orientalism   58
OT (Occupied Territories) *see* Palestine
outsiders *see* insider vs. outsider struggles

PA (Palestinian Authority)   22, 31–32, 39
PACBI (Palestinian Campaign for the Academic and Cultural Boycott of Israel)   1, 25–26
Palestine (Occupied Territories)
  anti-normalization movement in   29
  apartheid and   27
  civil resistance in   6–7
  Gaza flotilla raid   77
  Gaza Massacre   113–114
  occupation by Israel   1
  rights of refugees to return to   1, 23, 27
  see also Palestinians
Palestine Liberation Organization (PLO)   26, 31, 132
Palestine National Council (PNC)   33
Palestine Solidarity Campaign (PSC)   18–19, 69–70, 72, 84
Palestine Solidarity Movement (PSM)   24
"Palestine: Trial for Humanity" conference (2008)   121
Palestine-Info.com   38–39
Palestinian Authority (PA)   22, 31–32, 39
Palestinian Campaign for the Academic and Cultural Boycott of Israel (PACBI)   1, 25–26
Palestinian Center for Peace and Democracy (PCPD)   23
Palestinian Federation of Women Action Committees (PFWAC)   23
Palestinian Information Center (PIC)   38–39

Palestinian-Black solidarity   131–132
Palestinians
    basic rights of   27
    right to return of   1, 23, 27
    struggle of
        in general   27
        democracy and   65
        international struggle and   9–10
        Muslim struggle and   11
        siege of Sarajevo and   92, 99
        see also boycott, divestment and sanctions; boycotts
Palinfo.com (formerly Palestine-Info.com)   39
pan-Islamism/pan-Islamist movements   5, 21, 33–34, 43, 106
papci (bumpkins/hillbillies)   56
Pasha, Azzam   28
passivity *see* docility, of Bosniaks
Patel, Ismail   77
patriotism   93, 117, 125
pay inequality   45
PBC (Permanent Boycott Committee (Arab League))   28
PCPD (Palestinian Center for Peace and Democracy)   23
peace treaties   28–29
"peasantization"   56
pedagogical materials, on BDS   37–42, 64, 79
Permanent Boycott Committee (PBC (Arab League))   28
PFWAC (Palestinian Federation of Women Action Committees)   23
PIC (Palestinian Information Center)   38–39
piety, Islamic
    BDS and   2, 5, 10, 36, 63, 66–67, 68, 80, 86, 99, 126, 128
    BDS pedagogical materials and   64
    changing social and political conditions and   63–64, 78–79
PLO (Palestine Liberation Organization)   26, 31, 132
PNC (Palestine National Council)   33
politics/politicians
    in general   123, 128
    Arabism and   28
    BDS and   11
    distrust of   94, 103, 109
    in Egypt   29
    ethics and   4–5, 14
    fragmentation in   26
    Islam and   111
    Mladi Muslimani and   105–109
    in Stari Grad   57, 93–94, 101–103
    in Tower Hamlets   18, 49–51, 65, 67–68, 73, 76–80, 82
    umma and   35, 54
    see also under specific political parties
power, resistance and   7–8, 9
Preporod (monthly newspaper)   113–114
Presbyterian Church (USA)   24–25
primitivci (primitives)   56
private engagement
    with BDS   9, 13, 62–63, 65, 68, 101
    ethical practices and   14
    with Islam   14, 101, 110, 128
proto-nationalism   37
    see also nationalism
PSC (Palestine Solidarity Campaign)   18–19, 69–70, 72, 84
PSM (Palestine Solidarity Movement)   24
public engagement, Islamic   41, 59, 70, 82, 121, 128

al-Qaradawi, Yusuf   33, 34–35, 36, 37, 40–42, 119, 121
Qatar   31*n*2

racism
    against Black Americans   132
    against Muslims   47–48, 71–72, 73–75
    organizations combatting   77
    see also antisemitism
racist gangs   71
radical religious movements   15
    see also fundamentalism; Wahhabism
Rahman, Sheikh Mujib   69
Ramadan   52, 84–85
razbošnjačenje ("de-Bosniakization")   112
razmuslimovanje ("de-Muslimization")   112, 114
Red Card Israel campaign   77
reform movements, faith-based   66*n*1
religion
    knowledge of *see* religious knowledge

as mobilizing force   14–15
 see also Christianity; Islam; religious
  traditions, definition of
religiosity
 defensive   66–67
 of Muslims   95–96, 107–108, 122
 see also piety, Islamic; virtues, Islamic
religious authority   14–17, 41, 127
religious knowledge
 in general   16, 127
 of British-born Bangladeshis   81–82
 dissemination of   38, 41–42
 of younger middle-class Bosniaks   53, 101
religious movements, radical   15
 see also fundamentalism; Wahhabism
religious obligations
 BDS as   42, 86
 boycotts as   26, 32–33, 34–35
 fatwas on   40–41
 realizing piety *see* piety, Islamic
religious scholars, boycotts and   32–33
religious traditions, definition of   15–16
resistance, civil
 agency and   6–8
 BDS as   131
 emancipatory implications of   8
 ethnographies of   17
 online   33–42
 in Palestine
  in general   23
  Beit Sahour   30
  PA and   31–32
  transnational solidarity and   23–27
  see also boycott, divestment and
   sanctions
 power and   7–8, 9
 spaces of   9–14
Respect Party (UK)   49–50, 67
Rida, Rashid   119
"right to buy" policy   47, 74
right to return   1, 23, 27
rights frames   11, 131
Rihanna songs   98–99
ritual, Islamic   52, 80, 126
rural newcomers
 BDS activities of   96–97
 fundamentalist attitudes of   57, 88, 105

 vs. urbanites   55–57, 87–88, 94–95, 96
 "ruralization"   56
Russia   39
Rutgers University (USA)   24

Saff (magazine)   114, 118
Said, Edward W.   58
Salafi, use of term   119n12
Salafism
 Bosniaks and
  in general   57, 115–116
  AIO and   117–118
  IslamBosna.ba   118–120
Salvation Army   66n1
Salvatore, Armando   15–16
Sandžaklije (people from Sandžak)   56, 107
Sarajevo (Bosnia)
 King Fahd Mosque in   116, 118, 119n12, 121
 *madrasa*s in   53
 multiethnicity in   51–52
 politics in   57, 93–94, 101–103, 116–117
 population composition of   52n2
 siege of
  in general   51
  experiences of   20, 92, 99
  Palestinian struggle and   92, 99
 Stari Grad *see* Stari Grad
Sarajlije (people from Sarajevo)   55–57, 87–89
 see also urbanites
Saudi Arabia   31n2
Schiffauer, Werner   66
School of Oriental and African Studies
 (SOAS)   69
SDA (Stranka Demokratske Akcije)   93n2, 95, 106–107, 109–110, 111–112, 117
secularism
 BDS and   14–15, 130, 131
 Islam and   94–98, 109–110, 116, 121
 nationalism and   28, 33, 49, 61, 69, 75
self, authority and   14–17
self-reflection   97
self-sacrificing mothers   114–115
Selimović, Mehmed "Meša"   87
seljaci/seljačine (peasants or villagers)   56
separation wall (West Bank)   26
September 11 attacks   32, 38–39, 40

Serbia
    dividing of Bosnia between Croatia   105
    harassment of Muslims in   106–107
    nationalism in   107
    war with Croatia   54
Seventh Muslim Brigade   112
Shirazi, Mirza   34
Shomali, Amer   30
shopping   62
al-Shuebi, Hamoud al-Aqla   36, 40
shyness   53
sincerity   64, 82, 94, 95–96, 97, 126
Siniora, Hanna   33
Sistani, Ayatollah   41
SJP (Students for Justice in Palestine)   24
Smith, Jackie   130
SOAS (School of Oriental and African Studies)   69
sociability, BDS and   101–102
social conditions, solidarity and   10–11
social networks   46, 51, 69
solidarity/solidarity movements
    in general   3–4, 11, 79–80, 103–104, 123–124
    literature on   4
    local interpretations of   133–134
    Palestinian-Black   131–133
    racism and   73
    rejection of   28, 120–121
    in Sarajevo   3, 52
    social conditions and   10–11
    transnational   23–27
    see also boycott, divestment and sanctions; boycotts; under specific bds organizations
Solidarnost (Solidarity)   91
Sorabji, Cornelia   20n10, 52
Soroush, Abdolkarim   41
Sourani, Raji   10, 30
South Africa   27, 131
Spivak, Gayatri Chakravorty   9
Srebrenica genocide   3, 18, 104–105, 113–114
Stand for Justice
    in general   19
    aims of   102–103
    BDS as public engagement   121
    call for monitors in   100, 101
    Europe and   105
    founding of   98, 99
    opposition to   117
    protest organizers of   103–104
    supporters of   100
Stari Grad (Sarajevo)
    in general   88–89, 123
    BDS in
        in general   3–4, 17, 18, 19, 130–131
        generational differences and   125
        insider vs. outsider struggles and   55–57, 87–88
        of older middle-class   92–98
        organizations active in see under specific organizations
        social context and   10–11
        of younger middle-class   98–115
        see also Bosniaks
    population composition of   52n2
states, BDS utilized by   130
Stefansson, Andreas   55–57
Stop the War Coalition   77, 78
Stranka Demokratske Akcije (SDA)   93n2, 95, 106–107, 109–110, 111–112, 117
Students for Justice in Palestine (SJP)   24
subjectivation   8
supermarkets   65–66
suživot ("life together")   51
Sylhet   46, 60–61

taxes, refusal to pay   30
television, watching of   63–64
terrorist attacks   39
    see also September 11 attacks
Thatcher, Margaret   47, 74
Thrall, Nathan   22
Tobacco Protest (1891–1892)   34, 39
tolerance   84
Toth, James   14–15
Tower Hamlets Council   2–3, 76
Tower Hamlets (London)
    in general   44, 123
    anti-Muslim hate crimes in   45
    Bangladeshi community in see Bangladeshi community
    BDS in
        in general   2–3, 5, 17, 18–19, 130–131
        of British-born Bangladeshis   76–86

of first-generation Bangladeshi 62–66, 68
generational differences and 35–36, 61, 67–68, 77–78, 82, 126
insider vs. outsider struggles and 73
mass appeal of 64–65
organizations active in *see under specific organizations*
of second-generation Bangladeshi 68–76
social context of 10
see also Bangladeshis
Council of 2–3, 76
faith-based activism in 66
housing policies in 47, 71, 74
migration to 44–45
politics in 18, 49–51, 65, 67–68, 73, 76–80, 82
population composition of 2
racism in 47–48, 71–72, 73–75
religion as stabilizing factor in 45
unemployment in 45
white working-class in 2, 46, 47, 48, 71
trade unions 37
translocality 11–12, 17, 130–131
transnationalism 11–12

umma (Muslim community)
BDS and
in general 5, 44, 79, 119, 121–122
political rejuvenating of 18
collectivity and 76–77, 129
generational conflicts and 53–54
moral apathy of 104
politics and 35, 54
Srebrenica genocide and 18
Understanding the Qur'an: A Contemporary Approach (Mahmud) 107–108
unemployment 45
United Church of Christ (USA) 24–25
United Kingdom (UK)
BDS in 22, 25
see also Tower Hamlets
boycotts of 34, 39
colonial exploitation by 10, 47–48
culture of 73
migration laws of 48, 75
racism in *see* racism

United Methodist Church (USA) 25
United National Leadership of the Uprising (UNLU) 29
United States (USA) 22, 24–25, 132
University of California, Berkeley (USA) 24
University of Michigan (USA) 24
UNLU (United National Leadership of the Uprising) 29
urbanites
progressive attitudes of 88
vs. rural new comers 55–57, 87–88, 94–95, 96
see also Sarajlije
The Use of Pleasure (Foucault) 97n4

Velić, Muhammad 113–114
Veolia (French corporation) 2–3
victimhood 18, 19, 87, 114, 115
village networks 46, 51
virtues, Islamic
BDS and 32, 53, 64, 82, 87, 94, 103, 126
hypocrisy and 95–96
moral reform and 82–86
see also under specific virtues
Voice of Palestine (PA radio station) 39

Wahhabism 57, 115–116
WCAR (World Conference Against Racism) 24
websites 37–42
see also under specific websites
Wemyss, Georgie 47
Werbner, Pnina 68
West Bank barrier 26
white working-class 2, 46, 47, 48, 71
women
freedoms of 97, 121
roles in boycotts/BDS 35, 121
as teachers of children 63
World Conference Against Racism (WCAR) 24
World Council of Churches 25

Young Muslim Organization (YMO) 49–50
Yugoslavia 55, 58
see also Bosnia; Croatia

Zionism, movements against 70–71